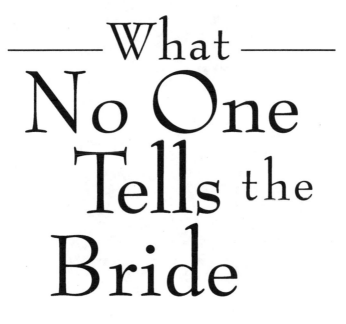

What No One Tells the Bride

Marg Stark

MJF BOOKS
NEW YORK

Published by MJF Books
Fine Communications
Two Lincoln Square
60 West 66th Street
New York, NY 10023

What No One Tells the Bride
ISBN 1-56731-361-2
Library of Congress Card Catalog #99-76032

Copyright © 1998, Marg Stark

This edition published by arrangement with Hyperion.
Cover illustration © Arnie Levin
Book design by Holly McNeely

Manufactured in the United States of America on acid-free paper

MJF Books and the MJF colophon are trademarks of Fine Creative Media, Inc.

10   9   8   7   6   5   4   3   2   1

For Mom,
who taught me a woman's life
is full of contradictions,
and rich because of it . . .

And for Duke,
who loved my contradictions
and enriched life all the more.

Contents

A Note to Readers   *ix*

INTRODUCTION: No One Had the Heart
to Tell the Bride   *1*

CHAPTER 1: Love's Identity Crisis: The Modern
Bride's Inner Turmoil   *19*

CHAPTER 2: From This Day Forward:
The Tumultuous Engagement and Wedding   *43*

CHAPTER 3: "You've Crossed Over
to the Other Side!": Making the Transition
Between Your Single and Married Social Life   *63*

CHAPTER 4: The Wedding Postpartum:
Finding Real Happiness When the Fairy Tale,
and Your Former Life, Fades Away   *87*

CHAPTER 5: For Richer, For Poorer:
Handling the Inevitable,
Momentous Squabbles About Money   *112*

CHAPTER 6: I'm Becoming My Mother:
What to Do When Your Marriage
Falls Prey to Stereotypes   *133*

Contents — viii

CHAPTER 7: What Have You Done for Me Lately?:
Destructive Mind-sets Left Over
from Single Life   *157*

CHAPTER 8: Sex and the Married Girl: Defying
the Odds with Lusty Monogamy   *178*

CHAPTER 9: Don't "Start a Family,"
Don't Buy a Dog, Not Even a Goldfish . . .
Until You Read This   *203*

CHAPTER 10: The Heart Grows Fonder:
The All-Important Balance Between
Time Apart and Time Together   *226*

CHAPTER 11: Let the Horse Pick His Own Path:
The Obstacles of Communication
and Criticism   *250*

CHAPTER 12: The Enormity of Love: Marveling
at the Changes Marriage Brings and Celebrating
Your Triumphant Moments   *274*

Recommended Reading   *294*

Acknowledgments   *296*

Index   *298*

A Note to Readers

I have always liked telling secrets. I don't mean that I like breaking confidences but that I like to say things most people are afraid to say, or have trouble saying. So when I got married two and a half years ago, I was struck by how many things go unsaid about the engagement and the first year of marriage. And I was amazed at how much pressure I felt *not* to talk about the things I felt, even with friends with whom I'd previously shared everything.

As much as I love my husband and wanted to marry him, I assure you that planning my wedding and leaving behind the single life I had enjoyed was not a trail of rose petals. But like most brides I know, I felt I had to characterize my wedding and my new marriage that way. I had to carry out the fairy tale.

Nine months into my newlywed year, I began to talk to one or two recently married friends about the mixed feelings I had, and I was relieved to find other brides felt the same way. We were all happy but, nonetheless, traumatized by how different married life was from single life, or from what we expected it would be. We all liked being married, but we worried that marriage would "swallow us up" and diminish our individuality. We all wanted to make marriage our own—different from our parents' marriages—but we weren't sure how to do that.

If we all felt this way, I was sure there would be books or research studies that made sense of this phenomena. So I started reading everything I could find in libraries and bookstores about a modern bride's experience of the engagement, wedding, and first years of marriage. What I learned was that very little research exists on the transition most of us experience today, having been single and on our own for a few years before we marry. The books and articles I read could also be extraordinarily depressing. They treated marriage clinically, as if it were an encroaching disease. None of them assumed the reassuring role of a country doctor, saying, "This is entirely normal. You're doing a great job. You just need to relax."

So I set out to write a reassuring book—one that tells brides that the vast majority of the anxieties and fears they experience in their journey from singlehood into marriage are normal. Feelings of ambivalence amid bliss are a normal part of the engagement. And arguments are a normal, even healthy, part of early marriage.

Of all the subjects I have written about in my career, none has struck the nerve this one has. I couldn't seem to write this book fast enough for the women with whom I talked about it. Everyone I met seemed to have a friend who had just gotten engaged and desperately needed to know she wasn't the only bride feeling the way she did—happy, crazy, scared, but mostly overwhelmed. Even women like my mom, who has been married for thirty-nine years, welcomed a book that clarified issues with which they still struggle.

My husband and I are, in many ways, your typical

bride and groom. We met four years ago, when we were twenty-eight, at an outdoor bar in Newport, Rhode Island. We actually had our first meaningful conversation in the Porta Potti line. Despite these mundane origins, my husband and I talk most about how *not* to live ordinary lives—how not to become complacent, how not to lose sight of what's important. And how *to* have a rich, meaningful life. How *to* have fun and keep our senses of humor.

It is this drive to live differently that shapes *What No One Tells the Bride*. I have chosen not to include some of the statistics you'll find in other books about how bad marriage can be for women. I fully acknowledge these facts, but I am far more interested in offering ideas and strategies for making marriage better, and for beating stereotypes.

I should remind you that this is a book by and for brides, so it will feel one-sided at times. The advice my friends and I offer, and the stories we tell, are from our points of view, not our husbands'. And while many of the lessons we learned will benefit both husbands and wives, some will mean far more to you because you are a woman.

Some of the ideas my friends, my husband, and I present in this book are endorsed by so-called marriage experts. More important to our way of thinking, these methods worked for us in our new marriages. By "us," I mean the fifty brides I interviewed or surveyed for this book. Some were in the throes of wedding plans but most were women who have been married five years or less. Many are friends, or friends of friends. Others I "met" through the Internet or through people who knew I was writing this book. Although many brides offered to let me use their real names, I tried to foster utmost candor and instead chose to identify them all by pseudonyms.

The brides range in age from twenty-four to forty-five, the majority of them in their early thirties. Most are middle class and college-educated. They come from diverse religious backgrounds and are pursuing wildly different careers or interests, from law to the arts to full-time motherhood. Most are experiencing marriage for the first time.

What they all have in common is that they broke a taboo. They were willing to tell you what no one usually tells the bride. They believed, as I do, that it only harms women to make the engagement into a fairy tale, and to shroud the first year of marriage in silence. We hope this makes *What No One Tells the Bride* a very human book. And a guide for all of those trying to forge new kinds of marriages—happy ones, for both women and men.

Introduction

NO ONE HAD THE HEART
TO TELL THE BRIDE

Six weeks before my wedding, a seamstress put a Herculean effort into buttoning the back of my silk shantung, Diamond Collection gown. Maria was a sweet Russian lady, brawny armed from carrying four or five heavy, beaded gowns at a time. She would sooner have stuck sewing pins in her tongue than make me cry. But I was already on the verge of tears when Maria let the unbuttoned back of my dress go slack and calmly entreated her manager to come to my dressing room.

The two of them took my measurements, as they had seven months before when I ordered the $1,800 gown, and the truth was inescapable. I had gained a considerable amount of weight. My wedding dress did not fit.

On the drive home, I was hysterical and inconsolable. It didn't matter that Maria was ordering another panel of fabric and would alter the dress in time for the wedding. It didn't matter that my mother trotted out reassurances she hadn't used on me since puberty. Nor that I was marrying a wonderful man, who upon hearing about the disastrous fitting, took me into his arms and told me again and again, "You're beautiful, you're gorgeous."

I was fixated on something a friend had told me earlier

about a bride whose wedding dress had to be altered dramatically. "No one had the heart to tell her," my friend said, "but the dress never looked the same."

No one had the heart to tell the bride. *No one had the heart to tell the bride.* The phrase resounded in my head. I couldn't imagine anything as mortifying as being the bride from whom such an enormous secret was kept, even if it were for good reason. And so it was that in the five weeks that followed, I lost so much weight that Maria had to remove the panel of silk shantung she had added, and a few more inches besides.

Of course I know this was irrational. At thirty-one, I should have been more "grounded." After all, the reason I had gained so much weight during my engagement was that I had mononucleosis. While I was sick, I had been cautioned not to exercise, and Wendy's chocolate frosties were the only thing that soothed my sore throat.

But I couldn't shake my pride. I wanted the wedding I had always dreamed about, and in the end, I had it. But little did I know that aside from what people *really* think of your dress, there is a great deal that no one tells the bride. For example, of all the things I would look at walking down the aisle—the stained-glass windows, my fidgety flower girl, my college drinking buddy sitting next to my former Sunday school teacher, or the blue hydrangea I spent a fortune to get in February—no one told me the finest sight would be the sweet, broad smile on my groom's face. But that was the one secret I was glad to unveil by myself, taking a step, pause, step, pause, toward a new life.

I could have used some help, however, with the other secrets that bewilder brides during the engagement and the first years of marriage. I didn't know that brides often experience growing pains and feel wildly disoriented in this, the happiest time of their lives. I didn't know that the adjustments to married life could be so hard. I didn't know that, consciously and unconsciously, my husband and I would bring certain expectations to our marriage, or that there were so many different kinds of marriages—all of them different from the one we would fashion for ourselves. I didn't know that we would grow so much closer in the process, or that I could be as happy and fulfilled in marriage as I am now.

I don't think this is a conspiracy. This isn't like childbirth, in which I'm told that if anyone revealed the gory details to you beforehand, you might never go through with it. It's just that very little research has been devoted to the modern-day adjustments of newlyweds. We presume that the honeymoon lasts a while, and that few problems arise before the seven-year itch. But divorce statistics demonstrate that marriages are more vulnerable in the first five years than at any other time. One British study found that couples who went on to divorce were already in serious trouble by the time they reached their first anniversary.

Dirty Little Secrets?

In this vulnerable time, brides and grooms are encouraged to be hush-hush about what is *really* going on in their new marriages, and about the difficulties of their passage from singleness to marriage. They are immediately isolated. In biblical times, a groom was given a year off from work just to tend to his marriage. Maria and Captain von Trapp enjoyed a whole summer's worth of honeymoon before returning to their musical brood—and the realities of war.

Even with just a week or two to honeymoon, couples

today learn that marriage, and particularly the first year, is a private matter. Parents and in-laws give the couple space, not wanting to be nosy or interfering. Friends don't call because they seem to think you are constantly having sex and don't want to interrupt. And for a year or more, people call you "newlyweds," an endearing term but one that creates a kind of aura, a signal that you and your husband are experiencing a bliss that sets you apart from regular life.

So what happens if things are not entirely blissful? What happens if the arguments over the wedding have made you actually dread your nuptials? What happens when you and your groom have trouble finding something interesting to talk about at dinner? What happens when you resent how you suddenly have to justify all your expenses to your fiancé or husband? What happens when you find yourself in the same kind of marriage your mother had, the kind you said you'd never be in?

Several of these things happened to me two and a half years ago when I married Darwin "Duke" Clark. I met Duke in Newport, Rhode Island, where I had a summer

---

BRIDE-TO-BRIDE

What do you wish someone had told you before you got married?

⚭ "That I wasn't going to get everything I had always wanted in one man."

⚭ "That if I wasn't happy as a single woman, I wouldn't be happy as a married woman."

⚭ "That marriage could be so delicious."

⚭ "That I could get pregnant on the honeymoon."

⚭ "That if you're happy fifty or more percent of the time, you're doing well; I was used to thinking that a fifty on a test was failure."

⚭ "That my husband and I would be as utterly foolish and playful as we are sometimes around the house, like little kids."

house with my girlfriends from Boston and he was in school as a U.S. naval officer.

A year and a half after we met, he faked a cramp in his leg on a ski slope in Taos, New Mexico, fell to his knees, and asked me if I would do him the ultimate honor and marry him. Fearing we were injured, the first people to congratulate us were the ski patrol.

Our relationship did not go downhill from there. It was, instead, a mixture of extreme highs and lows. From talking to other brides, I understand our engagement and first year of marriage were typical. We were in a predicament of bliss—a snare of both unprecedented pleasures and unprecedented confusion. The newlyweds I interviewed for this book told me that the first year of marriage, and the months before the wedding, were wonderful and awful at the same time.

I was lucky they opened up to me, because brides and grooms tend to keep these feelings to themselves. Couples fear that having difficulties in the engagement or early in the marriage means they have chosen the wrong people to marry or that they shouldn't be married at all. Just by articulating these fears, by allowing doubts to come into their heads, they feel they are breaking a faith or calling their vows into question.

Especially after they are married, brides don't feel comfortable turning to friends or family members. Isabelle, a twenty-eight-year-old bride from San Francisco, told me about a newly married friend of hers who broke tradition and told her single friends about the distress she was experiencing. After all, she'd left a great job to join her husband in a small town in New Hampshire where he was in business school. She had taken a considerably less challenging job at the college's admissions office and wasn't thrilled about having to traipse around in a foot of snow. But upon hearing this, the woman's friends began speculating that something was wrong with her marriage. That was when Isabelle came to the rescue, calming these single friends, offering the perspective of someone familiar with the difficult adjustments of newlywed life.

Obviously, there are some good reasons for brides not to talk to other people about their adjustments to marriage and about the panic they experience from time to time. For one thing, they don't want their friends to think badly of their new husbands, or of their marriages, having heard only one side of the story.

The Fairy Tale

However, there is usually a more compelling reason why brides don't talk about the less appealing aspects of their new marriages. Virtually all the brides I interviewed for this book were, to some degree, caught up in the fairy tale that is imposed on newlyweds. They didn't want anyone to think their relationships were less than perfect. They enjoyed the romance of the newlywed ideal at the same time as they loathed how isolated it made them feel.

After all, despite the prevalence of divorce, our society adores the idea of marriage. All kinds of traditions and folklore are heaped upon marriage, and Hollywood and Madison Avenue, in particular, make us feel that every wedding must be elaborate and every marriage flawless. Few of us are immune to fantastic expectations, even though brides today are older and more mature—the U.S. Census Bureau reporting that the average age of Americans marrying for the first time is higher than for any generation since the data was first recorded in 1890.

One bride told me that romantic movies make her uncomfortable because even though she is happily married, her relationship doesn't measure up to those in *Sleepless in Seattle* or *Bridges of Madison County*. Another woman said that registering was seductive, because picking out all new things—Waterford and Calphalon, bone china and damask linens—made her feel as though her life had to be impeccable. I remember the week after I got married, Oprah devoted her show to Martha Stewart's advice on weddings. I was transfixed by it, and somewhat disappointed, because despite having written a song for my groom that was sung at the wedding and having created many of the floral arrangements myself, there were still some details of the wedding that I could've paid more attention to (in the free time I had between Slimfast, working out, and recovering from mono).

I pray you are immune from this kind of perfectionism, but even if you haven't spent your engagement in a kind of wedding fog, tulle seemingly permanently attached to your eyeballs, think about the pressure you have been under. How many times during the course of your engagement did someone say to you, "What have you got to worry about? You're getting married!" Excitement over the wedding and the marriage takes precedence over everything else. And after a while, all those gentle admonitions that you're a bride and that you shouldn't have a care in the world build up in your psyche.

Turbulence on Cloud Nine

So when brides experience turbulence on what is supposed to be cloud nine, they feel they have no one to

BRIDE-TO-BRIDE

When were you most frightened during your new marriage and why?

ᴄꙅ "When my husband was diagnosed with a thyroid condition three weeks after we were married, the medical repercussions of which have been difficult. When we said, 'in sickness and in health,' I didn't think about problems coming so soon."

ᴄꙅ "Many times during the first year . . . over stupid arguments. I got as far as packing my bags and then I'd think, 'Where would I go?'"

ᴄꙅ "When I would feel alive and stimulated in conversations with other people and find conversations with my husband boring in comparison."

ᴄꙅ "When we moved to France the first year we were married so my husband could go to graduate school. I left my job, my friends, my family, everything."

ᴄꙅ "When my husband's college-age son from a previous marriage came to live with us for the summer, and I hated it."

turn to. And of all the things no one tells the bride, this is the most dangerous, because when I finally opened up to my husband, and to other brides, I learned that everything I was thinking and feeling was very normal. Duke and I were having arguments and power struggles almost identical to those our newly married friends were having, and all of us were afraid to talk about them.

If the experiences of women I interviewed are typical, assuming the posture of marriage is no small task. When you've spent a substantial amount of time defending your lifestyle, as single people invariably have to do, it's weird to find yourself on the opposite side of the argument, enumerating all the good things about marriage you once maintained were not essential to your happiness. When you've relied on and enjoyed very close, female friendships during single life, it's disconcerting to feel closed off from your friends and disheartening not to enjoy the same kind of intimacy with your spouse. When you've thought of yourself as a pioneer, as a solitary conqueror of urban life—putting up Christmas trees, negotiating with auto mechanics, and fixing toilets all by yourself—it can be devastating to hear yourself adopt phrases like "My husband wouldn't like that," or "I need to talk to my husband about it first."

You Are Normal!

These feelings are *very natural* and *normal* reactions to marriage. It doesn't mean you are going to have a bad marriage or that you are the last person on earth who should've accepted that diamond ring.

It's normal to have trouble adjusting to being someone's "wife." It's normal to chafe a bit the first few months you use a new last name or hyphenated name, and for it to take a year or two to adopt a vocabulary of "we" and "us" rather than "I" and "me." It's normal to resent your husband if he didn't come from a "rinse family" and plunks dirty dishes in the sink without a single thought of how food instantaneously hardens on them. And it's normal for the two of you to feel out of sync with your single friends and yet reluctant to embrace a "married couple" social life.

As a bride, I wish someone had told me that the doubts and fears I was experiencing were confusing and disorienting but not serious enough to doom my marriage, unless I let them get wildly out of control or out of proportion. I also needed practical advice and strategies to keep Duke and me from getting into what my friends and I call "the wheel," in which couples are entrapped in certain arguments and positions that repeat themselves over and over again. There was nothing more frightening to me than the idea that our entire marriage hinged on the habits Duke and I formed in our first years of living together and being married. So when I interviewed brides, I asked for "creative" solutions, the tricks they found to avoid the wheel, to avoid destructive and boringly monotonous behaviors.

Obviously, some marital problems require more than kind reassurances and helpful hints. If you find yourself married to someone who hurts you physically, who seriously manipulates you, or who is addicted to drugs, alcohol, or to a lifestyle that endangers your life and well-being, you need professional help, and you need it right away. You will note that even with less severe problems, some couples in the book benefited from going to see marriage counselors early on, when they felt their enthusiasm for the partnership had been squashed or when they were truly unhappy, not just disoriented in this momentous period of their lives.

Women and Marriage

Why is this book targeted toward brides? Aren't grooms just as clueless about the travails of new marriages? Absolutely. And yet the brides I interviewed were far more rattled by marriage than their new husbands seemed to be. I believe this is because women don't have a lot of confidence they will be happy in marriage, despite the fact that our society worships marriage and deems it the best life course for everyone. Medical research has documented that married men are happier and healthier than bachelors, but the same is not true of married women. And as many movies and books herald the wedding, Jane Austen's among them, few go on to herald the life of a wife.

I think "the movies" are just as afraid as women are to take the plunge. After all, we know what being a wife meant to many of our mothers, who were either unhappy or expected much less from life than we do. That is part of the reason I've chosen to address "brides" rather than "new wives" in this book. Few of us are comfortable with the word *wife*, probably because we still associate it with the past and with traditional gender roles of the past.

We are confused about how much happiness we can expect to eke out of what we know are going to be complicated, inundated lives. Divorce statistics and rates of depression among married women don't give us much reason to be optimistic, but we rarely consider that some marriages are succeeding as marriages have never succeeded before. In other words, some marriages are challenging convention, shaking up gender roles, and asking the Institution of Marriage to be far more meaningful and fulfilling than it was for men or women of any previous generation.

Keep that goal—a marriage that succeeds like none before it—in mind as you read this book and absorb its three central messages:

1. BELIEVE YOU CAN BE HAPPY IN MARRIAGE.

I'll never forget reading Laurie Colwin's book *Happy All the Time* shortly after I got engaged. I loved the book because the women in it—and in her other novels, which I soon devoured—were capable of a palpable joy in marriage and family life. And all of them were complicated, entertaining a myriad of emotions and ambitions at all times.

In this passage from *Happy All the Time*, a character named Misty muses about the night she and her fiancé, Vincent, announced their engagement to his friends Guido and Holly:

"Misty and I have decided to get married," he said. This engendered another spate of handshakes and kisses all around.

They drank a great deal of wine at dinner. Misty felt the candlelight reflecting in her eyes as she looked around the table. Everyone at the table looked beautiful and kind to her. Holly behaved as if she had simply incorporated Misty, but Guido seemed quite moved. There were going to be thousands of dinners like this, thought Misty. This is my place at the dinner table. This is my intended husband's best friend whom I am going to spend the rest of my life getting to know. Across the table, Vincent looked seraphically happy. Everything had a sheen on it. Was that what love did, or was it merely the wine? She decided that it was love.

It was just as she suspected: love turned you into perfect mush.

Until I read Laurie Colwin's books, I didn't realize how much I needed a vision that marriage could be extraordinarily good and happy, and that I could be extraordinarily good *at it* and happy *in it*. In her books, women fantasize about their bosses, leave their husbands for the solitude of monasteries upon learning they are pregnant, and wince at things they hear tedious women say at parties. But they always arrive at some kind of peace, a domesticity they can live with, that they hammer out and chip off of life.

Believing you can is the first step, a big step, toward arriving at some kind of peace, or a domesticity you can live with. As experts will attest and as you will see in the examples to come, married people need not stand behind life-size cardboard cutouts of husbands and wives, poking their heads into photographs of someone else's ideal. Happily married couples are too busy for this— busy pursuing partnerships that work for them.

2. CHALLENGE CONVENTIONAL THINKING.

With that said, it's true that the women I interviewed crave individuality almost as much as happiness. Brides today want to challenge conventional thinking, as they did by staying single longer, and as they continue to do by pounding on the glass ceiling, by telecommuting, and by combining motherhood and careers.

As newly married women, we seem to fear becoming clichés more than we fear divorce. (Of course, divorce is a cliché.) We like the feistiness and independence single life forged in us. As much as we want to share our lives with someone, we fear the undertow that marriage is famous for, the undertow that 83 percent of women polled in *New Woman* magazine in 1994 alluded to, believing that "wives submerge a vital part of themselves when they marry."

This is a very *real* fear. Even though she had dated her husband-to-be for six years, Elizabeth, a twenty-nine-year-old health care administrator from Boston, says the morning after she got engaged, she did not want to get out of bed. "I didn't want to face anyone," Elizabeth remembers. "I was so afraid I wasn't 'me' anymore."

Similarly, my friend Karla, a thirty-year-old director of a nonprofit organization in Baltimore, kept her maiden name when she got ·married two years ago because, she said, "I got married, I didn't get subsumed."

Karla's pithy remark says it all. Brides today are recognizing the dangers of going quietly into their marriages, of letting the Institution of Marriage confine or hem us in.

We're looking for something in marriage that is more like Lycra, something that stretches as well as it adheres.

In her book *Marriage Shock: The Transformation of Women into Wives*, Dalma Heyn says there is much about the Institution of Marriage to fear. Heyn argues that institutions in general—churches, academia, and the military—have not been very good to women. And yet, on a day-to-day basis, marriage does not feel like an institution to me, or to most of the women I know. More so it feels like two people slugging out a life and a love we want to last.

Nevertheless, Heyn makes a powerful argument that what *has* become institutionalized, or standard for women in marriage, is a crippling set of expectations— a perfectionism we impose on ourselves as generations of women before us have done. Heyn found that these expectations were born in the Industrial Age when, for the first time, men could overcome the class system and better themselves by way of work. As Jane Austen so often portrayed, women without wealth or privilege vied for the attention of men of means. And we began to offer ourselves up as partners of some "value," emphasizing what we might "do" and "bring" to a marriage to be worthy of it.

I did not realize forces of history and precedent were working within me during my engagement, during the first months I lived with my fiancé, or during the first year of our marriage. I knew that *something* was wrong, that *something* was so dramatically different that I didn't recognize myself when I looked in the mirror. In that fragile time, it felt to me as if I were constantly swinging at something, taking punches at Duke or at the air. I couldn't let any aberration in my or Duke's behavior go unnoticed. I kept remarking on the changes, saying

"Why do I feel guilty about buying things for myself now that I'm married?" or "Why do we always have sex when *you* want it?"

But even if I couldn't precisely identify the threat, I was keenly aware of what was at stake. I liked the head-strong single woman Duke had fallen in love with. She was a survivor. She looked good in my clothes. And she knew how to live well, and happily, no matter what the circumstances. She was, indeed, my soul.

The good news is that despite the precedent, despite the odds, *she* didn't go anywhere. Sure, she was lost for a year in yards of silk shantung and crinoline, and for another year in a jungle of things no one tells the bride. But just as you will, I emerged from the crinoline and the secrets essentially the same person I was before I got married, only much happier and much wiser. I can honestly say that I love being married.

Most of the brides I talked to said that sometime in the second year of marriage they stopped being so alert to the changes. They stopped being their own lifeguards. As a bride, or a bride-to-be, this may sound daunting. Does that mean those women were lulled into not caring about their own individuality? Or is it possible they simply stopped worrying as much about the undertow and let themselves enjoy the swim?

In the pages that follow, you will meet many brides who never knew they would, but who are enjoying the swim, strengthening their strokes, and finding that love buoys them. They are trying to defy what's expected, and they are richer for it.

Mara, a thirty-two-year-old writer from Vancouver, British Columbia, said she always thought of herself as a "lonely artist." There was no place in her identity for a house, for permanence, for lack of travel, or for giving her husband so much when, as a writer, she needed so much herself. "My dream was to pay off my last school loan and go off to Italy, even though I really couldn't afford it."

So when Mara fell in love with the man who is now her husband, she fought it rigorously. Never mind that this was the man who bought her earrings just because she had had a bad day; a man who, without being asked, folded three hundred flyers for a volunteer organization picnic she was promoting; a man who enjoyed the idea that she would have a more successful career than he would. Mara was still sure that she couldn't "be a good artist and be married."

Then a friend asked Mara to name her favorite writers, which she promptly did: Joan Didion and Margaret Atwood. Surprising herself, Mara admitted to her friend that both of these writers were married, and had been for more than twenty years. Now married herself, Mara says she is more content with her life than at any previous time. But it isn't a storybook. Their marriage is fraught with arguments, and if it isn't, she starts them. And, her dreams have not died or been subsumed. She still plans to go to Italy and to do it by herself, which her husband encourages, albeit for three months and not for a year as she'd prefer.

3. MAKE YOUR OWN MARRIAGE.

The third message of this book, and the best thing that no one tells the bride, is that there is no one method for marriage, at least not for happy ones. First, you plan a wedding that befits you. And then, by trial and error, you learn what works for you in *your* marriage, in your household, in the juggling of careers and finances, in the sharing of dust bunnies and rude and smelly bodily functions.

In essence, you sculpt your own union, a marriage as

devoted and as traditional in some respects as good marriages always are, but in other ways as zany and liberating as your experience of life when you were single. You throw out as much of the institution as you want to, or as much as you can, and you make your own marriage.

In the examples brides offer in the pages that follow, you'll see that many different kinds of marriages can be extraordinarily comfortable and happy. Each chapter begins with a reassurance and a pearl of wisdom—advice that helped my friends and me in a similar time of need. The chapters continue by giving you the lowdown on what no one tells the bride—about everything from money to sex to power struggles—and then our ideas for confronting the problems. Again, these are ideas, not a formula, because only you and your husband can come up with a formula for your marriage, and yet even when you do, you'll constantly be revamping it to meet the dynamic needs of your relationship.

Talking about her seventeen-year marriage to Phil Donahue, Marlo Thomas recently said: "I think what scared me away from marriage was the idea that there is only one way to do it. Then I realized you could design your own and it could fit your needs; you didn't have to fit into someone else's definition."

Women do not have to lose themselves or their freedom in marriage. We have to imagine, and then doggedly pursue, something better for ourselves.

Imagination, then, is our most powerful ally when conspiring against a life of clichés, against the institution, against divorce, and against unhappiness. My first inkling of this came on a bachelorette trip to Jamaica, when my friend Terry read excerpts of Thomas Moore's *SoulMates* to me out loud in the sunshine. She read, "A person in marriage who longs for freedom, finding marriage too limiting and confining, might best avoid the temptation to flee and instead work at re-imagining the marriage. [Her] notion of marriage is likely too limited."

My memories of Moore's words, the cadence of my friend's voice, and the safety of a seaside hammock have rocked me through many hard times over the past two-and-a-half years of newly married life. And I hope the following chapters impart the same calm and inspiration to you as you begin sketching the marriage you have on your drawing table.

Perhaps the most reassuring words my friends and I can offer, whether you are newly engaged or newly married, is that you need not remain in the dark. You need not fear the weird dreams you've been having or the unsettling thoughts you've entertained. Instead, breathe deeply, and believe that your venture into love will succeed. Between my husband and me, and fifty other new marriages we have come to know, we have summoned the heart to tell you what no one usually tells the bride.

WHAT NO ONE TELLS THE BRIDE ABOUT . . .

The bridal and newlywed experience:

∞ You'll feel shrouded in silence the first year of marriage.

∞ You'll feel self-conscious about having probelms and about asking for help.

∞ You'll worry about whether you can be happy in marriage.

∞ You'll worry about losing your identity in marriage.

∞ All of the above are normal reactions.

Our brides' solution:

∞ Believe you can be happy in marriage.

∞ Challenge conventional thinking.

∞ Make your own marriage.

Chapter 1

LOVE'S IDENTITY CRISIS:
THE MODERN BRIDE'S INNER TURMOIL

It's normal for brides to feel wildly disoriented. It's normal for your priorities to shift. But don't try to align your star with a fixed point in the sky. Let the things you cherish be a constellation, one more prominent in the sky one night, another brighter the next.

Unless you got married on the San Andreas fault, your wedding was technically not a seismic event. No matter how it felt to you, or to your mother, when the man in your life proposed, no Geiger counter leapt in a flourish of ink. And when your sister or your best friend stood in the back of the church and pulled a blusher down over your face, it's a safe bet that the ground did not actually rumble or split open.

But as a bride, you have undoubtedly experienced a kind of inner quake. While relatively little time has passed, the whole landscape of your life has changed. And though you invited this change and do not want to return to your former life, and though you have known the man you are marrying for a long time, it's likely that very little about engagement or early marriage feels truly safe or familiar to you.

As rare as it is that anyone talks about it, this is the

way many brides feel. Instead, we talk about the external chaos that surrounds brides—about families who turn into the Hatfields and McCoys over the simple matter of a guest list, and bridesmaids who go on strike demanding better dresses and an open bar after dinner.

Women on the cusp of marriage rarely snatch moments between bridal showers and gown fittings to consider their inner turmoil. This chapter is about precisely that. It is about the zillions of feelings you have about crossing a threshold—from what has defined your life since you left home to what will define your life in the future. These feelings sneak up on brides who think they are already fully formed adults, who haven't felt growing pains like this since adolescence or since they were first out on their own. But, as Dalma Heyn, the author of *Marriage Shock,* suggests, "Becoming a wife is, after all, one of the three critical life changes for a woman. It commands as profound an adjustment psychologically and emotionally as her earlier transition into puberty did and as motherhood will."

In the following pages, my friends and I will share how we fared in this disorienting time. Not so much how we overcame disagreements between our mothers and future mothers-in-law over the wedding. Nor about how we packed up our "single girl" apartments, the rooms hollow and echoing when we left. But how we *felt about ourselves* amid the arguments over the wedding, and amid the hollow, echoing walls of our former apartments.

The growing pains my friends and I experienced fell into the following categories:

You Have to Adjust to Your Own Happiness

Having someone love you and want to devote the rest of his life to you is life-changing in and of itself. It is especially so for women who are accustomed to having dating relationships crash and burn, and for those of us who, deep down, didn't believe that someone *would* love us this way. Frequently, it takes time for the reality to sink in—that this man is here for the long haul, that this man loves you *for you.*

I was very happy being single. I hit my stride with it, as most of my friends did, four or five years out of college. I placed a book on my coffee table called *Solitude* and touted the advantages of a solitary life, especially for a writer.

But then along came Duke, who loved it when I drank beer straight out of a pitcher, who wanted to get up and go to church with me the next morning even though he hadn't spent much time in church before, and who knew that the phone company turned off my phone because I paid for a plane ticket to Portugal before I paid my utilities. He knew all my foibles, the ones I hid behind my "composed career woman" exterior, and yet he was still crazy about me.

Having someone love me this much shook me up. Until he proposed, I'm not sure I really believed him. The night we got engaged, and all the nights thereafter, I slept like a dog in the sun. Something important had been settled, although I had denied, or ignored, for many years that "that something" was important to me.

Happiness is a tricky thing. Sometimes friends don't want to hear about it. Happiness feels frivolous, as opposed to angst, which is more substantial and inspires artists and heartfelt talks. Happiness also makes you paranoid. Many brides I know became fatalistic before their weddings, sure that an illness or a car or plane crash would prevent them from walking down the aisle.

I read this excerpt from Laurie Colwin's short story "The Lone Pilgrim" to the assembled at our rehearsal dinner the night before our wedding. Some of the guests were undoubtedly bewildered by it, but I know you will appreciate how alienated the narrator feels from her own fairy tale:

You long for someone to love. You find him. You pine for him. Suddenly, you discover that you are loved in return. You marry. Before you do, you count up the days you spent in other people's kitchens, at dinner tables, putting other people's children to bed. You have basked in a sense of domesticity you have not created but enjoy. The Lone Pilgrim sits at the dinner parties of others, partakes, savors, and goes home in a taxi alone.

Those days were spent in quest—the quest to settle your own life, and now the search has ended. Your imagined happiness is yours. Therefore, you lose your old bearings. On the one side is your happiness, and on the other is your past—the self you were used to, going through life alone, heir to your own experience. Once you commit yourself, everything changes and the rest of your life seems to you like a dark forest on the property you have recently acquired. It is yours, but still you are afraid to enter it, wondering what you might find: a little chapel, a stand of birches, wolves, snakes, the worst you can imagine, or the best. You take one timid step forward, but then you realize that

you are not alone. You take someone's hand—
[your fiancé's]—and strain through the darkness to
see ahead.

That which you and your fiancé will strain through
the darkness to see ahead is change, a virtual tsunami of
change, which brings me to the second growing pain
brides experience.

You Will Be Bombarded with Change

If you have dated or lived with your husband-to-be for
a while, marriage may feel like a natural and logical step
for you. But for most of the women I interviewed, marriage was not just a technicality. It often prompted a
makeover of their lives.

Natasha, a twenty-six-year-old bride from Portland,
Oregon, met her future husband, Israel, at a New Year's
Eve dance at church and married him five-and-a-half
months later. Natasha is white and Israel is African-
American but these differences didn't intimidate them,
having been raised to love all people and having the
support of a broad-minded church community. And yet
they couldn't have been prepared for the scrutiny they'd
endure as a biracial couple with the onset of the O. J.
Simpson media frenzy.

At her job as a corporate receptionist, Natasha was
appalled to have colleagues ask her "Does your husband
beat you?", or say things like "I don't do dark meat, not
even on Thanksgiving." Then, one time when they
were driving on the highway, they were followed into
a rest stop and chastised by a group of teenagers who
appeared to be "skinheads." Fortunately, Natasha and
Israel have been happily married for four years now, and

their relationship has been bolstered by the difficulties they have had to overcome. Nevertheless, the culture shock they experienced with marriage was immense.

Another bride I know experienced a vastly different form of culture shock, moving from Pennsylvania to China to join her fiancé, an American starting a business in Shanghai. Thirty-year-old Eliza learned Mandarin, found a job with an American company, lived with her betrothed for the first time, ate all sorts of things she didn't recognize, grew to love China and the people she met, supported her fiancé through the start-up of his business, and planned two weddings, one in China and the other in the States, all in one year. "Who needs a honeymoon?!" she laughs. "The whole engagement has been an adventure!"

I need a honeymoon just *thinking* about what she went through. And yet, on top of the monumental changes marriage often brings, couples dollop other changes, too. Right before or right after their weddings, many couples leave their jobs, move to new cities, buy houses or cars, get pets or have babies, launch businesses or change religions. I did this, too, leaving my home in Boston to settle on the blond coast, where Duke was stationed in San Diego.

Nearly every bride I interviewed made one or several of these major life changes in the midst of what was already a fundamental life change. In many cases, it seemed that people who stayed single longer felt compelled to "catch up" with peers who had been married for a while. And this is strange, because just months before, many of these brides and grooms were well-adjusted single people. They led busy, vibrant lives. It didn't appear as if their lives had been "on hold" for marriage at all.

Nevertheless, the decision to marry sends many brides and grooms charging out of the gate toward other life goals. During these vulnerable first years of marriage, we introduce even more stress into our lives. After all, planning a wedding is one of the top ten causes of stress, but so is moving to a new home. Having a baby makes the top ten, too.

My friend Morgan, a thirty-three-year-old artist from Portland, Maine, and her husband, Joe, were so worried she'd have trouble conceiving that they started trying to have a baby right away. They had not had a long courtship to begin with, but their desire to start a family was intense. (See Chapter 9 for more about timing any additions to your family.)

Morgan got pregnant two months after they were married, at a time when she and Joe were having agonizing arguments. Morgan was trying to cope with her disappointment that the marriage wasn't as intimate as she thought it should be. She couldn't believe that, such a short time ago, she had been a self-reliant, level-headed single woman. Newly married, pregnant, and unhappy, Morgan was as scared and as vulnerable as she has ever been.

For Morgan and Joe, the prospect of becoming parents forced them to slow down and start building a better foundation. She says, "It was incredible to find that we had a total commitment to finding a solution. The baby's coming really solidified things; there was no bailing out."

They made a difficult first call to a couples' counselor whom they would come to like and respect. Morgan read a lot of books and they had a lot of talks so that now, she says, "the marriage works much better for us. I've learned a lot and Joe met me halfway." Now their arguments are not nearly as bad because, Morgan realizes that, when they are over, "love comes back over and over again."

The marriage still isn't as intimate as Morgan would like, although having a child has brought them closer together. But she realizes that the closeness she desires comes with sharing experiences and overcoming problems together, something that builds over time.

For Morgan, pregnancy brought on *jamais vu*, the French translation of which is "never seen." This, I learned, is just one aspect of feeling lost in your own life, the third pang that newly married women, and women on the verge of marriage, experience.

You Feel Lost in Your Own Life

The opposite of déjà vu, which we've all experienced before, *jamais vu* occurs when, for a second or two, everything around you feels alien. Your husband-to-be seems like a stranger, the wedding plans a farce, and the prospect of lifelong commitment with this person the most insane of concepts.

I was very relieved to read there was a name for this phenomenon—and to find in my research that other brides had experienced it, too—because I had four or five incidents of *jamais vu*, one of which occurred shortly after I moved to California before we were married. Duke and I had flown from San Diego to San Francisco for the weekend to have dinner at the home of Carole Lynn, one of Duke's best friends, whom I was meeting for the first time. We had too much wine at dinner and afterward a rancorous political discussion in which Carole Lynn and I ganged up on Duke. Normally a very gentle and kind man, Duke was tired, fuzzy-headed, and pushed to his limit. So he walked out, presumably leaving me, at one in the morning, at the house of someone I barely knew, without money or the hotel key.

Of course, Duke didn't really leave me. He was waiting and cooling down outside. But in that instant I realized how utterly vulnerable I was, how much I risked by loving him and casting my fate alongside his. It was a defining moment. Because before the apologies were uttered, we chose one another all over again. We got into a taxi, stormed up to our hotel room, talked well into the night, huddled together in bed, and sheepishly called Carole Lynn the next morning to apologize.

Undoubtedly, you have had your defining moments, too times when nothing loomed bigger than your own vulnerability. As brides, we feel we could easily be subsumed by all the hoopla over the wedding and by the expectations everyone has of the newlywed year. It feels to us as if our very sense of self is threatened.

Author Dalma Heyn believes the Institution of Marriage—three centuries of traditional expectations and

> ### BRIDE-TO-BRIDE
>
> *What has been the most disconcerting change in you since you got married?*
>
> ∞ "I haven't been able to maintain my strict eating habits, so I'm gaining weight."
>
> ∞ "I have had trouble with the whole 'settled down' thing, you know: marriage, responsibility, your own home. I felt for a while that I wasn't fun anymore. But then I realized, I was happy being settled."
>
> ∞ "I used to travel alone for my job. Now that I'm married and living in a new place, I want my husband to go everywhere with me, even to the grocery store. I have become so dependent on him."
>
> ∞ "I feel pulled between pleasing my parents, my husband, and myself. It's hard to shift gears—to accept that what may be best for us as a couple may not be popular with my family."
>
> ∞ "Loss of freedom."

role models—closes in on a bride, distracting her with all the fuss over the wedding and exerting pressure on her to put aside her sexuality, her creativity, and her individuality to become an "ideal wife." She found that newly married women believed they had to "clean up" their sexual résumés, cut themselves off from their friends and their own feelings in order to meet this ideal. Brides she spoke to often expressed a fear of "going under."

This was true of the brides I interviewed. But I also saw my husband and other grooms I know do many of the same things, squirming in this adjustment period as if their manhood was threatened. Duke, for example, applied some revisionist history to his womanizing reputation while at the same time he laughed with friends that his marriage was a sign of the apocalypse. He made me go back to Goodwill and repurchase pint glasses of his I donated without asking him, and took great pleasure in telling his friends he had done so.

In the "You Won't Change Me" game we resorted to so often during our first months of matrimony, both of us played to win. And yet I do not believe the stakes in this transition were as high for Duke as they were for me, or that his questions ran as deep. He feared marriage would make him look weak. I feared marriage would consume me.

When I fell in love with Duke, it felt to me as if I had gone back to Sunday school, as if I was suddenly becoming reacquainted with the important virtues in life—honesty, goodness, kindness, and fidelity. Of course, that's how I knew that this was someone I wanted to raise a family with and spend the rest of my life with. But it also made me wonder what kind of heathen I was before. Had I gotten so far away from those values when I was single? Now that I was engaged, did I really need to disavow my entire single life, as it seemed so many married people wanted me to do?

These were the questions that bothered me most. Did I have to give up who I was to be married? I knew that, to a certain extent, it was natural for love to change my perspective and my priorities, but I also felt—and know many other brides who felt—this was a slippery slope. One wrong move and I might very well "go under," which brings me to the last growing pain brides experience.

You Will See Things Differently

A few weeks after I got married, I thought I had made that one wrong move. On a hot, San Diego day, I had spread wedding photo proofs all over the living room floor and was trying to whittle down the cost of our order—to live without just one of the dozen or so pictures of the adorable flower girl, or of Duke and me kissing—when it hit me.

The summer after I finished fifth grade, a camp counselor at a Presbyterian camp in Parkville, Missouri, urged me and my fellow campers to imagine that, God forbid, our houses had caught on fire. "You, your family members, and your pets will escape unharmed," she told us, "but you have time to save one item from your home. What would you save?"

For the past seventeen years, my answer to her question had remained the same. I would have saved my journals.

I have been keeping a journal since I was eight. Back then I called it a diary, and it was under lock and key. Today, I have more than fifty journals—the entire written record of my life—and believe it or not, I keep them in a fire retardant bag. I had never had any doubts about what I would grab if I awakened to a smoke alarm.

But as a recent bride, squinting through a loop to see who was sitting where in the pews of the church, the photos sticking to my sweaty, exposed calves, I realized that my answer had changed. I could no longer sweep up my journals and take the rungs of the hook and ladder by twos. The wedding album would come first.

I am ashamed to write this down. Just six weeks into my marriage, the record of one day in my life had come to mean more to me than that of the previous thirty-one years. Overnight, this one black album—bulky as it is, my new name embossed in gold on the front—had become more important to me than fifty books I had written myself. How could I already be putting the story of our union before my individual story?

Well, here's the truth. I have now looked at my wedding pictures so many times, and collected enough snapshots from friends, to last me for at least a quarter of a century. I have come back to my senses. I know that I could replace at least some of my wedding photos if they burned in a fire. But I should also tell you that since I've been married, I no longer keep a journal. I write letters to Duke when he is at sea, I write lengthy E-mails to friends, and I write articles for magazines. But only rarely, maybe three times a year, do I write purely for myself. Happiness is not the burning topic that thwarted love was. These days, when I am lost or hurting, my first instinct is to turn to Duke.

My journals were my identity badge. You undoubtedly have some of your own—medals from a marathon you run every year, a job you love, or a home you bought and restored. And the idea that your commitment to them or your interest in them may wane is very unsettling. Today the mere suggestion that a woman change for a man is heresy. A single woman's mantra is self-reliance, so the prospect of that self eroding, or changing in any way, is menacing.

But some of the identity we shore up in single life is defensive in nature. I didn't used to think so. When Duke and I first met, he had a difficult time getting me to fall in love with him. He blamed my "hard exterior," something he was sure had formed as a result of disappointments I'd experienced in previous relationships. I maintained that my trail of pain had nothing to do with it, that I enjoyed a full, stimulating life and wasn't going to drop everything for him. Today, I see the truth lay somewhere in the middle.

Shortly after I got married, I went to a friend's rehearsal dinner. When I asked some mutual friends who were bridesmaids about our friend's wedding gown, they rolled their eyes and said it was white and long and had daisies on it. Their contempt leapt out at me.

About the same time, I also talked to a college friend who had been married for five years. She couldn't understand why more of our classmates weren't married. I had to point out to her that perhaps they enjoyed being single or that it was difficult finding the right man. Even though this woman had served for a while with my friends and me in the trenches of single life, love seemed to have turned her into a total mush brain.

This, I think, is a modern bride's quandary. You still have some of your hard exterior, some contempt for the traditions the world tells women we have to adopt. You also enjoy the way love is softening you, the way you and the man in your life are infusing these previously loathed traditions with your own meaning. You just don't want to be completely co-opted by the

traditions. You don't want love to turn you into a total mush brain.

I remember flinching when friends and relatives said
I had a storybook wedding or a fairy-tale romance. I
knew these were supposed to be compliments. But to
me, the best thing about my relationship with Duke was
that it was *real*. Despite the passing of time, Duke didn't
turn out to be the psycho so many of my previous Prince
Charmings had been. To me, the best thing about my
marriage, and all the wedding traditions we would
choose to embrace, was that it truly was *my choice*, not a
canned destiny lent to me by a Disney studio.

This is the internal squabble every bride I know endures. In it, your identity badges square off against the
symbols of matrimony, as if they are fixed points on
opposite ends of a spectrum. You bash bridal magazines
at the same time you're stocking up on them, stealing
away to drugstores and magazine aisles. You *say* you
want to run off to Vegas and have Elvis marry you, but
you proceed to plan the world's most traditional wedding. And you run off with your girlfriends for one last
bachelorette weekend but pine for your fiancé while
you're away.

It is an exceedingly confusing time when, indeed, you
lose all your old bearings. And as you try to find them
again, you draw lines in the sand that marriage better
not make you cross, and that your husband-to-be and
his family had better stay far away from.

But what if love, not some tired traditional thinking,
is the catalyst for change? What if your heart expands
and you have to make room for new badges, for new
sources of identity? I am not denying the existence of
other threats, but I know that a year or two into mar-

riage, many women find their bearings again, and feel their equilibrium is restored. As was true for me, many emerge from wedding albums and gold-embossed fairy tales to make room for real love and real happiness. Eventually, the acute fear of "going under" goes away, not because the brides themselves disappear but because they learn to make marriage their own.

Managing Love's Identity Crisis

Until that day, you may ask, how is a bride to manage love's identity crisis and its pangs? How can you adjust to your own happiness, handle the bombardment of change, overcome the sense of being lost in your own life, and not be threatened when love begins to change some of your perspectives and priorities? Other than remaining prone in the arms of your lover, here is the advice my friends and I wish someone had given us.

1. GIVE YOURSELF A LOT OF REIN.

Horses need extra rein before they can jump five-foot-high hurdles. And couples need it to jump the broom, to lift the veil, and to stomp on the wineglass. A new marriage is a magnificent hurdle.

Katie, a thirty-six-year-old graphic designer whose husband proposed on a park bench in the Boston Public Garden, was not planning her wedding hastily enough for those of us excited for her. She wouldn't let anyone throw her a shower; she coveted her privacy.

Katie's wedding eventually unfolded, stunningly beautiful and meaningful at the Ritz-Carlton Hotel across the street from the Public Garden. But I realize now how wise she was to keep the revelry at arm's length, saying,

"When the time comes, Michael and I will have a great party. But for now I don't want to hurry anything. I just want to savor the feeling of being engaged."

Katie had been unhappily married before. And I think that with this wonderful second marriage, she was pacing herself, giving herself time to absorb the happiness of the event and the realization of so many things she had wanted in her life.

Few brides do this. In fact, I have known brides who bought their wedding dresses before they were even engaged. Most couples feel pressured to rush madly into the details, either because their parents are about to burst with excitement, because churches and reception halls are booked a year in advance, or because wedding planners urge them to get their ducks in a row. And as I said before, there's a propensity among newlyweds to rush headlong into other major life changes as well.

Like Katie, you need to give yourself time to enjoy being engaged. The traditional one-year engagement has many advantages in this respect; it gives both the bride and groom time to savor the celebration and sift through the emotional consequences of their decision to marry, to find themselves, and the centrality of their love, amid cake tastings and tuxedo rentals.

BRIDE-TO-BRIDE

What is the best change about you since getting engaged/ married?

∞ "Who I am when I am with my husband. He brings out the best in me."

∞ "Stability. I've always gone out too much, and taken on too many projects. It's better with the 'ole ball and chain.'"

∞ "I've become a better listener."

∞ "I feel secure in my relationship with my fiancé and I am really enjoying the deepening of our friendship and trust in one another."

∞ "I am more balanced and more at peace."

Resist the temptation to rush. Feel indignant when your nosy aunt asks when you plan to have children. Retell the story of your husband's proposal a hundred times because the fact that you have found him, and he you, should be splendid enough for people who love you.

Distance yourself from people who make you feel as though you are about to be stamped by a matrimonial cookie cutter, as if you should be feeling a certain way. Instead, give yourself permission to feel conflicting emotions—to entertain a real joy and a real sadness, both eagerness and fear, both utter peace and utter annoyance. Having conflicting emotions doesn't mean you shouldn't be getting married. It means that you are human.

2. DON'T NUMBER YOUR PRIORITIES.

Stephen Dunn writes in his poem "Traveling" that when the devil comes looking for companionship, the traveler recites for him a list of things he or she has learned to live without. That list, he writes, "is stronger than prayer."

Indeed, a single woman's dignity lies in the list of things she's learned to live without—namely, marriage and a family, which society still expects of women. So how do you cope with the emotional enormity of finding someone who enhances your life and your happiness? How do you incorporate into your world the very person you've denied needing without compromising yourself, your dignity, or your achievements?

For one thing, stop haranguing yourself for being happy. And don't force yourself, or let anyone else force you, to number your priorities during this vulnerable time.

I am sure my camp counselor was well intentioned, but brides are under enough stress without thinking that any minute the priority police, or perhaps I should say the priority firemen, are going to come along and force you to decide what comes first: your marriage or your career, your friends or your family, your bowling league or your synagogue, your armoire or his coffee table.

The brides I've met have made a tentative peace with their undulating priorities. They can make sweeping romantic statements like "I love you more than anything" and know in their heart of hearts, as their husbands do, that this is not entirely true. No one dissects sweet nothings, or at least no one should.

In their revolutionary study, *American Couples*, Philip Blumstein and Pepper Schwartz found that the happier working wives are in their jobs, the happier they are in their marriages. This is a far more revealing statistic than the one the Roper Organization put forth, in which 51 percent of the women who were polled would pick their careers over their families if they could not have both. Obviously, with the population they polled split down the middle, we can see that women prize both. Both these priorities contribute to their happiness.

Although we are no longer naïve enough to think women can "do it all" without feeling exhausted and conflicted, there is something really therapeutic about just accepting the presence of more than one first priority. That doesn't mean that in a pinch, come illness or hardship, you wouldn't rally around your husband and family, the more important priority at the time. That doesn't mean that it will be easy juggling a career and a marriage, walking the dog and training for a marathon. But after the initial adjustments, you'll be surprised to see that marriages can run smoothly. There truly are few drastic times in which you will be forced to divulge your ranking of priorities, in which you will have to prove something to someone. Amazingly, when you need some time to yourself, your husband will love you enough to give it to you. When you need to work late, he will understand, and vice versa. The two of you will have private negotiations and make your own individual pacts and trade-offs. In the presence of unconditional love, these priorities flourish, and swing back and forth, far more naturally than you'd think.

There will also be plenty of times in marriage when you will exercise the survival skills you learned as a single woman. Because, to be truly happy in marriage, you have to learn to live without certain things, just as you did before.

3. HOLD ON TO SOME IDENTITY BADGES.

The Japanese have a wedding tradition in which all the bride's girlhood possessions and playthings get thrown into a roaring bonfire. I have to hand it to them, because at least they acknowledge the identity crisis many brides experience, leaving one world behind to embrace another. But I think brides, and grooms, need some possessions from their former lives, some of their identity badges, nearby to help them feel safe in this vulnerable time.

Neal Cassidy, a character in many of Jack Kerouac's stories, liked women. He married twice but said he kept a packed suitcase under his bed so he was always ready to go. I would suggest the opposite may have been true.

Isn't it possible that his packed suitcase gave him the wherewithal to stay?

With a divorce rate that exceeds fifty percent, all of us who enter into marriage today are "wired" differently from previous generations who understood that marriage is a lifelong commitment. Often, this approach and its escape clause gives us permission to be lazy and unimaginative about marriage.

Instead of plotting your escape, try to envision a marriage in which your freedom, and the symbols of your freedom, are cherished. Let me explain. Most of the single people I know function with hand-me-down plates and bargain-basement silverware, but I have a set of Italian ceramic dishes I bought at Marshall Field's when I was in graduate school. Buying them was a great triumph for me because I didn't wait for a bridal shower to fill my cabinets; I cared enough about myself to set my own beautiful dinner table. Eight years later, when it came time to register, I told Duke I didn't want any new "everyday ware." And today, at the dinner table Duke and I share, these dishes still feel like a triumph to me.

The cusp of marriage is fraught with change, both physical and emotional. Some of the landmarks of your life will slip away, but some you should cling to as if your life depended on it. This may mean you have to hang your husband's poster of Comiskey Park in your living room. And he may have to stomach your grandmother's chintz chair.

Emily, a thirty-seven-year-old director of operations at a company in Salt Lake City, and Jonathan, her husband of a year and a half, began pinching pennies to buy a home and absorb the costs of a new baby. Months ago, Emily changed to a health club that was $100 cheaper

per month and encouraged Jonathan to do the same. Although maintaining his club membership didn't make a lot of rational sense, Jonathan was loathe to give it up, since he had joined there when he first moved to Salt Lake City and subsequently met many of his friends there.

Emily says, "He finally did switch clubs a few months ago, but it was a really hard decision for him to make." She also found it difficult to part with some vestiges of single life. This winter, when she was pregnant and Jonathan was away at a ski cabin they had rented, Emily went through her scrapbooks and found pictures of the man she had dated for six-and-a-half years, prior to her relationship with Jonathan. "By then, I was ready to throw all the photos away. Before, when we got married, I hadn't been."

Neither Emily nor I would suggest that fingering a picture of an old boyfriend is healthy for your new marriage, but sometimes, being surrounded by familiar things makes the power struggles, and the You Can't Change Me game you and your new husband will play, a little less threatening. In the absence of many of your old bearings, these symbols will be a great comfort to you.

Eventually, you'll grow confident enough in your new marriage that you won't need to cling to these symbols anymore. You'll make your peace with the changes marriage brings. But in the meantime, tell your mate what it is you treasure most about yourself. Encourage each other to hold on to some of those "sacred cows." In time, you may even fight for each other's right to preserve them.

That's why one husband-to-be did everything possible, including some discreet cutting and pasting, to get his future bride's sofa through the doorway of his apartment. And why another eschews time he and his bride could have together, insisting she maintain two part-time jobs that he knows are essential to her happiness.

When you keep some of your identity badges nearby, you are reminded of who you are. You don't try to align your star with some random fixed point; you become your own guide, taking the hand of your beloved and peering into the darkness. This is critical if you are to do battle with the conventions of marriage.

My friend Mara, the Vancouver writer who never dreamed she would marry, felt at first that her marriage was too volatile and too argumentative to be considered "happy." She described raging fights sparked by trivial things, like a comment her husband made while watching Olympic figure skaters. She told a friend her marriage was doomed because of it.

Mara's friend pointed out to her that Mara's marriage was the mirror image of Mara's life—rough and tumble. Mara had always thrived on doom. Her marriage wasn't a fairy tale because she didn't really like fairy tales. When life got too tame, Mara and her husband churned things up again.

WHAT NO ONE TELLS THE BRIDE ABOUT . . .

Love's identity crisis:
- You have to adjust to your own happiness.
- You will be bombarded with change.
- You will feel lost in your own life.
- You will see things differently.

Our brides' solution:
- Give yourself a lot of rein.
- Don't number your priorities.
- Hold on to some identity badges.

Having a friend suggest that her marriage matched her life, and was aligned with her personality, gave Mara permission to relax. She stopped feeling she had to change, and started enjoying the marriage for what it was: not everyone else's ideal, but a marriage that worked for her.

And this is what will eventually happen to you if you stay cognizant, not defensive, about what is at stake in marriage. Remember, Neal Cassidy's suitcase was stored under the bed. It was a quiet mainstay, a fixture he knew was there, without his flaunting it.

In my mind, this is the only graceful way to traverse the gulf between singleness and marriage. In this period of adjustment, give yourself time and space, refuse to number your priorities, and hold on to some treasured symbols of your independence. In time, "your world" will be turned upright again. As in a snow globe, the confetti will settle, the air bubble will again sit up on top, and village life will resume. It is at that point that you will most appreciate the following excerpt from one of Ellen Goodman's *Boston Globe* columns:

> There's a trick to the Graceful Exit, I suspect. It begins with the vision to recognize when a job, a life stage, a relationship is over, and let go. It means leaving what's over without denying its validity or its past importance in our lives.
>
> It involves a sense of future, a belief that every exit line is an entry, that we are moving on, rather than out . . .
>
> The trick of changing well may be a trick of living well. It's hard to recognize that life isn't a holding action, but a process. It's hard to learn that

we don't leave the best parts of ourselves behind
. . . We OWN what we learned back there.

The experiences and the growth are grafted onto
our lives. And when we exit, we can take ourselves
along. Quite gracefully.

Chapter 2

FROM THIS DAY FORWARD:
THE TUMULTUOUS ENGAGEMENT
AND WEDDING

It's normal for the engagement to be peppered with fear, tension, and discord. It's normal to feel inadequate compared to the fairy tale. But the only real source of splendor is faith, holding on to your groom's hand, and choosing the great unknown.

When I tell the story of how Duke proposed on that ski slope in Taos, New Mexico, I always leave one thing out. I call it poetic license; Duke calls it selective truth. But the fact is that about a half hour after we got engaged, we started arguing about the wedding.

We would have started sooner had I not been struck, the minute I got the ring, with the urgent need to go the bathroom. We skied down the mountain to the nearest lodge. Then, once I was in the privacy of my own stall, I spent a good ten minutes gawking at my ring. Holding it out in front of me. Holding it up to the light. Knowing someone would ask me if it was a full carat and wondering if there was any delicate way of asking Duke if it was.

Yes, it's true. These are the crass, inner thoughts of a woman who just got engaged. Like the arguments about the wedding that start almost immediately after you get engaged, they are not a well-publicized part of the fairy tale. They are what this chapter is devoted to, helping real brides-to-be—and those of you who think your marriage got off to a rocky start because of hassles over the wedding—evaluate what's truly important about this tradition-laden launch into matrimony. You'll see that engagements are often fraught with friction, bad dreams, irrationality, and fear. And that most brides are both seduced and intimidated by the "ideal" —a set of storybook standards that can keep you from enjoying the magic of the engagement and the wedding.

BRIDE-TO-BRIDE

During your engagement, when were you most frightened?

∞ "When my fiancé's aunt told me what patterns and cookware to register for and asked where I was going to get my dress and all these other questions I hadn't thought about the first ten days of being engaged. I was completely overwhelmed."

∞ "When my fiancé asked me about my finances. I had so much debt from school loans and credit cards that I thought he'd rescind his proposal."

∞ "When I felt ambivalent about getting married."

∞ "When I had a fling four months before my wedding. I feared my fiancé would find out."

∞ "Three months before the wedding when I got very cold feet. I wasn't sure I could be the 'perfect wife.'"

Trying Not to Blow Your Cover

I told my mom and a few close friends about the arguments I had with Duke about the wedding. But like the fact that months before he proposed, Duke and I had gone to a jeweler so I could point out rings I liked, it was something I wouldn't admit to acquaintances. It was my turn at the fairy tale, and I wasn't going to blow my cover. I wanted everyone to think Duke had exquisite taste in jewelry and a tremendous knack for secrecy, and that he wanted more than anything for me to have the wedding I'd always dreamed about. And of course, both of those things were true, except I had slightly more input than I let on.

When I say slightly more, I should clarify that at our rehearsal dinner, when I was thanking my parents for letting me plan the wedding myself, Duke yelled out, to the amusement of our guests, "As if they had any choice!" And although it wasn't the most flattering portrait, I will admit that when it came to our wedding, I was a controlling shrew. Compromise did not come easily.

Controlling shrew. Perfume advertisement in which a bride is surrounded by angelic flower girls dancing in the sunlight. Betrothed couple yelling at each other on the chairlift. TV commercial in which silhouetted couple embraces as the symphony music swells and the diamond glistens. You see the difference. There's a lot of pressure on brides to look as if everything were perfect.

Waiting for "This Is It!"

Like every bride, my friend Abigail, a human resources specialist in Vermont, wanted the perfect wedding gown. She had heard so many stories about women and their perfect wedding gowns that when it came time for her to buy THE DRESS, she kept expecting to try one on and have the "This is it!" sensation. She'd heard of women falling in love with the first dress they tried on. She knew that when she put on the right dress, she and her mother were supposed to dissolve into tears.

But Abigail found she had a favorite dress at this boutique and a favorite dress at another. None of the gowns brought tears to her or her mother's eyes, except maybe when they saw the price tags. So Abigail ended up having a dress made for her, a simple gown that nevertheless combined favorite elements of dresses she'd liked. And she went on with her plans for a summer wedding in Vermont with a pig roast rehearsal dinner, a reception under a tent in her best friend's backyard, colorful flowers in watering cans and music everyone could dance to. For her, this was a storybook wedding.

I was relating Abigail's predicament to a friend of mine who commented, "She shouldn't feel bad. I've never felt 'This is it!' about anything in my life!" The point is, brides are radically different, so we can't pipe our reactions out of a tube like a cake decorator does with icing. Many brides are simply unfazed by the fuss of weddings. One who hated shopping sent her groom to register and then watched his preferences—peculiar, albeit utilitarian—accrue in their home. "Who would have thought of registering for huge pots for ficus trees? Only my husband!" The same bride asked her mom to put together the same wedding her older sister had had months before, because she'd enjoyed it so much and because she cared very little about all the details.

Nevertheless, not measuring up to the fairy tale leaves some brides feeling slighted and inferior. You think to yourself, If I'm not feeling what I'm supposed to be feeling, should I be getting married? Or, If we're fighting this much now, what will we be like after the wedding? Or, If my fiancé isn't enthusiastic about the wedding or about getting involved in the planning, does that mean he isn't enthusiastic about *me*?

Ominous Signs, Worst-Case Scenarios

Right off the bat, I should tell you that most of my friends, and most of the women I befriended during interviews for this book, said their weddings caused more arguments during the engagement than anything did subsequently during the first years of their marriages. Even women in their thirties and forties, who took charge of their weddings more than younger women with controlling parents did, said that planning the nuptials caused many headaches. Once the wedding was over, brides said, much of the stress in their relationships disappeared.

Nevertheless, when you're engaged or in those first tender months of marriage, it's easy to read the worst into everyday situations, easier still to find ominous signs where there aren't any. For example, the winter I got engaged and made plans to move to San Diego to live with Duke, it snowed a record amount in Boston, my hometown. The *Boston Globe* reported that the total snowfall that year superseded the height of even the tallest Celtics basketball player. Most mornings, it was hard to push the front door of my apartment building open for all the snow swept onto the stoop. But one morning, when I must have been feeling particularly vulnerable, I opened the door to find icicles so long and so jagged they almost barred me from leaving. And I actually remember thinking, Someone is trying to tell me something. Someone is trying to tell me not to go to San Diego.

Of course, any normal person would have seen the icicles and said, "Enough of this already! San Diego, here I come!" But for brides, and grooms, too, this is a time when you're susceptible to a lot of worst-case scenarios.

Few brides escape thinking, Let's say I marry this guy and he turns out to be an ax murderer and I end up dead and he ends up collecting thousands of dollars in life insurance because everyone thinks he's such a nice guy. If you're like me, in your single life you dated enough men you thought were great but who turned out to be Satan incarnate that you may find it hard to believe in happily ever after, even when it is upon you.

Freaking Out

The weeks and months leading up to a wedding are a sensitive time, a time when many brides and grooms kind of freak out. Most do it privately. And that's possible because freaking out has many manifestations, the controlling shrew stricken with mononucleosis being just one of them.

Yvonne, a thirty-two-year-old from New Orleans, who contacted me via the Internet when she learned I was writing this book, said that she freaked out four months before her wedding and had a fling. Yvonne slept with an acquaintance of hers as a way, she rationalized, of being "sure" she was marrying the right man—the *other* man, her fiancé.

Almost immediately, Yvonne realized her mistake. She couldn't make a comparison between two totally different men. She had to decide on the basis of what she knew, not on the basis of all the other men there were to choose from. And after going through *pre caena* (the Catholic premarital workshops) and talking with her fiancé about her fears, Yvonne decided to go ahead with the wedding. To this day, her husband does not know about the fling.

Now, I'm not recommending a fling as the learning experience it was for Yvonne. But among the brides I interviewed for the book, Yvonne's experience is not that uncommon. Many brides contemplated one last fling, while almost everyone I know or interviewed, either in the engagement or early in the marriage, entertained such questions as, Am I doing the right thing? Did I marry the right person? Or, Am I even the marrying kind?

Revisiting Your Decision to Marry

Two months after my friend Janice, a thirty-three-year-old advertising executive, got married, she moved from Atlanta to France where her husband, Tom, had been admitted to business school. Janice had some reservations about moving to Europe in the first place. And without the job, friends, and family she'd relied on at home, and largely without Tom because he was consumed with school, Janice foundered in her new marriage, losing her sense of what their relationship meant to her. She thought about old flames, comparing her situation in France to life as it had been when she was single, and she asked herself, "Am I sure I want to be married?"

.Janice ended up taking a job in Atlanta during Tom's second year of business school. And while Janice enjoyed being back in a familiar environment and in an interesting job, her relationship with Tom proved even more difficult to maintain from three thousand miles away. The turning point came when Tom agreed to become a visiting student at a college in Georgia, where they could see one another more often. "Of course, it was not his first choice to move to Georgia for a semester and then back to France for one more semester," Janice says. "But I realized then the depth of his commitment to me, that he was willing to make such a sacrifice for me." And it was then, Janice says, that she felt the deepest peace she's known in her young marriage.

At one time or another, either during the engagement or during what's supposed to be newlywed nirvana, most brides and grooms revisit their decision to marry. But knowing that revisiting this huge decision is common doesn't make the feelings any less scary or unnerving. If you're already married and you are experiencing a crisis in confidence, the subsequent chapters offer a great deal of reassurance and advice. But for those of you who are contemplating the rightness of marriage even with the wedding countdown on, you need to know immediately whether your fears fall into the "normal" category or whether they are a sign that you should go nowhere near an altar anytime soon. Only once you know this can you quell the fighting, ease the irrationality, and get some semblance of the wedding, not to mention the marriage, you want.

Should I Call Off the Wedding?

There's truly no easy way to distinguish between the common "wedding jitters," which feel like convulsions to many, and doubts that are serious enough to cancel or postpone a wedding. But it seems to me, and to the counselors and clergy I spoke to, that you should not get married if (1) you are utterly preoccupied with doubts and are experiencing more anxiety than happiness about your upcoming marriage, or (2) you are counting on marriage to transform your relationship, to change you or your husband for the better, or to eliminate the significant problems between the two of you.

In either case, you need to talk to your fiancé about

these feelings and then approach an intelligent outsider for an objective perspective. A clergy member, coun-selor, or married couple whose experience you value can evaluate your concerns without having to consider how disappointed your par-ents will be if you don't go through with the wedding, or how big a nonrefundable deposit you have put down on the reception hall. De-pending on how you feel af-ter those discussions, you may then want to call off the wedding.

SIGNS YOU SHOULD CALL OFF THE WEDDING:

∞ You are preoccupied with doubts, and more anxious than you are happy.

∞ You are counting on mar-riage to transform your rela-tionship and to correct its significant flaws.

∞ After talking to your fiancé and other trusted confidantes about your fears, you do not feel relieved.

But if you are genuinely happier than you are anxious about the marriage, and if you know that marriage isn't going to heal all ills, the following four wisdoms, gleaned from my experiences and those of my friends, will ward off the usual panic attacks an engagement brings.

1. RELAX, HAVE FAITH.

If you find yourself revisiting your decision to marry, questioning your judgment or the promise of your re-lationship, repeat to yourself this quote from Susan Page's book *Now That I'm Married, Why Isn't Everything Perfect?*:

> Most decisions have to be made on the basis of insufficient data. If we waited until we had perfect data, we would not have to make decisions; they would make themselves. In other words, every commitment requires a leap of faith.

Or, to put it in a more positive light, you are as well equipped as any bride . . . maybe even more so, if you have a few years of single, independent life under your belt and have learned, through trial and error, how to make better decisions and gather better data to make major life choices.

The fairy tale of the blemish-free romance and the fret-free bride can make you feel you don't belong in the realm of the married. But as long as you have faith, which simply means that you trust in something you cannot see but that you believe in anyway, you are endowed with magic stuff.

Brides and grooms are rarely told this, but commitment in marriage often means choosing the great unknown over ambivalence, which is much different from choosing a golden carriage over a pumpkin. Faith may not seem like much in the face of ambivalence. But starting with the wedding, and continuing throughout the years of your marriage, you'll find faith buoys you, sometimes just by giving a bad mood a day, a month, or a year to work itself out, sometimes in far more dramatic ways in the midst of hardship.

Nothing works like faith, trusting in the common sense you had before you started lugging home two-ton bridal magazines and before you decided to do hand-calligraphy on all 350 of your wedding invitations, to steady you in this nutty time. But it works only when you ease up, only when you say to yourself, "Everything is going to work out. Our wedding is going to be paid for. And even if a few things go wrong, our wedding will still be beautiful. And my life with this wonderful man is going to be much better when all this wedding angst is over."

Just relax. And have faith. In God. In yourself and in

your decision-making ability. In the things you've learned about relationships that you're taking into marriage. And in the man you're marrying, who loves you and wants the best in life for both of you.

2. TRY TO FOCUS ON WHAT'S TRULY IMPORTANT.

Weddings always involve some compromises—compromises that can be particularly painful to a bride or groom who has dreamed of having her or his wedding a certain way. In the end, the best wedding you can hope for is one that preserves enough of what you and your fiancé originally wanted to make it happy and meaningful. This is not to say that it won't be a storybook wedding. It will just be *your* storybook wedding—a wedding that features the things that are truly important to you.

My friend Monique, a strategic planner in Minneapolis, did not have a storybook wedding or a storybook marriage. She wanted an intimate, formal wedding, but her future father-in-law, a professional fund-raiser, saw the wedding as a marketing opportunity. So Monique's fiancé, Alex, pushed for a larger affair at a country club.

When the two families convened with the catering manager at the appointed country club, Monique expressed her desire for a plated versus buffet dinner, and she wanted a vegetarian entree offered, since many of her relatives were vegetarians. But no one seemed to listen. Monique's father got so disgusted with the demands of Alex's family that he walked out only after he had declared that since they couldn't agree on anything, he would pay for the reception to have *everything*—every appetizer, every entree, every dessert, absolutely everything on the menu. That was his solution to the unending discord.

To Monique's chagrin, she had what she calls "the

buffet from hell" at her wedding reception. "It looked like something you'd see in a M.A.S.H. unit, an assembly line of food."

Accordingly, the wedding was only the beginning of the couple's problems. Monique has been divorced for ten years but recently got engaged to a wonderful man. With him, wedding planning has taken on new meaning. They remain focused on the most important aspects of the wedding—love, family, faith, and fun.

For me, one of the hardest parts about having a husband rather than the gaggle of girlfriends I had around me when I was single is that my husband will not "obsess" with me. Two days before my wedding, a group of some of my closest friends sat on the cold basement floor of my church and helped me stencil flowerpots for my reception centerpieces. Duke, and my more sensible sister and mother, insisted that the pots looked fine painted and did not need a stencil on top. But my best friend, Betsy, swept into town from Illinois and took over, literally following me down my trail of insanity, organizing the stenciling crew, and one by one, conquering my "to do" list without ever once saying I was being excessive or picayune.

But often during our engagement, Duke demanded that I emerge from my fanaticism. He would put his arms around me, which felt confining at first, and while he continued to hold me, he would repeatedly ask, over my jumble of rationalizations and excuses, "What is really important here?"

It was incredibly annoying. It made me really mad sometimes. After all, he wasn't doing the bulk of the work on the wedding, and he didn't seem to appreciate the level of detail that makes a wedding truly special. The only thing that redeemed his even asking such a question—in his very loving albeit seemingly patronizing way—was that he was absolutely right. It was a question the value of which we both came to appreciate during the first months and years of our marriage.

We learned that like smelling salts, the question seemed to "bring us to" when we got caught up in a malaise of distractions. This question was different from the one my camp counselor had asked, the one that demanded I pick one top priority over another. This question was reserved for critical times when one of us had *really* lost perspective, and it demanded the ultimate truth. So when Duke asked, "What is really important here?," I was forced to emerge from my obsessing and say, "We are."

And believe me, this is the best wedding present you'll receive. Because again and again, when the world pulls you every which way, you come home and realize that there is nothing more important to you than your partner and your marriage. You'll lose sight of what's important many times during the engagement and certainly during a lifetime of marriage, like all married couples do. Your jobs will demand ridiculous hours. Children can suck energy, and your sex drive, right out of you. It may be months before you find a weekend to get away together. It may be days before you're in the apartment together long enough to do more than kiss good-bye.

But then a lull will come, however brief, in which you have to look across a plate of burned toast and decide, What is really important to me? And when you affirm the marriage, when you say to another person, "You are what matters to me most in the world," and hear someone say it to you, love puts to shame our usual preoccupation with daily planners and "to do" lists, with promotions and deadlines, even with stencils and catering menus. The power of saying "We are" will take your relationship to places far better than your travel agent can ever recommend.

If you're lucky and stay focused on what's truly important, this is what you will feel on your wedding day: the power of love cannot be contained in a gazebo, in the chancel, or under any *chuppa*. It is quietly felt, and resoundingly true, over a lifetime, not of "I dos" but of "We ares."

3. MAKE THE WEDDING YOUR OWN.

With that said, I will never regret that Duke and I did so much to make the wedding our own. And the brides I surveyed and interviewed were emphatic that the best thing about their weddings were the vows they wrote themselves, and the things they did to make the service, in particular, personally meaningful.

It's critical that you wrest the ceremony and the party away from people and forces that would make it less sacred, and less festive, for you and your fiancé. And you're lucky because particularly in the case of couples who are marrying later, brides and grooms today are shaking up what used to be a predictable set of wedding festivities.

My friend Rachel, an editor in San Francisco, and her husband, Sam, both marrying for the second time, picked a field near a favorite hiking trail in Marin County for their ceremony. "Our wedding was perfect. We invited nobody, literally nobody," Rachel laughs. "We got a rabbi and we called the preschool nearby and asked them if they could spare two teachers for an hour the next Friday to be our witnesses. And they showed up with twenty of their two- to four-year-olds who were like our little cherubs. They had picked flowers for us and made us cards. Then they took turns taking pictures of us. It was all very private and very special."

Cindy, a thirty-four-year-old Los Angeles veterinarian I read about in my college alumnae magazine, hosted a remarkable "Mission Impossible" wedding in Las Vegas. She and her fiancé, Rick, sent wedding invitations that were accompanied by individualized cassette tapes, giving their guests "assignments," although you'll be reassured to know the tapes did not self-destruct. They went on to have a traditional church service, at the end of which shots rang out from the pews, the bride pulled a snub-nosed pistol from her bouquet, and the newly married couple and their guests were drawn into an evening of espionage.

Cindy and Rick wanted an "interactive" wedding—an evening their guests would never forget. Like many couples today, they got married in their thirties, by which time they had been to many weddings and knew exactly what they did and did not want.

Many brides I know now skip the bouquet and garter toss altogether. Many have cut down on the number of bridesmaids, making the ceremony simpler, while others have included more readings and recitations, enabling more friends and family to become involved.

Duke and I didn't like how single people are often demeaned, or made to feel left out, at weddings. Having been single ourselves for so many years, we were determined not to do this to our friends. So we agreed up front that even if we had to shorten our invitation list, each single person would be invited with a guest. And we talked to our minister, too. We told him we didn't want marriage held up as the "ultimate way" to live one's life, but as the very happy path we had chosen that we wanted to celebrate with our friends and family.

At one point in the ceremony, we invited our guests to use a pencil and paper inserted in our wedding bulletin to write two things: the name of someone who had taught them an important lesson about love for which they were thankful, and the name of someone whose life they could affect with a commitment of love and attention. In this way, we tried to make everyone at our wedding feel included in our vows and in our celebration, which in turn made it the kind of wedding Duke and I had always wanted to attend.

4. FIND SOME SIMPLER, SWEETER WAY OF CELEBRATING WHAT THIS MARRIAGE MEANS TO YOU.

Despite everything, weddings often spin out of control and turn into something very different from the wedding the couple originally wanted. My friend Amelia, a thirty-year-old fund-raiser from Princeton, New Jersey, had so many things go wrong that she says the best thing about her wedding was that "it was over!"

Amelia's wedding programs flew off the roof of her car, so she had to redo them the day of the wedding. Her sister-in-law was so sick she couldn't sing at the wedding as planned and a violinist had to learn new music overnight to fill in the gaps. Amelia and her husband spent their wedding night in a driveway trying to pry open the trunk of her parents' car to retrieve the luggage that was locked inside. Then, on their honeymoon, Amelia broke her toe and her husband lost his ring.

For Amelia, the realization of dreams did not come on her wedding day but afterward. She and her husband had not lived together before they got married, so she had fantasized about how great it would be to walk in and shout, "Honey, I'm home!" And in this, Amelia wasn't disappointed. "Marriage feels very natural to me," Amelia says.

Paul and Jamie's wedding on the TV sitcom "Mad About You" was marred with a misprint in the invitation, a succession of gravy-boat gifts, feuds over seating arrangements, and Jamie's nonstop eating, which made her gown too tight. But the night before the wedding, Paul and Jamie snuck out of the places they were staying to reassure one another and to say their vows in some sweeter, simpler way—before a justice of the peace whose other job was doing road work on the streets of New York City.

> **BRIDE-TO-BRIDE**
>
> *What was the best thing about your wedding?*
>
> ∞ "Writing our own vows and really expressing the reasons we were getting married."
>
> ∞ "When it was over!"
>
> ∞ "The moment before I walked down the aisle, I felt such extreme happiness."
>
> ∞ "We found a wonderful woman to marry us. And we put the ceremony together ourselves."
>
> ∞ "We let my mother plan the whole thing."
>
> ∞ "Being surrounded by family and friends."

Like Paul and Jamie, it's critical you reclaim some simpler, sweeter understanding of what your marriage means to you. Because the wedding is a test of one very important skill you'll need in marriage: your ability to let go of idealistic expectations and to recognize and enjoy the way love sneaks up on you.

Once you stop expecting goose bumps at bridal gown fittings, you'll be surprised to find your heart stirring at the sight of your mother in her curlers or your father shining his shoes before the wedding. At the speed with which your new husband signs the marriage license. And at the way everyone you know seems to have joined you on the dance floor at your own, wonderful wedding.

Two weeks before our wedding, having never managed to squeeze dancing lessons into our schedules, Duke and I pushed our coffee table aside and started practicing our "first dance" in the living room of our San Diego apartment. The CD player kept repeating our song—"Someone Like You" by Van Morrison—while we fumbled with the box step.

I tried to get Duke to loosen up, at the very least to look at me when we danced. Duke tried to get me to be coordinated, something my gym teachers gave up on long ago. Then, at one point, Duke got so uptight and nervous about the idea of dancing in front of a crowd that his breaths quickened, almost as if he were hyperventilating. Though I tried nearly everything, there was nothing I could say that calmed his nerves.

So I resigned myself to the fact that Duke was not going to be a groom who was comfortable making a stirring speech. He wouldn't croon with the band to some silly but charming rendition of "You Are So Beautiful." Nor would he gaze into my eyes on the dance floor as if no one else were there. Those were the things I'd dreamed a groom would do. And though I was a grown woman, it was disappointing to realize he wasn't that kind of man.

But I also wasn't prepared to learn what kind of man he really was, and what kind of groom he'd really be. Because at our wedding, Duke was so relaxed and so happy that to this day, I have never seen him smile wider. Though he hates having his picture taken, he submitted joyfully to the paparazzi. And when we were safely ensconced in our Ritz-Carlton room in our plush white robes, with a smorgasbord of wedding leftovers—an after-hours picnic we recommend you have your caterer prepare for you—Duke opened champagne and spoke from his heart about our future in ways he never had before.

Duke and I had had "Always" inscribed in our wedding bands. But because he had shunned the word throughout our engagement, I had begun to worry the word wasn't really in his vocabulary. On our wedding night, he proved me wrong. He said "always" again and again, and with great certainty. That he'd *always* love me. That we'd *always* take care of each other. That we'd have babies and grow old together, and that we would *always* work at our marriage to make it extraordinary.

It was the most passionate he has ever been about us, leaving me, the excessively verbal one, dizzy and speech-

WHAT NO ONE TELLS THE BRIDE ABOUT . . .

The engagement and the wedding:

∞ You will argue with your fiancé and your families about the wedding.

∞ You won't always feel what everyone tells you you're supposed to feel.

∞ Instead, you will feel pressure to look and sound happy all the time.

∞ You'll think the tensions mean you shouldn't be getting married or that your fiancé does't want to marry you.

∞ You will have had dreams and bouts of irrational thinking.

Our brides' solution:

∞ Relax; have faith.

∞ Try to focus on what's truly important.

∞ Make the wedding your day.

∞ Find some simpler, sweeter way of celebrating what this marriage means to you.

less. And it was then that I felt "This is it!" It was then, while Duke pulled endless numbers of hairpins from my headpiece, that I felt most like a bride. And could let fairy tales fall away for something real. For something sacred. For something so deeply felt that faith was the only way to reach it.

Chapter 3

"YOU'VE CROSSED OVER
TO THE OTHER SIDE!":
MAKING THE TRANSITION BETWEEN
YOUR SINGLE AND MARRIED SOCIAL LIFE

It's normal to cling to friends you had when you were single. It's normal to feel like a walking contradiction. But you can use these contradictions to make your marriage a home for both your independence and your love.

At my bridal shower, I remember my single friends recoiling in horror when I uttered the words, "Duke won't let me Rollerblade." What I meant was that Duke doesn't want me to learn to Rollerblade because I'm such a klutz. What they heard persuaded them I had already surrendered my identity, because before Duke came along, there was nothing I would have let a man tell me not to do.

Then it was *me* who recoiled the first time Duke and I encountered "board games" at a dinner party with married friends. This had been a running joke among my single friends and me: How we dreaded becoming "old married people" who played board games at polite dinner parties. Even though Taboo turned out to be fun, it was a guilty pleasure.

Not Fitting in Anywhere

This is every bride's predicament. You're betwixt and between two social circles and two seemingly different identities, neither of which feels entirely comfortable. It's a bit like adolescence, or the phase you went through a year out of college, in which you felt you didn't fit in anywhere.

At the heart of these contradictions is what experts tell us is the first big challenge couples face: the struggle for autonomy. And many marriage books talk about the fact that newlyweds successfully establish their marriages only when they separate themselves from their "families of origin," a formal way of saying they have to break away from parents, siblings, and their childhood homes. This remains a battle for many brides, like my friend whose mother-in-law came in and systematically rearranged items in my friend's kitchen cabinets while she and her husband were away.

Your husband's family and his buddies may very well interfere with your notion of happily ever after. This is something we'll talk about briefly in this chapter, but mostly we'll focus on your struggle with the past, specifically with the life you've built for yourself as a single adult. I'll talk about why breaking away from single life may be every bit as tricky as it was for previous generations to break away from their childhood homes, and then my newly married friends and I will share the ideas we have for making this inevitable transition easier.

Why Our Singleness Means So Much to Us

As prevalent as it is for college-educated, young adults to stay single longer, society has yet to appreciate how the years of singlehood figure into our development as adults. In fact, it's usually left to singles, in lengthy phone conversations with a mother who desperately wants to be a grandmother, to defend and define single life and its redeeming social values.

With the popularity of *Friends* and its TV knockoffs, perhaps this is changing. Perhaps society is beginning to appreciate what I believe is the hallmark of single people's lives: the way in which impromptu families form in the absence of customary family life. Of course, some blood relatives continue to figure prominently in our lives. But primarily, single people rely on "faux families" who dole out support, advice, concern, and love in many of the same ways real families do.

When my friends and I were just out of college and starting out in Boston, we shared a lot of meatless spaghetti sauce and a lot of circled want-ads. We borrowed cars and clothes, we moved each other in and out of fifth-floor walk-ups, and we took each other in during holidays.

Just as a neighborhood or hometown represented "home" to our mothers, my friends and I as single adults traveled in certain circles that came to represent something very important to us, namely, our independence. Over the years, you make friends with your dry cleaner, and you figure out who can get you Celtics tickets and how to get along with catty colleagues at work. You begin to master the elements of city and professional life.

All of this contributes to your sense of self. So when

marriage requires that, to a certain extent, you separate from the life you have carved out for yourself, and from the support network you consider "family," it can be very painful. And certainly one of *the* most confusing aspects of being a bride today.

From the Engagement On, Nothing's the Same

The confusion starts the day you get engaged. Only three inches of your left-hand ring finger actually crosses over to the opposite side of the engagement ring, but you notice almost immediately that people treat you differently once you decide you are getting married.

When Duke and I got engaged, his stockbroker wrote him to suggest they take a closer look at his portfolio now that he was "settling down." I thought this was strange because, presumably, Duke had been as interested in making money on his investments when he was single as he was now that he was getting married. But marriage is often viewed as a kind of graduation into serious life. Never mind that it may have been ten years since you last drank beer upside down from a funnel; people think of single life as one long pub crawl. And never mind that you may have your master's degree, a good job in a competitive field, own real estate, or have standing in your community. Nothing you have accomplished thus far in life holds a candle to the significance people place on your marriage. And when people put marriage on a pedestal, and create this fairy tale about your life, it feels as though they are pushing you, *the real you*, away.

Off the "List"

If you were single at least a couple of years, you were undoubtedly on the receiving end of numerous engagement announcements from friends. And no matter how happy you were for them, your mind automatically crossed them off a kind of list. The list was of single people, and probably women, against whom you compared yourself, because as long as you could name other women your age who were not yet married, you felt you were in good company.

The list served other purposes as well. It was a list of people you could call when you really needed to talk, without worrying you were interrupting or that there was an unsympathetic or impatient husband nearby. It was a list of those who still wanted to meet other single people, who would go to bars and parties, who would take tennis lessons and ski trips with you, and who would be available on Valentine's Day and New Year's Eve. Or, as I used to joke, a list of those who might still be available to room with me in a convalescent home.

Unfortunately, there's never a double standard around when you really need one. When my diamond came on the scene, I could almost hear the pencils making deep, black lines across my name. Meanwhile, my married friends were gleefully penciling me into their social calendars, with a chorus of "I-told-you-sos" about the engagement I considered a miracle and they considered a foregone conclusion.

I absolutely abhorred the sound of those pencils. My friends were ecstatic for me, but they realized our relationships would have to change. I kept trying to prevent them from thinking of me "that way." I didn't want to let go of my single friends, and I especially didn't want to become the kind of married person who was inaccessible or unimpressed by the lives of single people.

When Friends Seem to Push You Away

One night a few months before several of us turned thirty, I told my friends I wasn't dreading this fateful birthday. I was startled to have one of my best friends reply, "You're not worried about turning thirty because you know the ring is coming."

A comment like this deserved a rankled feminist reply. A comment like this deserved an all-out, impassioned, Marg Stark lecture. But I sat there, stunned.

It was the first of many times over the next couple of years that I would experience *jamais vu*, the feeling that everyone around me was a stranger. My closest friends, the people who knew me best, seemed to have decided my life was now settled and wrapped up in a bow. It felt to me that everything I had accomplished and worked for, leading up to my turning thirty, had been blotted out by the prospect of my becoming a bride.

Four months after my wedding, I had a similar experience. I was telling a single girlfriend about a mutual acquaintance of ours. I'd run into him recently and been reminded of how great he was. I urged my friend to give him a chance even though she didn't think she could be attracted to him. I told her that if I were single, I'd go out with him, at which point, she snapped, "Well, that's easy for you to say."

This was another blood-boiling comment. Even though we'd been giving each other dating advice for thirteen years, my friend didn't seem to want mine any longer. It didn't matter that before Duke came along, I could match, one to one, every dud boyfriend, every horrendous date, and every broken heart she'd ever experienced. It didn't matter that very little about my life right then was "easy," since my husband had already deployed on a ship in the Persian Gulf, and we'd spend four months of our newlywed year apart.

Neither of these friends meant real harm, and I know that deep down, both were genuinely happy for me when I got married. But at the same time, these comments placed an uncomfortable distance between us.

A Strange, New Social Life

In the absence of the predictable social set of our single lives, Duke and I, like all newlyweds, began to experiment with socializing as a couple. And it was a strange, new world to us.

At first, we hung out with my friends from Boston, all of them sharp-tongued and quick-witted, your typical crusty New Englanders. Duke's sense of humor is, on the other hand, entirely different—slow, dry, and full of metaphors you have to think about. You can imagine how these different manners clashed, and how I writhed in the middle, wanting Duke's jokes to go over, wanting my friends to like him, wanting Duke to be comfortable. I was miserable, trying so hard to make the situation work.

We also dabbled in the social circles our married friends belonged to. They kept saying how great it was to have a couple they could do things with. What we later appreciated they meant was how great it was to have married friends who didn't have children. Because married couples splinter into social subsets—those with children and those without—within a few years after marriage.

Like most newlyweds I know, Duke and I shied away from the "married with children" set at first. We didn't understand how you got together with people who had children. One key to socializing with couples who had children was giving them enough notice to get a sitter. But that might as well have been senior-level organic chemistry to us. We were still trying to figure out who called whom, who made arrangements with whom, and who had to clear it with whom.

Wives Make the Arrangements

Almost inevitably, my friends and I have observed, it falls to "wives" to make social arrangements for the couple. My friend Sarah, a thirty-three-year-old lobbyist from Jacksonville, Florida, declared right off that she wasn't going to be her husband's secretary. Matt's family assumed Sarah would be in charge of remembering birthdays and of sending cards and gifts when, in fact, she wasn't much better at it than Matt had been as a bachelor.

What Matt's family really wanted was for Sarah to be the conduit for the intimacy and affection they hoped to forge with the couple. Sarah came from a less demonstrative family, so her in-laws' efforts felt cloying and demanding. You can imagine the stand-off that ensued. Eventually, Matt's family accepted the boundaries that Matt and Sarah set, and the relationship between the couple and his family became much more manageable.

I took a somewhat different tack, not so much with family but with friends. I liked the control it gave me to make social arrangements. Besides, Duke didn't crave social interaction the way I did. For me, and for many brides I know, my satisfaction with our marriage often hinged on having a healthy balance of time alone with him and time with others.

But it took Duke and me a long time to adjust to the dynamic of "couples' socializing." We struggled through evenings in which we didn't jibe with one or the other individual in the couple. And we were surprised by how often men ended up talking to men and women to women. Duke and I could subvert this habit at dinner parties, but at larger gatherings, we were often the only ones breaking rank, entering into one another's gender groups of conversation.

Then, of course, there were our girls' nights out and guys' nights out. There was the awkwardness of "checking in" with your spouse at some point during the evening. We tested one another sometimes, staying out too late and forgetting to call. And we watched our previously free-spirited friends squirm through the ignominy of a bartender handing them the phone, a spouse having tracked them down.

BRIDE-TO-BRIDE

What do you miss most about being single?

∞ "The excitement that comes with going out, hoping you mill meet someone that night."

∞ "The intense moods and loneliness which, in my case, because I am an artist, seem to generate creativity."

∞ "Going out dancing with my friends."

∞ "Getting to smoke indoors in my own apartment."

∞ "The ever-present 'potential' French lover fantasy."

∞ "Making decisions without having to check with someone else."

∞ "More opportunity for spontaneity."

∞ "My independence."

A Change of Heart

Michelle, a twenty-six-year-old administrative assistant from Houston, imagined she and her husband would maintain the social life they had had when they were single. She had always tried to be the "cool girlfriend" who didn't mind when Todd played golf or softball, went fishing and hunting. "For the most part, I've never cared about his extracurricular activities. But now that we're married, I've started to care." Michelle says she's now frustrated that Todd is "into" so many things that take him away from time they could be spending together.

Marriage does change things. It may change the way you feel about your husband's social life. It may decrease the frequency with which you talk to your friends, since you find it harder to call them, wanting to spend evenings with your husband. You try to be cognizant of how "couple-ish" you and your husband act, remembering well what it was like to be lonely and single. And you try not to indulge in PDA—public displays of affection—or to talk a lot about yourselves. You don't want to make the differences between your life and your friends' lives so apparent. Although one bride I interviewed says that, a year into her marriage, she and her husband still enjoy "baby talking" to one another. It's their romantic language, and they don't care that it nauseates their friends.

Dolly, an accomplished musician from Washington state, became almost a champion for her middle-aged single friends. "Fat and turning forty, I snagged a thirty-year-old cute boy!" she laughs. Nevertheless, Dolly remembers well her years as a single mother, when marrying again seemed a remote possibility. So she tends not to say much about how wonderful her husband, Jake, is, at least not around those friends who don't have a man in their lives. She's found another outlet, saying, "It's easier at church where there are a lot of folks who are married, too."

Dede, a thirty-nine-year-old bride from Montana, runs an art studio with her husband, Michael. Dede also downplays her life with Michael when she's out with single friends. "I find myself either not talking about the good things in our relationship or telling them funny stories about the downside of living with someone, like how Michael will comment if I click my dish too much with my spoon, or if he sees me cutting vegetables without washing them first."

Breaking Away from Your Real Family

If you're used to telling your friends everything, you may take this diminished intimacy very hard. Faux family aside, if you remained close to your real family or developed a closeness with them once you were out on your own, the change in these relationships may also be disconcerting.

As is typical of mothers and daughters, my mom and I didn't stop yelling at each other until I was twenty-three. So my extended single life gave us an incredible gift of time. I learned to enjoy both my parents, not as people from whom I always needed money but as people who popped into town for a weekend, envying me my studio apartment, my pull-out couch, my dinners out, and all the glamorous accoutrements of single life they hadn't experienced, having married right out of college.

I also counted on my mom to come to my rescue as a best friend would. In my late twenties, when yet another of my major romances ended on yet another major holiday, my mom jumped on the train from New York to Boston to console me. But when I got engaged and married, I knew I couldn't involve my mom in my marital quandaries. I knew it would be Duke's voice, not hers, I would count on as the ultimate balm in a crisis. And while she and my dad would still be the backup, I would turn to Duke first for consolation, for prayer, or for encouragement.

This jolted my parents and me at first. I also despised not having time alone with them at holidays; I worried so much about whether Duke was having a good time with my family, and whether my family liked Duke, that I longed for the less-complicated Christmases when I was single. (Of course, I'd spent many of those Christmases longing for a partner, feeling like a fifth wheel since my younger sister had been married for years.) Only later could I relax and enjoy the different kind of holidays and family time that comes with married life.

When a new marriage is a second marriage, the couple's task is often to separate themselves from the first marriages. And at the same time, they must foster a relationship between themselves and children from a previous marriage, if there are any. Rachel, a forty-year-old editor in San Francisco, married Sam, who is seventeen years her senior, after being divorced and on her own for seven years. Rachel has no children and presumed she wouldn't have much to do with the children from Sam's first marriage because they were grown up and in college. "I forgot that kids come home from college in the summer and at Christmas," Rachel says. "I've never liked teenage boys. I didn't like them when I was a teenage girl. I felt like this sloppy teenage boy had been foisted on me. So I was angry all the time. I resented his presence and cried a lot. I probably should have had more empathy for the kid than I had pity for myself. But essentially, I just put up with it until it was over."

The "How to" of the Married Social Life

There are whole library and bookstore shelves devoted to the psychological aspects of separating from one's past, and to issues such as the one Rachel had to confront. Obviously, I've just touched upon a few of the strange and wildly different social circumstances newlyweds face. But lest you worry that you'll spend the next fifty years in this predicament of social estrangement, let me share the ideas my friends and I came up with to help you deal.

1. DON'T UNDERESTIMATE WHAT YOUR FRIENDS, AND YOUR SINGLE LIFE, MEANT TO YOU. HONOR THEM INSTEAD.

If you're reading this and you're not yet married, you have a tremendous opportunity to turn your engagement and your wedding into a love fest. The days in which it's cool for girlfriends to vie for "maid of honor" may be over, but you should still fill your engagement with friends, and with telling friends what they mean to you. Take one of your best friends along with you to shop for your gown. I took both my mom and dad with me on the all-important trip to Kleinfeld's, the world's largest bridal salon, in Brooklyn, New York.

If you're already married, you can still find ways to honor the people who prepared you to love someone for a lifetime. Write a friend and tell her how much you miss her now that you're married. Tell the people you care about how thankful you are for everything they have done for you over the years and how sorry you are that in the midst of the wedding madness, you didn't have time to tell them this.

If you worry that deep down your friends or siblings envy you your happiness, tell them again and again, "If this kind of blessing in life can happen to me, it can happen to anyone and it will certainly happen to you." Or, if that doesn't work, do what my friend Karmen, a thirty-six-year-old actress from Chicago, advises: "The few times friends have indicated I had something they wanted, I told them what my mother-in-law had done recently, which reminded them that the grass only *looks* greener on the other side. And sometimes the green is crab grass."

You'll need time to really persuade your single friends of these points. So I highly recommend taking a *Thelma and Louise* trip. I don't mean a plunge off the ledge of the Grand Canyon in a convertible, although when my wedding gown didn't fit this certainly seemed like a viable alternative. But take a trip, a weekend getaway, with a really good friend or a group of friends. Marriage counselors say that families benefit from three kinds of vacations: time with the kids, time for the couple, and time for each spouse to spend alone. Start this tradition early, before you have children, devoting some time off, even if it's only a long weekend, to different kinds of vacations and their different kinds of benefits.

If that's not financially feasible, take your friend, your sister, or your mom to dinner, to an afternoon of shopping, or have an overnight just like you did when you were a kid. Let your friend or your mom feel that there is no one more important to you, right at that moment, for the whole time you're with that person.

And try to remain attuned to the struggles of your

single friends. Respect times when you know that the last thing your friend needs is to be around a "happy couple." Remember the times that single life could be truly miserable. Duke and I did this last year by skipping a celebration of Valentine's Day. We waited until our anniversary five days later to pour on the romance so we could treat a single friend to dinner on Valentine's Day. This was important to us because our friend faced a double whammy, the fact that her birthday fell on this "couples' only" holiday, when almost everyone had other plans.

Equally important, keep your sense of adventure ignited. Don't let your husband tell you not to Rollerblade if you have a burning desire to do it. And every so often, suggest to one another that both of you take a weekend to do wacky things each of you has always wanted to do, which may or may not mean that you do them together.

> **BRIDE-TO-BRIDE**
>
> *What aspect of single life will you try hardest to preserve now that you are married?*
>
> ∞ "Creating my own happiness. I'm much more open to my husband's sweet gestures, and I love him more when I'm happy with myself."
>
> ∞ "My feisty, independent nature."
>
> ∞ "My friends."
>
> ∞ "Keeping in touch with myself. Being single, I got to know myself better and to know what things I wanted in life."
>
> ∞ "Keeping myself from becoming sheltered or isolated from reality so that if something happened to my marriage, it would not hit me like a ton of bricks."

In other words, take some time to savor the life you've led and the great life experience you bring to your new marriage. Consider this your trousseau, a host of adventures in which to clothe yourself for your new marriage.

At the same time, it's normal and healthy to mourn the inevitable changes marriage brings. I still regret, and I wonder if I'll ever stop regretting, that married life doesn't afford me the intimacy of relationships I enjoyed in single life. It is so difficult now to find the time and money to fly cross-country and be with my parents. And I hate that I no longer have the chance to sit on the floor the morning after a big party with five of my best girlfriends. I miss the bagels smeared with cream cheese, and the way we told stories, one after another, laughter overcoming body odor and morning breath until well into the afternoon.

You can tell me all you want about how childish I am for missing those mornings. And I'm not saying I would trade what I have, because my mornings now have their own incomparable intimacy. It never fails to amaze me that Duke's first instinct, before he's even awake, before he even knows he's doing it, is to reach for me. But don't let anyone tell you that you will not be acutely aware of what you've given up at the same time as you are acutely aware of what you've gained. Better than the Waterford or the Calphalon, better than any wedding gift you'll receive, are the relationships you enjoyed in your single life and the friendship of a lifetime you will enjoy in marriage. In good health and good conscience, you can, and you probably should, entertain both cravings in your heart.

2. DON'T "BUY INTO" THE NOTION THAT MARRIAGE MAKES YOU A TRAITOR OR A DULLARD.

My twenty-nine-year-old friend Lisa from Cincinnati is an ordained minister. And she had a really hard time getting used to the idea that, with marriage, she had "settled down." This cracked me up because one would think Lisa would have worried about a staid life when she became a minister. Yet it was marriage—the idea of being responsible to another person, of having a mortgage and a set routine—that made her feel she "wasn't fun anymore."

Of course, eventually Lisa realized she was happy with her "settled" life, and if other people thought she was boring, that was *their* problem. Certainly this is what most brides come to realize.

Yet there's something noble about brides wanting to retain the best parts of their single selves in marriage. It is crucial that women, in particular, safeguard their sense of independence and adventure, not only because those traits make you the person your husband fell in love with, but because then you'll recognize when your marriage falls into stereotypical roles or other undesired patterns.

However, you can't stand over your marriage with a hatchet, waiting for it to demean you. And you can't let your single friends, or the orientation you received in single life, persuade you that you are the Antichrist just because you delight in your husband's company.

When my single women friends said things like "You're not worried about turning thirty because you know the ring is coming," I came to a really important conclusion: The world in which we live gives women—and men, to a certain extent—very mixed messages. At the same time society worships marriage, it portrays marriage as a lifeless, boring choice. At the same time single people vaunt their solitude and self-sufficiency, they form faux families and enjoy nourishing relationships with the men and women in their lives.

As single women, my friends and I extolled the different arc of our lives. But privately we held marriage up as a status symbol and men as trophies. While my friends and I enjoyed the fact that we didn't *need* a man to have a full life, we still *wanted* one more than any of us let on.

It was not cool when we were single to need a man, maybe not even to want one. If a friend disappeared from our midst in the heat of a new romance, we attributed it to her weakness for a man, not her pleasure in being with him. But as emphatic as we were about not needing one, inside we seemed to fear we couldn't "get" a man. As strong as we were, as independent as we were, my single women friends and I often blamed ourselves for relationships that didn't work.

So when this fish got herself a bicycle, I saw for the first time how fervently my stubbornly single, self-reliant friends and I had wanted to get married. I saw how much we really wanted to be able to love and rely on another human being. And how much we privately feared, as I did before Duke came along, that we were in some way incapable of being loved.

With all these mixed messages, and mixed blessings, it is no wonder brides today feel confused by the transition from independent, single life to married life. If you feel like a walking contradiction, it's probably because you are. But the thing is, because you're a woman, you have been that way all along. And with all that experience with contradictions, you are well suited to blazing a trail in marriage, flaunting your union at the same time you flaunt your individuality, learning to trust and care for another human being at the same time you preserve some degree of your treasured independence.

3. SET BOUNDARIES. PRUNE YOUR RELATIONSHIPS AND PICK NEW ONES CAREFULLY.

My friend Janice, a thirty-three-year-old advertising executive who lives in Silicon Valley, lost a best friend to her marriage. Janice and Caroline had met in Atlanta when they were both single, and had been close friends for eight years. They told each other everything. They went everywhere together. They got the lowdown on whom the other person had slept with. They knew the bargain prices, and the not-so-bargain prices, of all the clothing and furniture the other person bought. Then, when Caroline moved to California, they kept in touch with letters and phone calls, their friendship never faltering.

Janice met Tom after Caroline moved to California, and soon Caroline was flying back east for Janice and Tom's wedding. Then, when fate and the job market brought the newlyweds to California, Janice and Caroline were ecstatic about being reunited.

But soon, Janice realized, Caroline wanted things to be just like they had been when Janice was single. She expected Janice to confide in her the same way she had before, except that now Tom was the first person Janice turned to. Caroline wanted them to pal around together and didn't understand when Tom and Janice wanted to be by themselves.

In the end, Caroline got resentful and mean-spirited. She would bring up Janice's old boyfriends in front of Tom, and mention things Janice had said about Tom when she had first met him. Janice says, "Tom is a very private person and he was embarrassed by this. But he saw immediately what Caroline was trying to do."

Caroline was competing with Tom, trying to demonstrate that she had known Janice before he had. After a while, it became clear that Caroline was not going to accept the changes that came with Janice's marriage. So Janice began to distance herself, and now she and Caroline are no longer friends.

For the most part, however, a bride's relationships with people she loves don't have to disappear, they just have to accommodate the marriage. You have to set boundaries.

Warren Molton, a marriage and family counselor from Kansas City, Missouri, says couples need to determine what kinds of relationships they want to pursue with their friends and relatives as early as possible, preferably before they are married. "You need to get a handle on family matters before you marry. It should be a source of alarm if your spouse is either very attached or completely estranged from his family."

Healthy autonomy, Molton says, lies somewhere between attachment and estrangement. "Try to develop an objective view of your own family, and appreciate what your family looks like from an outsider's point of view." Molton also encourages couples to distinguish themselves early, to indicate to their families and friends ways in which they intend to handle social situations differently from ways they had in the past.

He suggests that newlyweds treat, and encourage their families and friends to treat, the wedding as "the birth of the couple." With birth, Molton explains, comes a respect for something new and marvelous, something that is in the process of defining itself. When he was growing up, his family celebrated his parents' anniversary as the "birth of their family." So Molton encourages couples to treat their first anniversary, and all subsequent ones, as a very special celebration, one that "roots in your minds and in others' minds the significance of your marriage."

On other holidays, Molton says, establish the same boundaries of respect. "It is really important for a couple, particularly once they have children, to experience Christmas and other holidays in their own homes, and to begin to establish their own traditions."

Molton offers an example in which a single mom in Iowa held her three grown children captive to her wishes for many years. When one of those children got married, she made it clear that she expected the newlyweds to be with her in Iowa for both Thanksgiving and Christmas, even though the couple lived far away, even though they also had ties to the other set of in-laws. The couple felt trapped, unable to argue with a lonely woman who said, "I *need* you to come home; I deserve that much."

Boundaries are hard to set, especially with people who manipulate your emotions. And sometimes you will have a friend or relative who does not like your spouse, or vice versa. In these cases, the best boundaries may be those in which you see the offending friend or relative without your spouse being present.

And sometimes, as wrenching as it is to lose a friend, or to distance yourself from a family member you've grown up trying to please, there will come a time when you know cutting, or limiting, ties is the right thing to do. Think of it as pruning, heightening the potential of your marriage to bloom and grow.

In the future, cultivate friendships and relationships with people who want the best for you and your marriage. In their company, and in the burgeoning of the marriage so recently born, the pain of the loss and the limits on old relationships will pass.

4. LET YOUR MARRIAGE ACCRUE INTEREST.

If you and your husband spend every weekend with your single friends in bars, or if you and your husband have so many separate, extracurricular activities that you rarely do things together, you won't do what marriage counselors tell us we *must* do: establish the marriage as a wonderful, autonomous·entity. So occasionally you may find yourself playing a board game at a dinner party—and maybe even enjoying it. And occasionally it will hit you that an afternoon spooning with your husband on the couch and reading the *New York Times* is bliss incarnate. That doesn't mean you're boring, it just means you're well balanced.

When you graduated from college and had no money to enjoy the single life everyone told you was going to be so glamorous, you didn't know how much you'd eventually enjoy being single. And with a new marriage, it's the same thing. It accrues interest, your interest, over time.

A Wife's Best Friend?

Janice, the advertising executive who broke off her friendship with Caroline, had some difficulty calling her husband, Tom, her "best friend." She explains: "He called me his best friend, but it took me a long time to be able to say that he was mine. And this really bothered him."

Janice tried to get Tom to understand that men and women function very differently as friends. But she also admits that she withheld the title "best friend" from him. She felt more secure keeping something for herself. "I set it up that way, I didn't want him to fill that role."

A dear man, Tom asked if Janice could "teach him to talk like a girl," to share things the way women do, lingering over details and talking just to talk, not because any solution or action is needed. And Tom was very trainable, Janice says. "What I loved about him from the start was that he told me everything. He didn't hold things back like a lot of men do. But he can't really have a conversation the way a woman would either. He can take it for about two hours and then he's back to feeling he has to solve anything I bring up to talk about. For him, it's just not instinctual."

Now, three years into the marriage, Janice says, Tom feels more confident and understands he can fill his wife's needs of intimacy and companionship up to a point. He also encourages her to pursue close friendships with women because he understands how important they are to her.

Janice, too, feels more secure, and doesn't worry that Tom is trying to "take over" just because he wants to be her closest friend. They have gone through a lot together, and the time she needed to feel the intimacy with him she once shared with lifelong

---

WHAT NO ONE TELLS THE BRIDE ABOUT . . .

How peeole will perceive you differently:

∞ People will lend more importance to your marriage than to anything you've done before.

∞ Single friends will cross you off the "list."

∞ Married friends will add you and your betrothed to their list.

∞ Your family worries your marriage will change you.

Our brides' solutions:

∞ Don't underestimate what your friends, and your single life, meant to you. Honor them instead.

∞ Don't buy into the notion that marriage makes you a dullard or a traitor.

∞ Set your boundaries. Prune your relationships and pick new ones carefully.

∞ Let your marriage accrue interest.

girlfriends has now accrued. So at Christmas this year, Janice gave Tom a magnet that said "Happiness is being married to your best friend"—a gift Janice says made Tom very happy.

One of the cooking terms I most like running across in recipes is "Let the flavors marry." In this context, "marry" implies that time brings out the best and most delightful elements of a relationship. In Janice's case, it took three years to buy the corny magnet, to claim marriage as a companionship better than any other in her life.

Like Janice and Tom, you have to be honest with your spouse about what you can and cannot be for one another. And you have to set boundaries around the relationship, defining and protecting what you *do* have, and allowing the marriage to accrue interest—a fortune of shared experiences, traditions, and solutions. In this new life, there is room for contradictions, for friendship, for family, and for love.

Chapter 4

THE WEDDING POSTPARTUM:
FINDING REAL HAPPINESS
WHEN THE FAIRY TALE, AND
YOUR FORMER LIFE, FADES AWAY

It's normal to feel depressed and agitated after the wedding and the honeymoon. It's normal to find marriage isn't what you thought it would be. But you can stretch out the novelty of being newlyweds. Instead of rushing toward your next wellspring of happiness, savor happiness now.

Duke and I got married in Boston on Sunday, flew back to San Diego on Monday, and my husband the naval officer went to sea first thing Tuesday morning for the remainder of the week. We were not able to take a honeymoon until three months later.

In the ultimate anticlimax, Duke spent his first week of matrimony in the bowels of his ship, trying to find a fuel leak. I, on the other hand, nestled the top of our wedding cake into the freezer where it was destined for freezer burn and sat down at the desk in our empty apartment to try unsuccessfully to concentrate on the book I was writing at the time.

Is That All There Is?

It was far easier, I discovered, to dwell on the wedding. I called friends long-distance who had been there. I wrote thank-you notes and got my daily fix of frivolity from the UPS man who, for weeks, kept bringing wedding presents. I even picked fights with Duke about something stupid his best man had done.

This chapter looks at the reasons many brides get the blues soon after their weddings, and offers some suggestions to turn your angst in a more positive direction than I did when I experienced the "wedding postpartum." But you should know it's very normal to hit a slump when you come home, or come down, from the proverbial "happiest day of your life." As Thomas Moore writes in *SoulMates*, "Melancholy is a toning down of the upward rush of emotion, and therefore it may feel uncomfortable, or even like a disease, but from the soul point of view, it is simply the motion of settling down into the folds of actual life."

Normal Life

Some brides welcome "actual life," the calm of getting back into their routines. Others, like me, abhor the idea of life ever being "normal." But when a new marriage gets downright mundane, as it does when, for example, you find that your new husband blows his nose in the shower, few brides escape feeling some degree of disillusionment. You know then you're not at the champagne fountain anymore. Even though you weren't expecting perpetual bubbly from your marriage, the reality can be startling.

What no one tells the bride, or the groom for that matter, is that it often takes time to learn what marriage is and isn't. You have to acquire basic skills, such as fighting fairly, managing your money, and negotiating a social life. Even if you lived together before you were married and think you have these basics mastered, you and your husband may be inclined to reevaluate the routine now that you're in it for the long haul.

This is not to say that the first year of marriage *has* to be difficult. I've known people who dove in and swam, who made it look easy, as if they had gills. And I've known people who had violent reactions to marriage, as if they had no idea what they had gotten themselves into. However, the majority of brides I interviewed said that although the first year was happy, their marriages have gotten better and easier with time.

I believe that four myths are responsible for tripping newlyweds up, sometimes as soon as you cross the threshold.

Myth One:
All It Takes to Be Married Is the License

Technically, that's true. Premarital counseling often isn't much help, because teaching engaged couples how to be married is like trying to teach swimming without the water. Couples really do have to learn to be married, not in a formulaic way but in terms of finding what makes marriages work. The logistics of learning to live together are enormous. When it comes to things as rudimentary to your survival as sleeping, eating, and sharing the same space, you really should not underestimate the way a major change can throw you off balance, both physically and emotionally.

Getting in Sync

Two and a half years into our marriage, I am still struggling to become a morning person. Having lived on my own in New England for almost a decade before I got married, I was used to staying up late and sleeping in, the weather often being so bad that there was nothing to get up for. Duke, on the other hand, got up at 5:00 A.M. and was at work by 6:30 A.M. On weekends, he was rarely in bed past 8:00 A.M. because he was raised in southern California, where people bound outside practically in bedclothes, if not more scantily clad.

Once we were married, I realized that to see Duke at all during the week, I had to change my routine. I'm amazed at how few spouses do this, and maybe it's because, as I discovered, purgatory is preferable to the sound of an alarm clock at 5 A.M. I won't say that our breakfasts together that first year were necessarily "quality time," so unintelligible was I before sunup. Nor did I give up late night television very easily, pulling the covers up to my chin most nights at 9 P.M. to the purr of the VCR on "record."

But I did feel a mild satisfaction that sacrifices I made put us on the same schedule, making conversation, companionship, and sex possible in our otherwise hectic lives. I did feel, between yawns, that it was a noble cause.

Rachel, an editor in San Francisco who married again after being divorced and single for seven years, had to learn to share. Rachel came from a family that wasn't nearly as warm or generous as that of her new husband, Sam. "If I had a piece of pizza, a slice of cake, or some candy I liked, I would eat all of it," Rachel explains. "It never occurred to me that I needed to offer Sam any of it. Sam would say, 'You didn't save me any?' and I was always surprised that I was supposed to have."

Now when they go to the movies, Sam asks Rachel three times if she is sure she doesn't want her own popcorn. "Because he knows I will start eating his popcorn, and that eventually I'll eat it all," she laughs.

But it wasn't just sharing food that was the problem. Sharing space was also an issue. "When we first got married," Rachel says, "we had this huge apartment, but we still kept bumping into one another. Every time I turned around, I was elbowing him in the stomach. He was constantly underfoot. If it hadn't been so upsetting, it would really have been amusing."

Now that Rachel and Sam have been married for a few years, she says their relationship is "delicious." Primarily, she says, they had to overcome radically different views of what marriage was. "Sam's view of marriage was to share everything. My idea of marriage was to have a date on Saturday nights, for weddings, and for New Year's Eve. It was an adjustment for me to see marriage as a full-time proposition. And he's adjusted to the fact that I need space and solitude, time to just space out and do nothing. I've learned to announce to him, 'I'm going into the living room to meditate, or do my yoga, or just lie around and do nothing,' and then I won't be interrupted. Before, he treated my solitude as a signal that I was ready to play with him."

Different Eating and Exercise Habits

Some of the most disconcerting changes brides report are in their diet and exercise routines. As much as they have tried to fight the stereotype that married women "let themselves go," they have learned there are specific reasons this can be true.

Elaine, a twenty-four-year-old newlywed from Albuquerque, New Mexico, is cooking and shopping for her husband while at the same time trying to maintain the strict diet she had been on when she was single. As a result, she's struggling with her weight. "It seems that having to eat meals together and especially fixing dinners, even though I'm cooking low-fat meals, I am eating twice as much as when it was just me." When she was single, Elaine kept "nothing in the house that would tempt [her] to overeat" whereas now "there is too much food around!"

To compound this problem, in 1996, University of Alberta researchers found that "slipping on a ring can mean slipping out of a regular schedule of exercise." The experts discovered that women often leave their fitness routines at the altar, shifting their leisure activities to match those of their spouses, even if the spouse is slothful.

I did this when Duke and I were first married. On weekends, I liked to take long walks around the bay. After sitting at a computer all week in our two-bedroom apartment, I felt as though the walls were closing in on me. But Duke was chief engineer of a ship, a job that kept him in its bowels and engine rooms for hours on end. In his limited free time, he wanted to sack out on the Adirondack chair on our balcony, or consume the living room floor with his outstretched limbs. Guess who stayed home?

But it didn't take long for Duke's and my waistlines to demand we settle on a better exercise plan. Duke changed jobs, we bought hiking boots and started hiking together on weekends, and we worked out separately during the week. From my experience and that of the women I know, I believe that if the Alberta researchers followed up on the brides they initially studied, they would find that after a while the women returned to something closer to their premarriage workouts.

Sharing a Home

In the beginning, couples do what porcupines do. They experiment with the amount of distance they need to be together and enjoy one another, without hurting one another. Karla, a thirty-year-old director of a nonprofit organization in Baltimore, married Charles, an assistant store manager and dj, with whom she had had a long-distance relationship for several years. She knew that long-distance relationships were artificially romantic; she knew that Charles went to great lengths to clean his apartment before her visits. But once they were married, Karla was nevertheless startled to find "an additional tax write-off growing in the shower," since Charles's normal routine was to "clean once a year, you know, around the holidays."

But turnabout is fair play because Charles found, once they were married, that Karla was a "wonderful person"—after she brushed her teeth, went to the bathroom, and showered. Thus, Karla says, the key to surviving the first year of marriage and cohabitation was finding an apartment with two bathrooms.

Yvonne, the thirty-two-year-old bride from New Orleans, owned a home before she got married. Two months before their wedding, when Yvonne's fiancé, Ken, moved into her condo, things got dicey.

"What an invasion of my personal space!" Yvonne says. "My six-hundred-square-foot, one-bedroom apartment was plenty of room for *one* but a very tight squeeze for *two*." Then Ken "insisted on bringing furniture with him. So we had to rearrange and cram it all in there.

Whatever pieces didn't fit we reluctantly put into a storage center that charges us a monthly fee. This was all very trying on our nerves."

In Ken's defense, he quit smoking before he moved in with Yvonne. He does his own laundry, goes grocery shopping if given a list, and—here's the kicker—also hangs up his clothes. But it took a while for Yvonne to relax and realize Ken wasn't going to "destroy everything [she] had built." Eventually, she says, she even learned not to begrudge his leaving beard shavings in the bathroom and dishes in the sink. Meanwhile, they are looking for a larger home.

A Name Change

For others, finding middle ground is much, much harder. Six weeks before their wedding, thirty-five-year-old Chicago freelance editor Tamar Goldstein and her fiancé, David, are still in a "name change" stalemate. "I appreciate how nice it is for everybody in a family to have the same name," Tamar says, "but to me, the tradition in which a woman changes her name relates to a time when a woman became a man's property upon marriage and didn't have rights of her own."

Tamar says David "has the same attitude that a lot of men who think they are liberated do—in other words, he thinks it's fine for me to keep my name as long as the kids have his name." This being unacceptable to Tamar, she has proposed numerous alternatives. Hyphenating "Goldstein-Cohen" proved too cumbersome, and David rejected the notion of shortening the two names into one name, or of changing both of their names. "He doesn't want to change his name," Tamar says, "which of course makes me say to him, 'Now you know how I feel.' "

The worst part is that David *doesn't* seem to understand how Tamar feels. "I keep instigating arguments over this and he thinks I'm just being a contrarian. He doesn't grasp that this is a very deep-seated belief for me." David's father has also expressed his disappointment about Tamar's choice not to take the family name, only exacerbating the problem.

Like Tamar and her fiancé, Duke and I had to reconcile our last names—Stark and Clark. Years before, my sister had married a man whose name was Corn and I had a great time razzing her about her hyphenated name, singing "Cathy Stark-Corn and I don't care . . ." This would all come back to haunt me when I fell in love with someone with a name that rhymed with mine.

Because of the rhyme, hyphenating was out. So we agreed on a somewhat complicated solution: Legally and professionally, I kept my name though I took Duke's name for social purposes. When we have children, our son or daughter will be a Clark but inherit a Stark family name as either a first or middle name.

For me and many other brides, these are not just logistics. Surrendering a name or an address is emblematic of much larger sacrifices women fear marriage will require of them. As wonderful as it is to conceive of a new life together, merging the emblems of your previously independent lives often proves to be a very difficult emotional adjustment.

These are just the logistical changes that new marriages require, all of which have their own giant emotional adjustments. But if you had different things in mind when you thought about "playing house" with your spouse, the process of learning to be married, and of finding solutions that work for both of you, can be very jarring.

Myth Two: "He Will Be the Perfect Husband"

The second myth that infests brides is the ever-popular notion that "The man in my life is going to be the perfect husband." I'm not suggesting that most of us sit around, fancying notions of sensitive, bicep-bulging, master lovers who propose marriage to us under an arbor of climbing roses. But when we dream about success in our careers, we picture a great man accompanying us to cocktail parties and company picnics.

The more years women spend single, the more we think we're being careful in selecting a mate, and the more we believe we're not going to have to compromise. And during much of the courtship and engagement we try to stuff the men in our lives into the suit of armor we believe a white knight would wear, only to discover in marriage that husbands resist all our efforts to change them.

Often, *we* don't even realize what we expect, so deeply ingrained and unconscious are the messages we've acquired about marriage and marriage partners. The same is true of our spouses, whose impressions only materialize in marriage when all of us start "acting out" things we saw our parents do.

It's true that love does change people, often bringing to the fore our best qualities. And it's fine to expect that your husband will bring his best self to the marriage, and that he will work harder to accommodate you than he did his roommates in a bachelor pad. But beyond that, expecting marriage to metamorphose the flawed human being you committed your life to is a recipe for the blues.

Dreams That Disappoint

Dolly, a forty-five-year-old musician who lives near Mount Rainier in Washington state, has recently married for the second time. She met her thirty-year-old husband, Jake, at a folk festival. But even though they used to sing and perform together, Jake's interest in continuing to do so has diminished since they got married. Dolly is very hurt that he doesn't want to share something they had enjoyed so much. She once fantasized that she and Jake would become a "hot new musical act," but now has resigned herself to the fact that this is never going to happen.

Rescinding dreams is very hard even if, somewhere inside, you know the dreams are not feasible. When you're nervous about your new life, as most newlyweds are, you tend to make your spouse jump through hoops to prove his love for you. And when your husband won't, when he chooses simply to be himself and to be loved, it can be downright maddening.

Cindy, the veterinarian from Los Angeles who had the "Mission Impossible" nuptials, is a health-conscious person; her husband, Rick, is a diabetic whose health depends, to a degree, on being active and fit. Cindy expected that, after they were married, Rick would start an exercise program and take better care of his health. "I thought he would do this as a way of proving to me that he was committed to a long-term future with me. But he will not do it. He is simply a couch potato." Cindy has had to accept Rick's behavior, and to remind herself that Rick's refusal to exercise doesn't mean he doesn't love her, though it could shorten his life.

Luckily, most of the accommodations we make for our new husbands are not as complicated as this one.

But when you come home from paradise—from a honeymoon in Hawaii or the Caribbean—you're still in a sandy flip-flop fantasy world. It is startling to feel the slap of the words "compromise" and "acceptance" on your face so early in your marriage.

Myth Three: "I'm Going to Be the Perfect Wife"

Perhaps even more startling than having to accept your groom's idiosyncrasies is having to accept your own foibles, the ways in which *you* do not meet the expectations you had for yourself in marriage. Usually it takes a few months for this myth to take shape, but it almost always does, because no myth is more pervasive among brides than believing they will be super-wives.

Janice, my friend who works in advertising, thought that as a wife, she'd be a cross between haven maven Martha Stewart and Italian sexpot film star Gina Lollobrigida. "But alas, I'm human," Janice sighs. "So sometimes we have Chinese takeout twice a week and, oh well, sometimes I'm not the love goddess I'd like to think I am."

Martha Stewart's name came up a lot when I asked brides what they expected of themselves when they first got married. Most aspired to do all the traditional things their mothers had done well, at the same time as they enjoyed help from their husbands, kept up their careers and their social lives, and looked dewy and fresh.

My Early Mistakes

For over a year in my new marriage, I served gourmet dinners, never once resorting to leftovers the following night unless Duke was out of town. As a result, not only did Duke and I gain ten pounds but I turned into a weepy Mary Tyler Moore to his confounded Dick Van Dyke if he did not lavish my efforts with compliments.

Then the meals became more of a chore. And then, finally, when my workload grew, they became impossible. But I remember the precise night, the disgrace of it all, when I served the same meal for the second night in a row, and Duke greeted my guilt with an unobservant, "Great dinner, honey."

My perfectionism that first year has come back to haunt me in more ways than one, because now, when I ask Duke to do more of the cooking, he is intimidated by the meals I have served. I keep telling him I'd be happy with scrambled eggs and ketchup, with spaghetti straight from the jar, or with anything I don't have to plan or serve. But so far, he won't take the initiative. I have to provide a recipe and the ingredients for him to make dinner.

Michelle, the twenty-six-

BRIDE-TO-BRIDE

What did you expect of yourself when you first got married?

∞ "I expected to always be happy and in control of my emotions and to keep everything perfect. Then I realized, 'Yeah, right.' My husband does not expect this of me so why should I?"

∞ "To be an equal partner in the marriage, maintain my own identity, and stay true to the goals I had for my professtional life before I got married."

∞ "I thought I would be better at saving money. Now I realize it takes a lot of willpower and determination."

∞ "I expected I would be this wonder-wife . . . cook, clean, and so on. And that my husband wouldn't have to do a thing. It's really a team effort now. I have happily lowered my standards."

∞ "I can't say I expected anything of myself in terms of marriage. I didn't have any particular standards for myself; neither of us did."

year-old administrative assistant in Houston who started coveting her husband Todd's time once they were married, is confused by a lot of the things she expects of herself now that she is married. Michelle's parents divorced when she was four, so she doesn't believe she had any preconceived ideas about marriage or her role in it. And yet, from the beginning, Michelle felt a lot of pressure to be something she wasn't. "I hated planning the wedding," she said. "I didn't have an opinion about the dress or the flowers. I borrowed a friend's dress. And we let my mom and Todd's mom plan it. I didn't really care about all the details. I just loved sharing the wedding with Todd and all my friends. I loved the honeymoon, taking a cruise with Todd."

But it was hard for Michelle to move into the home Todd owned. "I had come over every weekend for five years but it was still *his* house. It was a big deal for me to move out of my apartment; I felt as if my independence had gone right out the door. It took a long time for his house to feel like home to me."

Now that she has adjusted to living with Todd, she feels other inhibitions. She misses going out with her girlfriends. She feels guilty about spending money on herself because her husband makes twice as much money as she does. She would like to have sex more frequently and she'd like to try different techniques, but feels funny about talking to Todd about it. She is reserved around Todd, suppressing anger that she expresses freely with friends. And for a while, Michelle felt she had to "make it look like [she and Todd] had the perfect relationship."

Michelle says, "Every day I love my husband more. He makes me feel good and I am more comfortable around him." Nevertheless, she thinks she might shock or embarrass Todd if she told him how she really feels about sex, intimacy, and other subjects.

Michelle balked at some of the expectations of her as a bride, refusing to care as much as some people thought she should about what she viewed as the superfluous details of her wedding. But now that she's married, she's having trouble, as many of us do, wrestling the notion of "the ideal wife" to the floor.

For most of us, this process isn't pretty, because sometimes, in the wrestling match, you become the nag you swore you'd never be. And sometimes you gain weight when you've loathed the thought of "letting yourself go." And often, you're hardest on yourself when you can least afford to be, amid adjustments as major as those that come with marriage.

Myth Four: "We Are Going to Be the Perfect Couple"

As if a triathalon wasn't enough, there's a fourth myth that inspires newlyweds to impractical feats. It is the myth of the perfect marriage. The marriage that produces simultaneous orgasms every night. The one that generates jewelry every anniversary and flowers regularly. The one that photographs well, ages well, and always looks intimate and fond. When in reality, in every marriage, there are arguments that go nowhere. Things that get said that should never be said. And lapses of sex, of conversation, and of courtesy that you wouldn't have imagined you'd ever experience in *your* marriage.

One Big, Happy Family

My friend Teresa, a thirty-year-old retail manager in Denver, cherished the idea that marriage brought together two families as one. But the month before the wedding, the weekend of the wedding, and for months afterward, Teresa had to contend with her mother-in-law being critical and demanding. For the first couple of months she and Blaine were married, Teresa "protested, nagged, and analyzed"—all in an attempt to get Blaine to take her side against his mother. But Blaine just felt torn, withdrawing from Teresa because he couldn't handle her anger.

It took one nasty confrontation with Blaine's mother for Teresa to decide she had to back off. She set certain boundaries in her mind that her mother-in-law could not cross without crossing her, but otherwise bit her tongue and tried to be pleasant. And she vowed never to bad-mouth her mother-in-law again, even though Blaine's mother bad-mouthed Teresa constantly when Blaine spoke to his mother on the phone.

Then, unbeknownst to Teresa, Blaine stood up to his mom, saying, "I married Teresa because she was a strong person who would be a great mom and a good wife. You pushed her too far and she has had enough. If you continue to bad-mouth her, you will force me to have to choose between the two of you. And I warn you, if you make me choose, I won't choose you." His secret ultimatum worked, and his mother stopped being so critical. And months later, when Blaine felt the situation had improved, he told Teresa how he'd confronted his mother on her behalf.

Teresa never imagined she'd become embroiled in vicious arguments with her mother-in-law. And Michelle didn't envision herself being hemmed in by marriage, even as she herself began to feel like "hemming in" her husband's activities. The surprises marriage springs on us frequently do not correspond with our dreams and ideals, even as passionately as we may try to make our new marriages and families better than the ones we grew up in, or observed.

Your Skirmish with Myths

So you're a newlywed. And as the weeks go by, these myths erode the assurance with which you and your new husband strutted down the aisle to the applause of guests. The UPS man comes less and less often with wedding gifts. And you no longer carry the wedding album with you to friends' houses, or hoist it onto the laps of people who come over, because everyone has already seen it.

If only you had something to look forward to. If only you had something that occupied your thoughts the way the wedding did. This was the bait I took as I started madly decorating the apartment. I started buying furniture, reupholstering furniture, and planning what to buy next. Other brides I knew did the same thing, except they threw themselves into work, or went off the pill to have a baby, or started circling ads for houses in the real estate section. Even with rice still in our hair, we went charging toward the next rite of passage.

The Motorcycle v. the China Cabinet

Then one night, Duke and I stopped on the way home from a party to have a drink at the Hotel Del Coronado, a fine old hotel on a gorgeous San Diego beach. We were in a dark, mahogany-paneled bar with Kahlua in our coffee. It was late and we were proud of ourselves for doing such a romantic thing rather than heading straight home to bed.

Duke was telling me something he'd heard at the

party, about how this guy saved up for a motorcycle but ended up spending the money on a china cabinet his wife wanted instead. And as we did to one another so many times early in our marriage, Duke goaded me, trying to see how domesticated we'd become. Would you make me buy the china cabinet? he seemed to ask. Would you make me conform and be a browbeaten husband when what I really want to be is a daredevil? Is this my suburban destiny? Are we going to be like everybody else?

Maybe it was the Kahlua. Maybe it was the late hour of the night. But I started thinking about the Villeroy & Boch we had in boxes in hall closets. And the crystal on the shelf above the refrigerator neither of us could reach. So I took his disdainful challenge, and said, yes, we really need a china cabinet.

Duke didn't want a motorcycle. Nor, deep down, did he really believe that we'd conform and become a cul-de-sac couple with a minivan anytime soon. But that night he reacted to me as if I'd said something far more poisonous, which, I later learned, I had. Because not only was our bank account still obliterated from our share of the wedding and honeymoon costs, but my determination to move on, to feel as special again as I had as a bride, and as purposeful, said something devastating about our new marriage: that it, in and of itself, was not enough for me.

Duke didn't say it precisely that way. What he did say, with considerable annoyance, was, "Why don't you take time to enjoy the china before you have to have the china cabinet?" Why, he seemed to say, do you have to rush us into the next stage of our lives instead of enjoying the honeymoon phase? Why aren't you satisfied with us as we are?

To a certain extent, Duke's challenge to me represented his own lack of comfort with the idea of being married. We were both doing the porcupine dance, trying to find a comfort zone that only more time as a married couple would lend us.

The Ammunition You'll Need

Duke proved his military training that night because he knew exactly what to arm me with. Though he may not have known that he was doing so, he gave me what I needed to battle the myths that both of us brought into marriage, but that I struggled with far more. And now I can share those insights with you.

1. SAVOR WHAT IS REAL AND PRESENT IN YOUR MARRIAGE. LOOK FOR SMALL WONDERS.

Savoring the good in your marriage means choosing another way to view your reality. It does not, however, mean you should abandon your high standards. After all, as Judith Wallerstein and Sandra Blakeslee write in their landmark book *The Good Marriage: How and Why Love Lasts*, "in happy marriages, the high expectations of courtship are modified . . . but never entirely given up."

Kathryn, a thirty-year-old attorney in Washington, D.C., finds great peace in quiet dinners with her husband, William. She couldn't name one thing he did that made her happy recently, but said there were hundreds of little things William did every day that thrilled her. Just that William is himself is the best, she says.

I want to strangle Kathryn, because she's already got it; she already knows what it takes to make a marriage work. *She* wouldn't have squirmed through her drink at a glamorous setting perched on the Pacific with her handsome husband. She would have seen his dimples in the candlelight. She would have tasted the Kahlua. She would have taken snapshots of the moment in her mind.

BRIDE-TO-BRIDE

What has your husband done recently that made you really happy?

⅒ "He let me sleep in on a rainy Saturday while he went out and did all the errands. Then he brought muffins home."

⅒ "He bought me a bracelet I've been coveting. It was a big sacrifice for him."

⅒ "He included me in a big decision about changing jobs. It is really nice to be part of a team."

⅒ "At the end of a busy day, he noticed I had cleaned the house and said how nice it looked. That acknowledgment was better than flowers."

But the perfectionists and workaholics among us know more about work than we do about enjoyment. We exhaust ourselves preparing for dinner parties, or for the holidays, so we don't truly enjoy them when they occur. And we approach marriage the same way, as if our happiness lies in fabric swatches and mortgage payments, parenting classes or the next item on our "to do" lists.

Marriage is, instead, about taking care of each other. Researchers at the University of Washington tell us that couples who are satisfied with their marriages report a five-to-one ratio of positive to negative moments. And while calculating your "moments" could be destructive, too, it is true that the tiniest components of our marriages—the smiles, the kind words, the kisses hello and good-bye—make all the difference.

Though I haven't found the source, I once heard of research that said that married couples who tell each other they love one another every day have a greater chance of staying together than those who don't. As corny as this may sound, Duke and I have always said

"I love you" to one another five, sometimes ten times a day, not because of any research but because the words come naturally. When Duke hits the snooze button and first kisses me in the morning. When we finish speaking on the phone during the workday. When I'm fixing dinner and he comes over to see what's cooking. When a commercial comes on during a sitcom and we look at one another across the room. And especially at night when the lights are off, and we don't want to let go of the day, or the last conscious thought of one another.

These "I love you's" arise from real feeling, from a real presence in each other's lives. And I've learned to sustain the shivers those words can produce. They don't come in blue Tiffany boxes. Nor are they for public consumption, like most of the wedding plans.

2. STRETCH OUT THE NOVELTY OF BEING A NEWLYWED.

Many brides get deluged with attention during the engagement and wedding, and when it's over, they miss it.

However, people with really good marriages learn how to fuss over themselves. They learn to make everyday life sacred and festive. Wallerstein and Blakeslee put it beautifully in *The Good Marriage*, saying the identity of the marriage is the first child the couple produces and "like a real baby it brings real joy."

Forging the identity of the marriage is the fun part of being a newlywed. And you can do it in many ways. By recounting to yourselves and to your friends the story of your courtship. By using your new china and silver for Friday night dinners. Or by returning to the place where you spent your wedding night now and again.

Dolly, the musician married to Jake, says they celebrate everything, and they do so in a number of ways.

Dolly and Jake prize the spiritual side of themselves and joined the Greek Orthodox church before they got married, even though neither of them was Greek Orthodox before. In part, they chose this religion because it was laden with ritual and tradition.

Because they like the way the ancient church and mythologies gave time meaning in the form of calendars, Dolly and Jake have made their own "love calendar." Each year, they celebrate the day they first met at a folk festival, the time when they started falling in love, the night they first made love, in addition to the anniversaries of their engagement and marriage.

Teresa, the Denver newlywed who struggled to get along with her mother-in-law, and her husband, Blaine, went to a Christmas store soon after they were married to buy a lighted angel for the top of their own family Christmas tree. While Elaine, the bride from New Mexico struggling with the changes in her diet since she got married, and her husband "make a big deal of every month [they] are married, getting cards and balloons for one another." They make a point of saying each time a holiday passes that this is the first one they have spent together as husband and wife.

But it isn't just big holidays and anniversaries that need celebrating. A friend recently challenged Duke and me to make our entire St. Patrick's Day dinner green. So I made green Irish soda bread and a herb-crusted swordfish while Duke saturated mashed potatoes and apple sauce with food coloring. Sure it was tame compared to the way we used to spend St. Patrick's Day when we were single, but it was the idea that counted: we could imbue holidays with our own traditions, and every day with a sense of sacredness and merriment. Over time, you stop looking to outside landmarks as your source of happiness, but find resources within.

3. WAIT FOR THE WAVE TO COME.

Duke understood much better than I did that, as new-lyweds, we were on a learning curve. It would take months, and perhaps years, for us to develop our style of marriage, and for much of the way we'd be taking baby steps. Sometimes even backward steps.

That Duke was a southern Californian was a big help in this respect because the beach has a way of sapping overzealous tendencies out of people. He already knew how to relax, how to sit on his surfboard and bob up and down until the right wave appeared. He knew that eventually it would come.

As I said in the previous chapter, marriage is often about choosing the great unknown over considerable ambivalence. And the honeymoon stage is a particularly vulnerable, tentative time. You worry a great deal about preserving your identity, and about your marriage turn-ing into the drab, predictable life you spent your single years trying to avoid. And you don't trust that your part-ner has your best interest at heart, which most likely is true because he is also liable to be worrying about pre-serving his identity and keeping the marriage out of the doldrums.

But like Duke, I had to learn to bob around and wait for the right wave, for the stride that we would soon adopt. It took several incidents of me giving Duke the silent treatment, and Duke not noticing, to persuade me that my husband really wasn't a mind reader and didn't know what was upsetting me until I told him. It took months before my family felt they knew Duke very well, and months before Duke's family began to accept me. No amount of work I could do would have hurried those natural processes along. No amount of haranguing myself or Duke would have made the transition any smoother.

My writer friend Mara is the Vancouver bride who learned not to expect her marriage to match someone else's ideal, but to accept that, like her, her marriage would always be rough and tumble. However, things got a little more rough and tumble than she would have preferred just eighteen months into her marriage. She and her husband, Clint, had just bought a home when Clint was hurt in an accident at work. Clint had been a "grip" in the film industry for many years, hanging lights and doing other kinds of physical labor involved in preparing scenes. Once he was disabled, Clint lost his job. And what came next was "pure, unadulterated hell," Mara says.

Having worked eighteen-hour days most of his life, Clint was now recovering from a back injury, lying around the house, depressed and in pain, watching TV, eating and gaining weight, and leaving the house a mess. "I went berserk," Mara remembers. "We fought every night. He said I didn't understand how much pain he

---

WHAT NO ONE TELLS THE BRIDE ABOUT . . .

Four myths we bring to marriage:

☞ Myth One: All you need to be married is a license.

☞ Myth Two: He's going to be the perfect husband.

☞ Myth Three: You're going to be the perfect wife.

☞ Myth Four: You're going to be the perfect couple.

Our brides' solutions:

☞ Savor what is real and present in your marriage. Look for small wonders.

☞ Stretch out the novelty of being newlyweds.

☞ Wait for the wave to come.

was in. I felt he was wallowing in it. All I did was work and write, and we had no money at all. I was so resentful."

But four months later, Clint emerged from this, the biggest crisis of his life. If he couldn't work on films the way he had before, he decided to go into computer animation, and he began a work/study program to learn about the field. Today, he and Mara are back on their financial feet, still stirring things up when life gets too easy, but appreciating, too, the way that only time can compel us to action, to compassion, to forgiveness, and to love.

There are many phantoms that emerge in the first year or two of marriage. And I hope these three adages—appreciating small wonders, celebrating your new love, and waiting for the wave—drive some of them away. At the worst of it, when you're most afraid, or most in denial, or when you ask yourself, "Is that all there is?," you'll at least have some ideas of how to extricate yourself from the malaise. You'll know that just as was true of the wedding, all you can do, to a certain extent, is take your new husband's hand and believe that something better is in store.

But different than before you were married, now it really is up to you to create something better. You will find within him the small wonders that sustain your hopes. You will find within yourself the patience to let your budding marriage grow.

Chapter 5

FOR RICHER, FOR POORER: HANDLING THE INEVITABLE, MOMENTOUS SQUABBLES ABOUT MONEY

It's normal for you and your husband to be worlds apart when it comes to money. And it's normal to find that even in the haven of marriage, money equals power. But as distasteful as it may be, work together to form healthy habits, and do the unexpected by trusting one another, utterly and completely.

My friend Pam, a thirty-two-year-old software designer from Phoenix, bought a new car shortly after she got married. She loved the car, but there was one little hitch. Pam had been independent and self-sufficient for so long that she had never thought to consult her husband, Michael, about buying the car. When Michael saw her new acquisition in the driveway, he was so angry and hurt that Pam thought he might leave her. He didn't, but Pam says it was the most frightening point yet in their marriage.

Amelia, a thirty-year-old development director in Princeton, New Jersey, married a man who loves to fish. But when Dean bought a $600 fly rod without asking *her*, Amelia was, if you'll excuse the pun, fit to be tied. They had a horrific fight, which concluded with the newlyweds deciding that "the only way to avoid conflict

about money was to talk, talk, talk about expenditures
in advance!"

The Leading Cause of Arguments

Experts tell us that money is the leading cause of arguments among newlyweds. Money may even cause more
friction for us than for our predecessors, since most of
us who now vow "for richer, for poorer" have a financial history—a few years of experience in which we have
acquired credit ratings and debts, mortgages and loan
payments, gold cards or dunning notices.

There's nothing so unromantic as balancing a checkbook. And it pains me to be pecuniary this early in the
book. But the fact is, not only do newlyweds argue most
about money, but these arguments can escalate. Citibank
conducted a survey and tells us that 57 percent of divorced couples cite financial disputes as the primary reason they didn't get along.

This chapter reveals how prevalent and how painful
arguments about money are among the betrothed and
recently wed. You'll learn whether or not a spender can
live happily ever after with a saver, and how modern
couples are handling money differently from previous
generations. And I'll talk about the ugly truth that even
in a loving union, money equals power, and how you
and your husband can use that power to the marriage's
advantage.

Fiscal Opposites

When we got married, Duke and I were fiscal opposites.
I lived hand to mouth, paid the minimum every month

on my credit cards, and never had any savings. I also believed in "the freelance fairy," an invisible protector who saw to it that a magazine or freelance client mailed a check to me just when things were getting desperate.

Duke, on the other hand, had ridiculous amounts of money in his checking account, along with a bloated savings and investment portfolio. He didn't believe in credit cards, and carried $200 or more in his wallet at all times. Without a lapse, Duke had been paid on the first and the fifteenth of the month, every month, for nine years.

You can imagine that considerable head butting preceded Duke and my coming to a "meeting of the minds." In fact, in the four years we have known one another, the only time Duke and I have intentionally gone without speaking was because of money.

We had gotten a notice from the bank that eight checks from our joint account had bounced. With my business acumen, it logically should have fallen to Duke to oversee our finances. But because Duke's job takes him to sea so often, he wanted me to handle the bills and the checkbook. So I was the accounting wizard Duke looked to for an explanation when the checks bounced. And according to my math, there was plenty of money in the account.

Duke had also failed to mention to me that his security clearance—the permission the U.S. government gave him to be involved in matters of national security—could be revoked if he bounced checks. In other words, his job depended on his having an unblemished financial record. If it were otherwise, the government would deem him too vulnerable to bribes or lucrative offers to betray his country.

Now it wasn't just a matter of the bank tacking on a

$10 fee for insufficient funds. It wasn't just a matter of having to make a humiliating phone call to my landlord or to Bloomingdale's, explaining my "innocent mistake." Suddenly my bouncing checks was a matter of national security.

Duke was furious—he had never had a check returned. But I had good reason to be furious as well. First, I had begged Duke to handle our finances when he was home. I was no shrinking violet, I could figure out the checkbook when he went away; in the meantime, I preferred to be accountable to him. Second, because we'd never really evaluated how best to bank once we were married, we maintained an overly complicated system, a savings account at one bank (to which his paychecks were automatically deposited) and a joint checking account at another bank. I was constantly switching money from one account to the other, usually mailing deposits so as to not spend hours away from work running errands. And third, I certainly would have set up overdraft protection with the bank had I known that our bouncing checks could have career-ending repercussions.

It turned out that a large deposit I made to checking had been lost in the mail. And without talking to each other, we spoke to an agent at the bank to straighten things out. Once we were on speaking terms again, Duke and I consolidated our accounts and checked our balances much more frequently to prevent future errors.

Power, Influence, and Control

But other than the fact that Duke's job depended on it, why was an argument over money more intense than any other? Because, you see, arguments about money are never *just* about money. They are, according to Howard

Markman, the director for Marital and Family Studies at the University of Denver, about "power, influence, and control." Markman has studied 150 couples for ten years, starting when they were newlyweds. He says that while friend and in-law problems plague couples early on, they taper off quickly; money problems, on the other hand, cause conflict immediately and linger for years. Why are money problems harder to resolve? There are several reasons.

One is that our sense of security and autonomy are often intimately tied to the income we make, or the savings we have. Sure, single people identify with and draw self-worth from their faux families, friends, and colleagues who take the place of their families of origin. But the day a single person feels truly free—your personal Bastille Day—is more likely to be when you claim financial independence from your parents.

Milestones of Economic Freedom

The longer you are single, and the longer you have to establish yourself, the more you are apt to forget the important milestones in your financial independence. Remember the minuscule paychecks you got when you first started out? The first apartment and the landlord who demanded your parents co-sign? The first piece of furniture you saved up for? The car loan that was, miraculously, approved? The department store credit card with the $200 limit? The shopping spree you paid for with checks? The bid you made on a condo? The first trip to Europe you financed? And the Merrill Lynch stockbroker you thought would laugh at the amount you had to invest?

In marriage, we are quickly reminded what those

milestones meant to us. Like when a husband comes home sweaty from basketball and sinks into that treasured, saved-for chair. Or you have to move out of the single pad that symbolized your emancipation. Or his money starts mingling with your money, his expenses with your expenses, in ways that seem uncouth.

The Downside of Exercising Our Choices

The worst of it, for many brides I met and talked to, is that women often make major life changes simultaneously with their marriages. And usually these changes leave them at a financial disadvantage, or what they perceive to be a financial disadvantage, because they must depend on their husbands for money. Some women move to accommodate their husbands' careers and have to look for work in a new place, which can take months and months. Many leave jobs to start home-based businesses or to pursue careers they couldn't have without their husband's salary to fall back on. Some take time off, either to plan a wedding, to start having children, or to reconsider their career paths.

I made a major change, too. Because my job was the flexible one, I left Boston, my freelance writing contacts, and my part-time job to join Duke in San Diego. Duke was very generous, paying for my move, some of my debts, part of the wedding, and he subsidized my full-time work on a book for months before I received a publishing contract or compensation.

As a result, Duke's overstuffed checking account dwindled, and his savings began to shrink. Of course, this made him very tense. He didn't believe that my freelance fairy would come through. He didn't believe that this was an unusually expensive transition and not my normal pace of spending. Duke simply was not comfortable with a smaller financial cushion.

Meanwhile, I felt I had to justify any money I spent on myself, emphasizing the *low* price of any item I bought. I nudged him to take over the finances so he would feel more in control. I got mad that he wouldn't accept our circumstances. And I felt he blamed me when he made jokes about how, as a bachelor, he'd withdrawn $200 at a time from the ATM whereas now that he was married, he took a meager $40 or $60 and had to check the balance even then.

I have heard dozens of brides, not to mention women who leave work to become full-time moms, express the same frustrations when they suddenly became financially dependent on their husbands. I'm not trying to lend credence to the stereotype that women are always the "spenders" in relationships, smuggling new clothes into their closets when their husbands aren't around. After all, plenty of brides I interviewed have higher salaries, better credit ratings, and more conservative spending habits than the men they married. One bride I know works three jobs to help her new hus-

---

BRIDE-TO-BRIDE

Has money caused problems in your new marriage?

∞ "It took the whole first year for us to move from an attitude of 'mine' and 'yours' to 'ours.'"

∞ "It only does when I let it. I feel bad about spending money because I'm not working. My husband has to remind me it's our money."

∞ "I like to shop—who doesn't? But my husband has taken away my credit cards. Still, I know that, in the long run, he's right."

∞ "Money? What money?! When I moved to Hawaii with my new husband, I left a $30 per hour job. Now I don't have a job and the most exciting thing I do is go to the grocery store."

band pay his debts since he declared bankruptcy right
before their wedding.

But by and large, it seems women who provided for
themselves when they were single felt less pressure to be the
primary breadwinners once they got married. With the
support of their mates, these brides explored their choices
—whether to go back to school, pursue a riskier dream career, stay at home with kids, or work at something less than
full-time. As a result, many of these brides experienced a
loss of self-esteem. They felt guilty spending money they
didn't make, or contribute equally. They felt their opinions
didn't, or shouldn't, count for as much in decision making. And they resented feeling this way.

The Pressure of New Responsibilities

On the other side of the coin are brides and grooms like
Duke who find it terribly uncomfortable being econom-
ically responsible for someone else. My friend Lisa and
her husband, James, who live in Ohio, bought a car
shortly after they got married. Lisa had the better credit
rating, so the car needed to appear in her name. James
wasn't bothered by this but Lisa felt "stressed out" that
she was legally responsible for the car, even though James
was making equal payments on the vehicle.

Looking out for someone you love who is less skillful
at managing money, or who thinks about financial matters in a radically different way, can be very stressful.
Cindy is the veterinarian from Los Angeles I mentioned
whose husband filed for bankruptcy right before their
wedding. She and Rick are now starting a business together, a prospect Cindy is excited about, yet at the same

time she's frightened. "My biggest fear about the future is that the business will fail or have difficulties because Rick will not take his part seriously." Rick contributes a lot around the house, doing all the cooking and cleaning, while Cindy works three jobs so they can launch their business. Nevertheless, Cindy feels incredible pressure, knowing she cannot get pregnant and they cannot go ahead with plans to have a family until the business is established. And until Rick takes charge of it, which she worries he never will.

Obviously, when you are just cutting your teeth on marriage, biting off more than you can chew is not advisable. But my point is, newlyweds are frequently traumatized by changes in their economic status, and by having to share financial decisions that have enormous practical, legal, and emotional consequences.

Financial Baggage, Family History

Then, just to make money more of a sticky wicket, add the fact that one's spending and saving habits are usually steeped in family history and tradition. Duke, for example, grew up with a father whose family lost their business in the Great Depression. His father distrusts the stock market, stores up money in the bank, and got his first credit card in years when he traveled to our wedding.

I grew up in a Presbyterian minister's family in which money was tight but no financial hurdle seemed insurmountable. My mom would do the taxes and caution that we had $150 to eat on for the month, but then take us to a sale at Macy's the next day and load up the credit card. My parents drove jalopies, one of which burst into flames minutes after my father leaped out of it, but they sent both my sister and me to expensive private colleges.

It was no wonder Duke had trouble adjusting to a smaller surplus of cash, and no wonder that, given my parents' propensity for making things work out, I believed money had a way of just appearing. Part optimist, part spending fool, I've had to adhere to a more conservative approach.

Financial histories and family habits play a game of peek-a-boo in new marriages, popping up unexpectedly. My newlywed friend Teresa, the retail manager in Denver, grew up in a family in which long-distance phone calls were considered a luxury. So she was annoyed when Blaine called his mother across the country a few times a week. Once Teresa and Blaine talked about it and found that family values had caused the rift, Teresa began to enjoy a much closer relationship with her parents because Blaine encouraged her to call them regularly. As a new family, the two of them decided family ties were worth the added expense.

Married Money Management Tips

Arriving at strategies that work for you is the key to surviving these momentous money squabbles, according to the brides I interviewed. The following four tips helped us to reorient ourselves to the teamwork involved in married money management:

1. TALK, TALK, TALK ABOUT YOUR VALUES, GOALS, AND FEARS. MAKE RULES THAT WORK FOR YOU. This is the key to resolving ugly money skirmishes and to relieving the "shock of the new" that you and your

groom may experience in your economic partnership. As Amelia said in the beginning of the chapter, "talk, talk, talk" about your individual values, goals, and fears, and then construct a plan for your new family.

Maybe you'll need rigid budgets and computerized record keeping. Maybe you'll call upon a financial adviser to project what you'll need to buy a house, to start a business, to send kids to college, or to retire comfortably. But in any case, set up rules that work for you, by which I mean, both of you.

A lot of people think a marriage isn't a marriage unless you combine bank accounts. Phillip Blumstein and Pepper Schwartz's 1970s landmark study, *American Couples*, found that couples who combined and shared their money were more likely to think of their marriages as permanent covenants. Those who believed marriage could be something less than a lifetime commitment were less apt to pool their funds.

The majority of brides I interviewed, however, reported a slightly different approach to sharing money than was true in our parents' share-and-share-alike generation. These women advocated a joint account for shared expenses and bills, plus "his" and "her" accounts so that each has some degree of spending freedom. Amelia and Dean embraced this method after coming to blows over his unapproved purchase of the $600 fly rod. Now Dean can buy fishing stuff without asking her and Amelia can buy work clothes without hiding price tags from him.

There are downsides to having separate accounts, such as double the amount of record keeping and less of a shared vision. And separate accounts work best when both husband and wife have similar incomes. They don't resolve battles such as Cindy and Rick's, in which Rick contributes nonmonetary support of the marriage by manning the household chores while Cindy works outside the home. In those cases, different rules apply.

Many brides suggested an agreement between spouses that you talk about any purchase over $100, or whatever monetary limit you set. And many suggested monthly meetings so that both partners stay informed about the couple's dynamic financial status. One bride said she and her husband have a weekly "Sunday financial summit."

Most important, make rules that suit you and that take into account what may be your and your husband's different approaches to money. Rex LeGalley and Teresa Garpstas of Albuquerque, New Mexico, received national media attention for their "premarital agreement," a wide-ranging set of rules they formulated while driving long distances for the business they owned together. Both Rex and Teresa were married before and believe that careful planning will help them avoid the problems of their previous relationships.

The agreement spells out exactly what they expect of each other, namely: Rex will handle the finances and both of them will live within a budget. Teresa will always work off a list when she goes grocery shopping. Each of them will receive a $70 weekly allowance for haircuts, eating out, gifts for friends, and spending money. They will always buy supreme unleaded fuel and never let the gauge go below half a tank. They will stay one car length's distance behind the car in front of them for every ten miles per hour of speed they're traveling. Lights in their home go out at 11:30 P.M. and they must wake up an hour and a half before they have to be somewhere.

Rex and Teresa's rules go on and on. And to be honest, Duke and I would *drink* supreme unleaded fuel before we would burden our marriage with these kinds of regulations. But for Rex and Teresa, two engineers who like things spelled out and orderly, these rules may relieve the guesswork, deceit, panic, and anger that undermine a marriage, especially in the financial realm.

It may take some long talks to come to financial agreements by which you can both abide. Your solutions may be as simple as keeping your own accounts and credit cards, or as complicated as taking note of everything you spend and reporting back to one another regularly. But eventually, after really listening to one another and considering what it is you value and fear about money, you will formulate your own plan. You'll reevaluate your plan hundreds and thousands of times over the course of your marriage, but hopefully not just when eight checks bounce and your spouse is biting his lip.

I recommend you merge your assets in at least one account. With joint accounts, the incentive is there for you and your partner to have to grapple with issues of trust early and often. And scrapping and negotiating is healthy, even if it sounds as appealing as a tax audit.

Nevertheless, when you start celebrating financial milestones in your marriage—say, the first month you manage to keep $200 in reserve in your checking account, or the first time you and your husband buy a car together—you'll feel an unexpected joy and relief at having met a shared goal. Not the same joy you might have had buying the cashmere sweater you wanted when your husband insisted you stick to the budget. Not the same joy my husband would have had if his mountain of money had never diminished in the first place. But, God forbid, a more grown-up joy, one borne of plans and dreams, of sacrifices and compromises, and of working with someone you love, in whom you also have trust.

2. Delay making changes that will dramatically alter your financial status.

While you are developing that trust and formulating your plan, you and your husband should delay, if at all possible, making changes in your lives that could dramatically alter your financial status. If you are planning a wedding, moving in together, and putting a household together, you are already in the middle of an expensive transition.

I particularly caution women against making decisions that leave them at a financial disadvantage so early in a marriage, because there is some evidence that even when women work, they feel guilty about their expenditures, especially about money they spend on themselves. Author Dalma Heyn documents this phenomenon, suggesting that women hide their purchases and fiddle with checkbook balances because we believe denying ourselves is part of being a good wife and that exposing our expenditures to our husbands might make us, in some way, unlovable.

I believe that my mother's generation suffered more from a reluctance to spend money on themselves than is true of women today. My father, sister, and I have spent hours in dressing rooms and in aisles of department stores, imploring my mother to buy things for herself. And yet, today, my mother reports much greater freedom to spend, albeit in her conservative fashion, because she works and makes her own money.

Nevertheless, women are, to a certain extent, predisposed to guilt about money, because we are often raised to subjugate our own needs and desires for the sake of others. And although good, trusting marriages can overcome this predisposition, I think new marriages need to pace themselves, tackling this one when the foundation of the marriage is stronger.

Obviously, many times in new marriages, dramatic economic shifts are unavoidable. But if you happen to be reading this in time to plan ahead, come into your marriage with as much financial stability as you can manage. Then, particularly in the first year, move slowly and cautiously, and make modest financial goals together. Work as a team toward any big job or lifestyle changes.

3. DON'T FORCE YOUR SPOUSE TO DO SOMETHING HE OR SHE IS NOT GOOD AT. SHARE FINANCIAL RESPONSIBILITY.

I don't know any married couples in which both partners are high rollers or spendthrifts. And I know few marriages in which the partners are really simpatico about how much to save and how much to spend. But in cases in which one partner truly has less self-control and fewer money management skills, Seattle financial planner Karen Ramsey says, "Couples shouldn't force each other to do things they're not good at."

This is a pearl of wisdom that has profound implications for a marriage, and I'll talk more about it in a chapter to come. But in essence, unconditional love means accepting a person's flaws. You can't allow your husband to squander your money, but you can't expect to teach him fiscal responsibility, as you define it, either.

Duke and I ran into this problem several times. I once suggested that he should carry my credit cards; that way

I would have to consult with him before I bought things on credit. But Duke rejected this idea, saying it didn't get to the root of the problem—my spending. Here I thought I had taken this really big, grown-up step, but Duke wanted all or nothing.

In marriage, all or nothing is a losing proposition. It doesn't make sense to entrust all money matters to a person who has never in his or her thirty-three years on this earth taken them very seriously. Nor should a more pecuniary bride or groom have to "parent" his or her spouse, or be the "bad guy" in the relationship who says, "No, we can't afford to go out to eat," or "No, we can't afford to buy the house you want."

Frequently, this is the way Elizabeth, a twenty-nine-year-old bride in Boston, feels. She says her husband, a medical student, is clueless about their financial status. He thinks he's contributing equally to their living costs because his army stipend pays for his schooling when, in fact, it is Elizabeth's full-time job that pays for their condo, their car, and all their other expenses.

"My girlfriend and I just laugh at our husbands because both of them are so oblivious," Elizabeth says. Turning the stereotype on its ear, she laughs, "We just let them *think* they know what they're doing."

It's healthier in financial matters to meet somewhere in the middle. Have the more financially savvy person pay the bills and keep the checkbook, while the other spouse balances the checkbook every month. Experiment with solutions to see if they promote better habits, and then reevaluate how those solutions worked or didn't work for both of you. Most of all, check back regularly with one another, not because you distrust one another but because you want to work as a team.

4. USE TRUST TO SURPRISE THE SOUL.

In our society, money talks. And in relationships, money can speak in very surprising and wonderful ways.

Take Amelia, for example. Dean, her fishing aficionado husband, "does not believe in jewelry." A $600 fly rod is utilitarian in his eyes but baubles are excessive. So imagine Amelia's delight when Dean bought her, out of the blue, a bracelet she'd been coveting. Not for any important occasion. Just because.

In marriage, it isn't necessarily the money you spend that matters. It's the way in which your soul stretches to delight and please your partner. But because common wisdom holds that we should prepare prenuptial agreements and guard our money even more than we guard our souls, it often means the most to us when we, as partners, use money to extend ourselves.

Ken Reich, a Cambridge, Massachusetts, marital therapist and psychoanalyst, recently reminded me of a dramatic moment from *Les Miserables*, the book/musical. Jean Valjean escapes from prison where he was serving a life sentence for stealing a loaf of bread, which he took because he was starving. A priest takes Valjean in and gives him food and shelter, but desperate for money, the escapee steals candlesticks from the altar of the priest's church.

When he is later caught pawning the candlesticks, Valjean is handcuffed and escorted back to the church where police ask the priest if he wants to press charges. Surely, Valjean will face the gallows if he returns to prison. But instead of renouncing the thief, the priest denies that Valjean took the candlesticks and says they were a gift. Then the priest goes one step further, handing Valjean a gold chalice and saying, "Here, you forgot the wine goblet I also gave you."

Reich articulated for me the value of doing the unexpected in relationships, and of *undoing* the rote, repetitive patterns of responses and behaviors that couples bring to and engender in marriages. Doing the unexpected is a theme that will come up again in this book, but as it pertains to money, doing the unexpected can do wonders for relationships.

Last week, for example, I heard myself say to another woman, as women so often do, "My husband has no idea what bedding costs, and I think it's better to keep him in the dark." When I thought later about this blithe, off-hand comment, I realized it had far more serious implications. I had chosen deceit over trust, stereotype over surprise.

Because I have a love affair with beautiful sheets and comforters, I assumed that Duke would object, when, in fact, I can think of very few instances when Duke has said no to anything I really wanted for which I could make a good argument. He's never once told me to take anything back. More often,

---

BRIDE-TO-BRIDE

How do you make financial decisions now that you are married?

∞ "The first year we kept our finances separate. Then we gradually moved into sharing finances."

∞ "I gave my input, but because I'm not working, I often allow him to make the final decisions."

∞ "This hasn't changed much. I still function independently."

∞ "We talk about purchases over $150, not including gifts for one another or my clothes."

∞ "I gave him a card on my Visa account, he gave me a card on his American Express. So we each take some responsibility, but don't have separate accounts."

he's encouraged me to go back and buy something I hesitated buying.

Often, pat little phrases like this come out of my mouth as if from some woman I don't know. But they are telling, because they represent my unconscious expectations of marriage, of how I think I'm supposed to act as a wife. And they help me identify when to do the opposite.

So the next time I buy the sheets and comforters, I'm going to take Duke with me, show him what cotton sheets with a thread count under two hundred feel like, and introduce him to a world in which good linens don't come cheap. He'll be unfazed. He won't know why I felt compelled to show him. But I'll know I've done something radical by trusting him, by giving him the wine goblet, instead of believing what mainstream culture would have me believe—that I have to hide my spending and that Duke has to revile it.

Duke also surprises *me*, outstretching his hand when I expect him to draw it back. Shortly before we were married, I was offered an opportunity to co-author a book. But my co-author could not pay me, nor was there any guarantee that we would get a publishing contract. Even if we could sell it, I had never written a book before and, without a track record, the proceeds would probably be meager, not nearly enough to cover the cost of a year's work.

This was a particularly big risk because of the kind of person I am. I have never really understood money very well, once asking financially knowledgeable friends of mine if the banks went around trading gold bricks at the end of the day to balance the books. I have always liked beautiful things; I have always liked buying other people beautiful things. And when I was first out on my own,

I lived way beyond my means. My parents had to bail me out of several credit card fiascos, and it took me a decade to get over the shame of having to ask them to do that.

So when I presented the book option to Duke, a big part of me didn't believe I deserved his financial support. It was if tapes played in my head, saying, "You aren't to be trusted, you aren't to be trusted."

But Duke trusted me, utterly and completely. He hardly had to think before he said, "It's your first book, we have to take a chance." With that, he supported me, at the same time as he covered our share of the soaring costs of our wedding and honeymoon. And for eight months, he watched the bank balances fall.

Then something miraculous happened. So many publishers liked the book that our agent held an auction to handle the sale. By the end of the auction, it was clear Duke and I would reap enough from the book contract to restore the money he had invested in me, and to keep me

WHAT NO ONE TELLS THE BRIDE ABOUT . . .

Marriage and money:

∞ Money is the leading cause of arguments among newlyweds.

∞ Arguments over money are not just about money but about power, influence, and control.

∞ Your sense of security and autonomy may be intimately tied to your income and/or savings.

∞ The way you think about money often stems from the way your family handled money.

Our brides' solutions:

∞ Talk, talk, talk about your values, goals, and fears. Then make rules that work for you.

∞ Delay making choices that will dramatically alter your financial status. Share financial responsibility.

∞ Don't force your spouse to do something he or she is not good at.

∞ Use trust to surprise the soul.

paid for another two years of writing, including the year I would need to write *this* book.

Duke could have attached conditions. He could have asked me to get a part-time job; he could have made me promise to pay him back. Those conditions would have made him feel secure. As someone unworthy of being trusted, I expected some conditions. But even before we were legally bound to one another, he made his money mine. And my dreams his.

This enormous risk bound me to him more than any ring or any piece of paper. And this is what the trust you place in one another can do, more often in simple, less dramatic ways. It may hurt at first. It may be all you can do to keep from attaching conditions or qualifications to your trust. But go ahead, defy convention, defy your spouse's biggest hopes, and do the unexpected.

Like me, most brides I interviewed were loathe to share their money or their trust at first. But when they sat down with their new husbands and began to make plans and budgets, they found they enjoyed the teamwork, the shared goals, and the shared milestones. Carefully, they worked through problems—times when money made them feel guilty or overburdened, and times it wove power, not love, into their relationship. Ultimately, they had to trust one another, surprising one another the way only trust can. By doing so, they enriched their marriages a hundredfold.

Chapter 6

I'M BECOMING MY MOTHER:
WHAT TO DO WHEN YOUR MARRIAGE FALLS
PREY TO STEREOTYPES

*It's normal to see yourself saying and doing things you
saw your mother say and do. The clay you start with
will surely be the model of the marriage you know best—
your parents'. But it need not be the marriage you make
from now on, if you learn how to sculpt it.*

My mother is a professional woman and not a culinary
maven, and yet, the recurring images I have of her from
childhood are of her doing dishes. In my mind's eye, she
is either on tiptoe putting away bowls in high cabinets,
or round-backed over the prone appliance door with a
box of Cascade in her hand.

When I first got married, this was what I was always
doing, too. Morning, noon, and night, I was now the
drone. Round-backed or on tiptoes. Rinsing before
loading. Unloading the plastic cradle of silverware. And
lingering in the kitchen after everyone else had left.

I could not believe this was my fate. Like my mother,
I was both cooking dinner and cleaning up after it. I
stood at the kitchen counter, like housewives of old, and
was sure that this was God's way of getting back at me
for all the times I didn't help my mom with the dishes.

Duke said he'd clean up, but for the first year of our

marriage, his offer was punctuated with the word *later* as in "I'll clean up later." Which meant that the residue of boiled potatoes had all evening to cling to the All-Clad. And the burned cheese around the edge of the lasagna pan became what a barnacle is to a ship. So the next morning, when Duke left for work, I wanted to Brillo his face as I made my way through the mess he'd been too tired to get to.

Trouble in paradise, you ask? You betcha. I had become my mother, and I was not pleased. From the interviews I've conducted, it is clear this was not the life other brides imagined for themselves either. One said, "I'm nagging him to help around the house, just like my mother did with my dad," while another barked, "Argh! I thought I had exorcised these traits—my mother's tendency to take on too much responsibility and then get angry about it."

After years on our own, in which we distanced ourselves from the rumble of Maytags and the complaints of overburdened mothers, it is terrifying to make a marriage in which both are seemingly reborn. In this chapter, I'll expose this sorry fact of marriage while at the same time assuring you that your union can shed its familial skin. And we'll see the extent to which early patterns of behavior, such as who does the dishes, become lifelong marital habits.

Thirteen Bedmates

The morning after the wedding, marriage counselors tell us, the bride wakes up with thirteen people in her honeymoon bed—her husband, her parents, her grandparents, his parents, and his grandparents. As unsavory a mental picture as this is, it's true that we all get hand-me-downs from our families. It is not just gender roles—dad takes out the garbage, mom does everything else—that are encoded in us, but many underlying messages of marriage, including how we argue and how much happiness we expect to find in our relationships.

Morgan, an artist from Maine, had been single for a decade after college; during this time she rarely argued with people, at least not in any passionate or prolonged way. Then she got married and started fighting with her husband, screaming and yelling at him. She had grown up in a family in which there were "ugly, nasty scenes," but presumed that after so many years of being away from home, she'd become a different person. This was Morgan's unfortunate dowry.

Her husband, Joe, had to confront his inheritance as well. Joe was the strong, silent type, and when he came home from work he "just sat down and ate, only mildly interested in my chatter," Morgan says. "He did not know how to keep the ball bouncing, you know, the fundamentals of keeping a conversation going." Morgan later realized this was because Joe had had three sisters and a very verbal mother, a bevy of conversation makers who hardly let him get a word in. "So we had to practice at dinner," Morgan says. "He would try to give me details about his day. But sometimes it was disappointing. Thirty years of his habit of 'just eating' were hard to break."

During their courtship, Morgan's penchant for screaming and Joe's for silent dinners hadn't emerged. But in daily life, and in the magnified scrutiny of the newlywed year, these traits not only surfaced, they became major points of contention. Of course, not all the attributes we inherit are bad. After all, we fall in love in the first place with characteristics bred in us by our families, either by nature or nurture.

Repetition Compulsion

Don Childers, a couples counselor in Indianapolis, says that because "the American family is so broken, people come out of families very wounded, ready to repeat the same patterns" in their new families. He adds, "The problem with repeating those patterns is that often, what we've been taught was wrong." And even if you're lucky enough to have come from a family in which communication was healthy and unconditional love was plentiful, you may not be equipped to tackle a "companionship" marriage, the challenging partnership of equals many of us aspire to today.

Psychologists call our tendency to repeat what we learned from our families and from our culture "repetition compulsion." Ken Reich, a marital therapist and psychoanalyst, says the concept is humorously illustrated in the movie *Groundhog Day*. In the film, Bill Murray is held captive by his own inability to change, when time after time, he tries to get things right with the character played by Andie MacDowell. Sigmund Freud would say that Murray doesn't remember what he has forgotten but acts it out anyway, which is precisely what we all do, to a certain extent, in marriage, Reich explains.

We often act without memory of a conflict, Reich says. We may have been able to push aside thoughts about a painful event from the past, but when something in daily life evokes this event, we are destined to feel the pain and vulnerability again "until we find a way to respond to it differently." Murray has this kind of epiphany in the movie, and we can, too, when, Reich says, our spouses support us and help us acknowledge and grieve over whatever pain it is that we aren't addressing.

Breaking Painful Patterns

This need not happen in therapy, although with traumatic events in one's past, or with wounds that are particularly stubborn, counseling can do a world of good. In good marriages, however, the healing of old wounds takes place constantly. Using a calm, moderate-volume voice, Joe can argue with Morgan—the product of "screamers"—and she learns to appreciate other ways of expressing anger and disagreement, ways that feel safer and saner to her than did her family's arguments.

My husband, Duke, is the product of loving parents but also of a rancorous divorce and custody battle. Because, as a child, he was shuttled between two families, he grew to dread Christmas and other holidays. Later, as a naval officer, he often came home from sea right before Christmas, when the commercial hype was at its peak and when he had to elbow people aside to buy presents. By now, he hisses year-round at the sight of anything remotely Christmas-like.

But I find he's coming around to Christmas, since I've begun to show him how great it can be. I'll admit that the tradition he likes best is a house laden with mistletoe, and that the midnight Christmas Eve service is a tougher sell. Still, I've taken over the Christmas shopping, even for people on his list, because I really enjoy doing it. And I've waited, as year after year, holiday after holiday, our traditions have accumulated meaning for him. Good memories have pushed aside the bad to the point where last year he volunteered to serve as the Easter bunny for a children's egg hunt I helped organize, and this year, believe it or not,

Scrooge succumbed and gave me a star for the top of our Christmas tree.

The Power of Marriage

At the risk of delving too deeply into psychobabble, I was amazed to learn that psychologists believe that marriage represents the nearest adult equivalent to the parent/child relationship. It makes sense to me that the caretaking we do in marriage is unparalleled by anything but the parent/child relationship. But marriage also allows adults the freedom to regress and to excavate the feelings we had as children, our tenderest enjoyment of love and safety and our tenderest fears of abandonment and vulnerability. In marriage, we have the opportunity to give birth to something different and better, to nurture kindness and integrity in one another as good parents do.

Obviously, marriage is very powerful. It calls forth reactions and behaviors that even a full single life may not have, which is scary and disconcerting to people who think they long ago left behind their adolescence and childhood.

Falling into Traditional Roles

Of all the things bequeathed to them by families or by cultural osmosis, traditional gender roles disturb brides the most. And different from pains buried deep in the psyche, brides walk down the aisle entirely conscious and very fearful of having to do more work in the marriage than their grooms do. Unfortunately, in the majority of cases, their fears are confirmed because independent women, and their progressive husbands, fall into these traditional roles as if they were grooves etched into the floors of their apartments and town houses.

Experts tell us that no more than 20 percent of dual-income couples share domestic work equally. And Dr. Clifford J. Sager, director of the Marital Therapy Clinic at New York Hospital–Cornell Medical Center in New York City, says that it's women who do most—by some estimates, 75 percent—of the household work. Newly married women, Sager says, argue more about cooking, dishwashing, and the like than anything else.

Exhausted, Overworked Brides

The brides I interviewed were nearly unanimous in saying that they were more tired now than before they got married. This surprised me because single people are usually very active, and because the women I interviewed said they were more tired now than when they were engaged, when wedding planning and celebrating made life very frenetic.

The vast majority of the women I interviewed did not marry chauvinist pigs. They married men who at least professed to believe in and desire equal partnerships. Yet, in my experience and in my research, two other factors—the expectations women had of themselves and the assumptions men and women make almost unconsciously—determine whether a woman will do the lion's share of the housework.

The "super-wife" mentality dooms women to dishpan hands. And if we can't trace the roots of this mentality back to our families, then it's a safe bet that magazines, movies, and TV shows made us believe our homes had to be beautifully furnished and maintained, that we should select special gifts for people and deliver them on time, and that the care we take in making meals is a reflection on us.

A Bride's Expectations of Herself

But husbands, by and large, do not expect this level of perfection. Sheila is a thirty-three-year-old nurse practitioner from Orange County, California, who has been married three years. "When I got married," she says, "I expected to maintain my career and the house, plan the meals, and look great without missing a step. Now I know that Tim didn't marry me for that. He married me because he loves me and wants to share my life. He didn't marry me for what I could *do*."

But Sheila described almost a two-step process to letting go of her compulsion to "do." First, she realized her husband loved her no matter how dirty, in her eyes, the house was. Then she had to throw off her own meticulousness. "I started off in the marriage spending any time I had off from work cleaning the house or gardening. There was little time to just enjoy one another. So I had to learn that a little mess was okay."

And when asked what Tim had done recently that made her happy, Sheila said, "At the end of a busy day, he noticed that I had spent a good portion of the day cleaning the house and he commented on how nice the house looked. Because he's more relaxed and has different priorities than I do when it comes to the house, his acknowledgment of my efforts was better than flowers."

Undoubtedly, women expect too much of themselves because society expects too much of them. But it was a revelation for most brides to learn that their husbands had much lower standards for the conduct of the household than they did. Why this should surprise us, I don't know, since bachelor pads are notoriously dirty and smelly. But even if a man is a neat freak, he's rarely also a gourmet cook, an executive secretary, and a flawless dresser. These are *our* expectations, not theirs.

In addition to finding that most husbands don't expect all these attributes, brides soon discover they can't do it all *and* enjoy their lives. Karmen, a thirty-six-year-old actress from Chicago, says, "I really thought I was going to be Martha Stewart. And although I still enjoy doing things to fix up the house, I am more realistic. The biggest thing I did was just admit that cleaning wasn't my thing in the first place, and with a full-time job, I didn't have the time or energy to do everything, so we hired a cleaning service. But it took me a long time to admit to friends that we hired a housekeeper. I felt guilty. It seemed like a strike against my womanhood."

Many brides feel the way Karmen does—that asking for help, or lowering their expectations, is a strike against their womanhood. But once women get over feeling that way, once they realize their standards are unattainable, they free themselves and their husbands to enjoy the marriage and the household much more.

Societal Expectations

I should not be glib about this. Most women spend their entire lives shooing these expectations out of their homes and out of their heads. And it is not just a little internal voice that says, "Stay up till midnight making a Christmas wreath out of fresh cranberries," or "Maniacally attend to your child's runny nose even though your husband is standing next to the child and the Kleenex box." It is also an insidious voice that both husband and wife respond to, whether or not they know that they are doing so.

A few weeks ago, our landlord had a new furnace installed in our home, and the workmen forgot to reignite the pilot light. It wasn't until the next morning, when there was no hot water, that Duke and I identified the problem. Automatically, without even so much as a pause, both of us presumed that lighting the pilot light was "a guy thing."

Now you must understand that, different from some marriages, my husband goes to sea for six months at a time, so I don't always have a man to count on to change a tire, take out the garbage, or fulfill any of the other hackneyed ideas of what comprises "a man's job." Regardless, mentally assigning this to Duke was instinctive. I didn't give it a second thought. . . .

Until about five minutes later when I realized the cliché that Duke and I had perpetrated, and I couldn't get to the water heater fast enough. I read the directions on the heater gleefully; once again, I was the pioneer woman, the single girl who wasn't scared of anything, the one with the match in her hand, ready to set the world on fire.

BRIDE-TO-BRIDE

Now that you're married, what traits of yours remind you of your mother?

∞ "I do more than my share of the work, as does my mother."

∞ "I nag my husband more. I am pickier about the presents he gives me. These are traits of my mother's."

∞ "When I am angry, I want to lie silent and deal with it like my mother always did. But she kept it bottled up so long, she divorced my dad."

∞ "I immediately noticed my tendency to have brief outbursts, like my mother did, and I'm fighting hard against it."

Thinking I was angry because he hadn't gotten to the chore soon enough, Duke rushed to my aid. But breathlessly, ecstatically, I explained. So that together, squatting in our slippers, peering into the cylinder and the blue gas light, we communed with a poison. The poison of our own assumptions—and the leak of conventional ideas into the marriage we like to think of as bold, defiant, untamed. . . .

That's what the *new* marriage—one that doesn't rely on another generation's assumptions—requires. Not resentment, but vigilance. Not perfection, but realism. It *does* take a man who loves a feisty, independent woman. But it *also* takes the feisty, independent woman refusing to give in.

The Silent Treatment

It is often all too easy to give in to habits we've learned from our mothers. Amelia, the development professional from Princeton, New Jersey, is using the silent treatment on her husband the way her mother did to her father. "Even though I hate it, I find myself doing it. Unfortunately, I also find that it works. Because my husband gets exasperated after a while and will do anything to make me talk. And while I'm silent, I finetune what I'm going to say so that once I begin speaking, I'm well-spoken and my arguments hold more water."

Again, Amelia is doing what most new brides do, borrowing from a dated rule book of behaviors. Essentially, she's trying to gain the right to be heard by not speaking. And at the same time, Amelia is polishing up her argument, as if her feelings are not important enough on their own to deserve her husband's attention.

It could be that Dean comes from a family in which

the silent treatment was common, or that he has been indoctrinated to believe that women's arguments are often irrational. Or it could be that Dean hates the silent treatment, too, and would prefer a more honest form of communication with his wife, whose opinions he values. In either case, Amelia has chosen an indirect route of expressing discontent or anger that may work, albeit manipulatively, but which doesn't promote the ideal of a relationship of equals.

I tried the silent treatment, too, at first. When Duke asked if anything was wrong, I gave him a curt "nothing" while I banged pots and pans around the kitchen and went out for long walks or drives by myself. Hours would pass while Duke read the paper or sunned himself on the deck, oblivious of my growing rage, taking me at face value when I said, crisply, "nothing" was wrong.

In part, I didn't want to tell him what was wrong because that would be romantic blasphemy. As my soul mate, he was supposed to know what was wrong, and know just what to do in response. But in part, I employed the silent treatment for the same reason that I think many newly married women do: I wasn't certain the feelings I had were rational or reasonable, and because I presumed, as a result of my feminist conditioning, that Duke would underestimate these feelings.

Surprise, Surprise

The wonderful thing about marriage is that there will be times when your argument holds no water, when the thing you are upset about *is* lunacy, and when your partner will see this and still love you immensely, maybe even more than before you made yourself so vulnerable.

Believe me, this is not a gender-specific malady. Both you and your husband will sometimes present ridiculous, seemingly hormonally induced complaints. And whether you choose to coddle one another, or gently guide your temporarily insane partner back into the real world, the power of this deed will persuade you that marriage is a very safe cave.

Susan Lucci, who plays Erica Kane on the soap opera *All My Children,* remembers that early in her marriage to restaurant executive Helmut Huber, she was prone to volatile outbursts. "I was pretty hot-tempered when I was younger. During the first year of our marriage, I dumped a plate of cold cuts on my husband's head. Another time, I threw a Lalique ashtray at him. I didn't want to hit him, I just wanted him to feel the wind."

But even though Huber felt the wind, he didn't hold it against his wife. Eventually, Lucci says, "I grew up—I mellowed—which surely must have been a relief to him."

In her book *Secrets of a Very Good Marriage: Lessons from the Sea,* Sherry Suib Cohen describes her own turn with irrationality in the context of the difficulties she had embracing her husband's passion for fishing and his fishing boat. She writes: "I have to keep reminding myself that I'm not a murderer every time I lift a flailing flounder out of the water." One night, Cohen woke in a cold sweat from a nightmare in which she says a red, scaly mullet "has looked [her] in the eye and forgiven nothing." She characterized her husband's response this way:

Patiently, seriously, he listens, forcing his eyes to stay open. Because he loves me, he will not trivialize what I feel. He knows this is no laughing matter.

We don't fish for mullet, he says when I'm all done . . . Strangely, I'm comforted, and I can sleep.

This is the art of the unexpected—the surprise, surprise of unconditional love. That even when you're nuts, someone loves you. With this, the traumas and pains of childhood, or of unknown origins, can often be healed.

Eventually you acquire another skill that makes the silent treatment unnecessary. Author and host of a syndicated radio talk show, Dr. Laura Schlessinger often tells callers that a mature person does not expect every emotion she has to be affirmed, only the important ones. Some of our thoughts and feelings are, after all, selfish or downright wrong. And I think "Dr. Laura," as she is known, is right that women, in particular, expect this of relationships, instead of appreciating that mature men and women sort through their thoughts and feelings to assess which ones are truly important.

In our zeal to be taken seriously in the world, perhaps women confuse the issue and want *everything* we think and feel to be taken seriously, which a loving, patient partner will do. But over time, love's assurance enables both partners to separate the wheat from the chaff, to pick our battles, and to limit the number of times we ask our spouses to indulge lesser laments.

Preparing for Battle

There is, perhaps, no problem more vexing for modern brides than history repeating itself in what are supposed to be modern marriages. And as tiring and as aggravating as this battle will be, brides tell me they have found ways to fight and, sometimes, to win. These are our suggestions:

1. ACT LIKE AN EQUAL. AND DEMAND HELP.

To build better marriages than previous generations had, I believe women must first act like equals. We have to cultivate and then enjoy the safe cave marriage can be against the backdrop of a world in which we are not yet always treated as equals.

Let me explain. Recently, a woman I don't know called me to check a reference on a pet-sitter Duke and I had used before. The woman and I started talking about our dogs, and about how much work they can be, when she said, "My husband was the one who wanted this dog but I'm the one who is doing all the work." It was the kind of thing women say to each other all the time, an intimation that women bear the work of the world, especially in child-rearing and household chores.

But it struck me that unless this woman's husband was a tyrant, she probably had equal say in whether or not they got the dog in the first place. She had characterized herself in unflattering terms to a complete stranger, making me believe she had, you'll forgive the puns, bowed to her husband's wishes and allowed him to bow out of all the work of caring for their dog.

Women frequently depict themselves this way. And to the extent that it empowers us to return to our marriages and demand something different, I don't have a problem with it. But marriage should be a sanctuary in which you know your partner respects and cherishes you as he does himself, in which case pretending we don't have equal say, or characterizing ourselves as passive, is really just a cop-out. It is our way of avoiding confrontation. We wink at one another and say, "This is just the way it has always been" rather than stirring up the status quo, asking our husbands to do more, making ourselves do less, or believing our marriages are strong enough to withstand these tests.

How we detest the idea of becoming a "nag." In the surveys I gathered, I asked brides if there was anything they said they would never do that they had already done in their new marriages, and the most common answer was "nag my husband." But what is nagging really? Unless you are pinching your nose and whining nasally "Honey, this is the third time this week I've had to pick up your underwear," nagging is, simply, demanding help. And when a man demands help, no one calls it nagging.

Francine Deutsch is a professor of psychology and education at my alma mater, Mount Holyoke College, in South Hadley, Massachusetts. Deutsch has been studying the domestic division of labor and has found that women in marriages in which work is truly shared have a common trait. Whether or not they identified themselves as feminists, Deutsch says, "at some deep level they believed they deserved equality. They didn't feel guilty about asking for help."

In Deutsch's study of sixty-six married couples with infants, the men doing the most housework were typically those whose wives made comparable salaries and whose wives *asked* them to take responsibility for household chores. Thus, Deutsch believes it is crucial that women fight for what's fair. "Sometimes equality comes at the cost of a struggle, but there are costs to not engaging in a struggle as well. It's not necessarily bad to fight over who does the dishes."

Deutsch found that there are three approaches men

take to household labor: "I'll do it if she asks me," "She assigned me this job and I'll do it," and "I'll think ahead about what needs to be done and then take care of it." Deutsch confirmed what I have found maddens wives most: men are least likely to take the third approach. They simply cannot seem to anticipate the needs of the household, or of children, the way a woman does. And Deutsch says that in situations where wives did more parenting, husbands weren't opposed to doing more, "they just couldn't figure out how to carve out a role for themselves."

I wish I could sugar-coat this reality, because not only must brides battle perfectionistic tendencies society has ingrained in us—not only must we constantly be on guard for assumptions and patterns we've inherited—but we must also take initiatives around the house and assign priorities to tasks for our husbands. I know this isn't fair. I know I've largely put the onus on brides to keep marriages from conventional pitfalls. But if you cherish the woman you became in single life, if the feeling you have when you conquer problems on your own is almost electric, I am sure you would rather fight than acquiesce.

Remember, you're fighting archetypes, not the man who loves you. You're demanding help, not assigning blame.

Maybe it will help to point out to your husband the Deutsch study in this chapter. Traditionally, men respond better to "research statistics" than they do to personal stories and anecdotes, as Deborah Tannen, Ph.D., documented in her book *You Just Don't Understand: Women and Men in Conversation*. I can tell you that the night after I read Duke this chapter, he cooked dinner for us and scolded himself for forgetting to put napkins on the table. He was trying so hard to see what I see, and know what I know, about the details of running a household.

2. EMPLOY THE "WHO CARES MOST?" RULE. THEN FORCE YOURSELF TO CARE LESS.

It is difficult for me and most women I know to "let go" of the high standards to which we hold ourselves and our households accountable. Then, because we can't, and our husbands don't see the merits of our meticulousness, we take on too much responsibility and wind up resentful.

Duke once came home in the middle of a "briefing" I was conducting with a team of pet-sitters. He cut me off mid-sentence—somewhere amid my typed, three-page list of instructions—to interject sarcastically, "Marg, Lucky is a *dog!*"

That was the last time Duke treated me condescendingly in front of other people. He blundered by upstaging me, especially when I had made all the phone calls and all the arrangements so the two of us could leave town. He had a lot of nerve since not once in the year and a half we've had the dog has he checked a pet-sitter's references, made a kennel reservation, or taken the initiative to do *anything* with the dog so we could get away. And don't get me started on who makes all the vacation plans, airplane and hotel reservations, and car rentals!

Then again, I've never asked him to. Chances are, given his proclivity toward procrastination, waiting for him to do it would make me crazier than doing it myself. Besides, to him and lots of men like him, a dog is a dog, theater tickets are theater tickets, a hotel room is a hotel room. And if I left these arrangements to him, I'd have to take a sleeping pill to become as relaxed as he would be about the outcome.

Therefore, some division of marital labor can only be decided by the "Who cares most?" rule. But the problem with this rule is that women are conditioned to care about social pretenses and traditions, about appearances, and about fostering good feelings among families and friends. And caring more about all of these things is onerous work in what is supposed to be an equal partnership.

You remember my friend Sarah, who swore she wouldn't become her husband's social secretary? I talked to her last week and she told me she's ended up doing it anyway. Her husband thinks it's acceptable to send a card to his dad on Father's Day even though they got a present for his mom on Mother's Day. Sarah can't live with this, so she ended up coaxing gift ideas out of her husband for *his* father's Father's Day.

Before I was married, a friend of mine and I had an ongoing bitch session about the lackadaisical way the men in our lives handled *their* lives. Both of us confessed to being somewhat controlling, but we didn't know how these two men could function so well at work and be so sluggish about life's other details.

Then one time my friend and her boyfriend went hiking in Colorado. They picked a very ambitious climb, near the top of which my friend almost collapsed from exhaustion. She didn't think she could finish, but her boyfriend took her pack and gathered enough energy to lead both of them to the summit.

It was the first time, my friend admitted, in what was perhaps a seven-year relationship, that she had *let* him take charge—the first time she had surrendered control and let him take the lead. And, she told me, it felt absolutely fantastic.

It shouldn't take oxygen deprivation to get women to

let go. We deprive ourselves of much, much more by being so controlling and by expecting the world of ourselves. Obviously, to get anything done, sometimes you have to let the person who does it well take the lead. And sometimes that may mean you fall back on traditional gender roles. But even more often, it's critical to stop caring as much about social pretenses, about perfection, and about doing the right things.

After all, sometimes the best vacations are the ones you conduct without guidebooks or four-star-restaurant recommendations. Sometimes the best afternoons are hatched, not planned. And sometimes the proper gift is the one we give ourselves when we surrender control, when we relax our standards, when we let others lead.

3. DON'T WORRY, MARRIAGES CAN CHANGE. AND CHANGE MAY TAKE TIME.

As if there wasn't enough pressure on newlyweds, brides and grooms worry that the patterns they establish early on will be with them for life. For their book *The First Year of Marriage*, Miriam Arond and Samuel L. Pauker, M.D., recruited seventy-five people—married, divorced, or widowed—who reflected upon the first year of marriage from a perspective of three to sixty years later. And the people they surveyed overwhelmingly agreed that the first year of marriage had set patterns for what had followed—in everything from sex to modes of arguing to sharing money.

But at least in the domestic division of labor, Francine Deutsch found that "equality isn't something you establish and that's it—it's an ongoing process." She expected that couples who shared housework equally would have negotiated this early on, but found this wasn't the case. It was sometimes only after the birth of a second child, when household needs skyrocketed, that a husband became an equal partner. In some marriages, Deutsch found that couples had discussed the division of labor a great deal, while in others, the division gradually and quietly evolved.

The first year Duke and I were married I cried often and entertained many fears that I had set myself down in a carbon copy of my parents' marriage. Now, my parents have been married, and extraordinarily happily so, for thirty-nine years, and they enjoy more equality than most marriages of their generation. My father considered my mother his intellectual equal years before my mother believed this herself. Yet it's natural for children to want to distinguish themselves, and as happy as my home life was, I had designs for my own marriage, new ways I wanted to fashion it, and holes I wanted my marriage to fill that my family life hadn't.

My dad, like most dads of his generation, was away a lot. Because he is a minister, weeknights and weekends were not sacred, at least not sacred family time. His work consumed him. So my mom spent many evenings with us or alone. Sometimes my dad missed events that were important in my life: a dad's day at preschool and, much later, the high school basketball game when he was supposed to escort me, a queen candidate, onto the court. Sometimes he missed events that were important to my mother, like an election returns party when she ran for public office.

I was in college when I finally confronted my father about this. It wasn't easy to do, because he is an urban minister, and he was often away because he was helping people far needier than we were. But I told him I just wanted to *know* him. And then we cried, hugged, and began to work at building a much better relationship than we had ever had before. Now that my father is in his sixties, I know he loved us much more than he loved his work, and mourns the years he didn't get to spend time with us.

But I'll be darned if I didn't marry a naval officer. Despite my vehement attempts to ward off a long-distance relationship, I ended up loving Duke from afar, seeing him once every three or four months for nearly two years. For six months of our engagement and four months of our first year of marriage, Duke was in the Persian Gulf. For weeks at a time we had no phone contact and only sporadic mail. Even when he was home from sea, he was chief engineer of a ship, and he worked all but a couple of waking hours of every day.

My new husband was so exhausted and headache-prone when he was home that he balked at running errands and didn't want to spend much time socializing. I did all the housework and cursed him for it. I remember several Sunday afternoons when all of this closed in on me, when I was paralyzed by my own foolishness, afraid to tell him what was wrong because the feelings ran so deep. No matter how fervently I believed I was

BRIDE-TO-BRIDE

What one person, besides your new husband, has taught you the most about love?

∞ "My grandmother. She always put others' needs first. She truly loved people and did not give to get."

∞ "My parents—I can't say one or the other—and the model they provided for a lasting relationship. They argue but they still love and enjoy each other after thirty-two years."

∞ "My mother, because no matter how mad she was at me, she always told me she loved me."

∞ "My father. He taught me to respect myself and that to receive the type of love I want, I have to be myself."

equal, I had ended up in a traditional marriage, and nothing I could say seemed to change the reality.

Then two incredible things happened. One was that the cloud lifted. Duke got a new assignment that was far less demanding, and he gradually became the person I had wanted to marry. He started doing the laundry and cooking dinner on occasion, to the point where now that I am in the throes of writing this book, he is doing much more than his share of the household work. I see now that stress forces marriage into certain patterns, and that when stresses change, so do our reactions to them. And I see that circumstances sculpted my new marriage in my parents' image more than we, as individuals, did.

But before the cloud lifted, and before the circumstances changed, I learned something

my mother probably always knew but to which I had no access as a child. Because no matter how far or how long work took my dad away, home was where he passionately wanted to be, even when he was so fixated on his career that he couldn't name his priorities. I only know this now because of the way Duke threw himself

WHAT NO ONE TELLS THE BRIDE ABOUT . . .

Traits she'll inherit:

- A tendency to repeat behaviors learned in childhood
- Painful, knee-jerk reactions that result from some past ordeals
- Modes of arguing she doesn't recognize or like
- Traditional gender roles, in which the woman does more of the housework and does not think of herself as an equal partner

Our brides' solutions:

- Act like an equal. And demand help.
- Employ the "who cares most?" rule. Then force yourself to care less.
- Don't worry, marriages can change. And change may take time.

into my arms, into my cooking, and into the nest I had created while he was away. I only understand now, because I am married, why my dad sometimes leaves church retreats, after full days of leading discussion groups and camp songs, and drives two hours to spend the night at home with my mother, only to turn around the next morning and drive two hours back to the church retreat.

The good news is that marriages change and evolve. And that only from the inside will you come to know the intimate trade-offs all marriages make in one way or another. Once you know these trade-offs well, and the passions they represent, they won't scare you as much.

It is, nevertheless, crucial to address problems early in marriage, to experiment with new ways of resolving conflict, and to teach one another what feels good, either in lovemaking, homemaking, or marriage forging. When brides and grooms learn and share their life stories early on, they give their partners crucial information on how to respond appropriately and lovingly in everyday interactions. After all, we can only do the unexpected if we know what our partners expect.

But it is reassuring to know that in many cases, marriage is a sculpture-in-progress, and that your hands will always be wet with clay. There are also conundrums of marriage that take time—a layering of kiss upon kiss, talk upon talk—to solve. Especially when the conundrums have evolved over generations, healing and rebirth also take time to evolve.

Chapter 7

WHAT HAVE YOU DONE FOR ME LATELY?: DESTRUCTIVE MIND-SETS LEFT OVER FROM SINGLE LIFE

It's normal to have habits left over from single life. But as soon as you can, stop dallying in the past. Start loving for the sake of loving.

Like tin cans dangling from the bumper of the honeymoon getaway car, we clank along on our journey from singlehood to marital bliss. We think we've driven away from our families and from our bachelor/bachelorette lives, leaving them on the sidewalk in front of the reception hall when, in truth, all our demons are hiding in the trunk.

In this chapter, we'll talk more about these demons—the habits left over from single life. These mind-sets are, by and large, a natural outgrowth of single life, because if dating isn't the most vulnerable thing we do in life, then it certainly is a top contender. And to spend years dating and pursuing romantic relationships as a single person, you have to develop some armor, some tactics to survive.

The Three Mind-sets

In my experience, and in that of my friends, single people bring three mind-sets into marriage. These are the rules and standards they used when they were dating but which do not apply to marriage. In the second half of the chapter, my friends and I will suggest parameters that are healthy for a growing marriage.

The Fifty-Fifty Standard

The most common of the three mind-sets is the fifty/fifty standard, which demands that each partner contribute equally to the relationship. Think about it. Dating is conducted as a series of transactions, and dates turn into relationships only after many tentative expressions of interest are met with reciprocal expressions of interest. Most people I know, myself included, had very few long-term dating relationships, but we did have many that petered out quickly because an expression of interest was not met with an equal expression of interest. Over time, then, single people become affection accountants, wary of dispersing too much of themselves without reciprocation.

But unlike other accountants, the affection types do not have objective means by which to measure the contribution a partner is making to the relationship. It is as if, as John Gray writes in *Men Are from Mars, Women Are from Venus*, men and women come from different planets but have no recollection from whence they came. Thus, we expect one another to act in relationships as our species, or gender, would.

In this new world of marriage, the affection account-

ants continue the sassy anthem of single life, "What have
you done for me lately?" Women, for reasons we talked
about in the last chapter, are particularly prone to keeping score. They don't want to do all the work in their
marriages, as their mothers did. They want things even-
steven, give and take.

Kathryn, a thirty-year-old attorney from Washington,
D.C., says that she and her husband, William, were "hy-
per-sensitive" about how they "divvied up" chores
when they first got married. "I would look at other couples and think we had to explicitly make it even as to
who did what in our relationship." But as time went
on, Kathryn says, "We've become more relaxed about
this. We try to be fair but we don't have to tally everything up."

The words Kathryn used—divvied, explicit, even,
tally—are typical of the newlywed vernacular. They represent the couple's attempt to establish a balance of
power in their relationship.

Michelle, the twenty-six-year-old administrative assistant from Houston, would like her relationship to be
more balanced, too. She wants her husband, Todd, to
share things with her the way she does with him. "A
co-worker of Todd's will announce that she is pregnant
and he won't think to mention it to me for three days,"
sighs Michelle. "Or we'll be out with his work friends
and something will come up in conversation that has
been bothering him. And this will be the first time I
hear about it."

Michelle can drive home from a party and have a
million things to tell Todd about the conversations she
had and the nuances she observed during the evening.
But Todd is apt to be silent, never saying another word

about the party they just went to. If she's like most brides I know, Michelle will bang her head against the passenger side window, trying to cajole Todd to talk more. Maybe that's because, as John Gray would say, she's a Venusian and Venusians carry on witty repartee on the way home from parties. Or maybe it's because she's accustomed to the way men and women act on dates, when they are especially motivated to talk to one another. Or maybe it's because that's what Michelle expects married people to do.

Ultimately, when faced with spouses who won't say or do what we want them to, brides take one of a predictable number of steps. We become nags, in the true sense of the word, pleading for more. We withdraw, suppressing disappointment until it boils over at another time. We become stingier with our affection or attention, trying to teach our spouses a lesson. And perhaps worst of all, we become jaded. So that even if our husbands do come through for us in the end, we don't enjoy it.

The Standard of Comparison

It is when brides feel jaded that we are most susceptible to "the standard of comparison." We start thinking about other men we dated, other couples we know, or other relationships that appear to function better than ours. This is also a side effect of single life. Because when you're single, there's always the possibility that a better relationship awaits you. And there's always the chance that a romance from your past will emerge, smarter and happier than the first time around.

Of the brides I surveyed, all but five said they still think about, and sometimes even pine for, old flames. Brides were most susceptible to fantasizing about other men when things were not going well with their husbands. But they also snapped out of these fantasies quickly, knowing that in the end, these relationships would not really work.

Thirty-three-year-old Maine artist Morgan explains, "Before I met my husband, I was involved with a man—another artist—who was passionate. And he and I used to finish each other's sentences. Our conversations would last five hours at a time. I've never felt so alive or stimulated. But life wouldn't have worked with him. I wanted children and he didn't. And he was not ambitious, not someone I could rely on."

Morgan's husband, Joe, on the other hand, "made his life work. He knew how to handle life's obstacles. And he adored me, he loved me." Morgan concedes, however, she's had better sex with other men, and more meaningful connections in her life, mostly with women. "My best friend, Lisa, is really the love of my life, although obviously not in a sexual way."

Still, Morgan cannot deny the feeling that she's missing out on something. She says, "I still believe these types of passionate, deeply connected relationships exist somewhere out there in the world, although the idea of that bothered me deeply at first. Books, movies, folklore, all of it focuses on the idea of the soul mate, the one true love. And it may very well exist here and there. I can't talk to my single friends

---

BRIDE-TO-BRIDE

Who, if anyone, do you still pine for, and could you be happily married to that person?

∞ "One old flame I was more sexually compatible with, but that was our only strong suit."

∞ "No one."

∞ "My high school boyfriend, who was the quintessential dreamboat and very kind but materialistic, shallow, and not very bright."

∞ "John F. Kennedy, Jr. I think we'd be a happy couple, especially because I love having my picture taken."

about this, they don't understand. They still have that hope of finding that relationship. Married people are just much more pragmatic."

Pragmatism isn't the stuff of screenplays or miniseries. Give us a priest and his torrid affair with an Aussie lass. Give us Romeo and Juliet, or any number of love-struck, tortured souls. Give us characters on whom the camera lingers so we know the instant change comes over them, the instant they resolve their lifelong search, the instant they lay eyes upon the one, true love of their lives.

But drastically different from the movies, only a handful of the brides I interviewed said they experienced love at first sight. Some said they thought love at first sight was a man's disease and that women are just too analytical for it. I believe women experience it even less as they get older, and spend more years dating. The brides I know and interviewed said they had come to distrust the first rush of emotions when they met someone. Being smitten made them feel too vulnerable.

Once they had fallen in love, however, brides felt ill at ease if their passions didn't come forth in the classic fashion. If they didn't experience the butterflies or the head rush, brides feared that they had "settled" for something less than the ultimate relationship.

Veronica, a bride I met through the Internet, is twenty-nine and lives in New York City. She says, "I think by the time I met my fiancé, I was too level-headed about the whole thing to fall head over heels. I really wanted a partner, not a white knight. But it freaked me out the first months we were engaged that it wasn't like the movies."

It took Veronica a while to stop second-guessing herself, to relax and enjoy her relationship with her fiancé on its own terms. That's also the plight of brides and grooms who presume that marriage should meet the "thrill standard" of single life.

The Thrill Standard

In her book *Marrying Later, Marrying Smarter*, Tracy Cabot coined the phrase *thrill whore* to describe women who become addicted to the tension of bad relationships. When you date someone who doesn't call when he says he will, or who is hot for you one minute and a cold fish the next, you are constantly agitated. You are worked up over what will become of the relationship, so your body is always swimming in adrenaline.

I think the term *thrill whore* is brilliant, but I would define it more broadly. Both men and women become addicted to "the chase" of dating, the "newness" of new relationships, the "scene" of the singles scene, and the adrenaline of uncertainty. And the brides and grooms I know who were still addicted to these aspects of single life when they got married had the hardest time adjusting to marriage. Or at least they were the most vocal about their difficulties.

I don't mean to be harsh about the addiction, because Duke and I were as addicted to single life as any two people could be. When we met, we were adamant about our independence and about the potential that we might stay single all our lives. With droves of people in their twenties and thirties staying single longer, single life has, in many ways, been transformed into a viable, fun lifestyle that rivals marriage. There are many happily single people. Even those who are at first unhappy develop skills, and faux families, that make single life easier.

Among one's faux family there is a "group think" that makes settling down seem uncool. Once you adapt to

single life, married life seems boring by comparison. After all, happy, fulfilling relationships leave you very little
to talk about with your friends. There is a constancy and
stability to good relationships that doesn't produce
adrenaline, that doesn't keep you up at night, and that
doesn't require consultation with fifteen girlfriends before deciding what to do next. Engagement rings, "the
rush" of wedding planning, and the camaraderie of bachelor and bachelorette parties can extend the thrill, so that
it really is in the first months of marriage that many
brides and grooms go through withdrawal.

Single people enjoy a free-wheeling, pleasure-seeking
social life. But once you're seriously committed to someone, and certainly when you're married, you have to
concern yourself with how comfortable your spouse is
and how well he is being perceived by the social world
in which you have defined yourself. Because of these
concerns and other expectations you and the world have
of your "married" self, the social life you once enjoyed
may not be as much fun anymore.

For five years before she got married, Michelle lived for
Friday nights. Every Friday, Michelle and her best friend,
Pam, whom she had known since elementary school,
went to a country-western bar in Houston. Her boyfriend,
Todd, now her husband, is seven years older than Mich-
elle and preferred to work late and go home on Fridays.
Besides, Todd isn't a dancer, so he never minded that
Michelle wanted to paint the town with Pam.

Michelle and Pam got to know so many people at the
club that it became "their" hangout. They danced, they
flirted, and had innocent, but tantalizing, fun. Michelle
says, "We had so many friends who were great-looking
guys. And it was good for my ego, knowing I could turn
a head."

When Michelle and Todd got married, they talked about the fact that she "couldn't go out and party as much." Todd didn't mind if Michelle went dancing with Pam now and again, but Michelle all but eliminated "girls' nights out" from her life. Even when she did go out with Pam and her girl-friends, she didn't have as much fun as she used to.

As a result, one night early in her marriage, Michelle hit rock bottom. She was de-pressed and began question-ing her decision to marry. Most of all, Michelle missed the intimacy and compan-ionship she'd shared with Pam. It hurt that Pam's life now centered around her of-fice friends. But Michelle also craved the fun they'd had and the attention they'd at-tracted, dancing and banter-ing until closing every Friday night at their hangout.

> **BRIDE-TO-BRIDE**
>
> *What habits or traits of yours are left over from single life?*
>
> ∞ "I forget that I have a part-ner to help out—with flat tires, finances, fixing things, and so on."
>
> ∞ "I still read myself to sleep sometimes, which throws us off our routine of saying prayers together and then having sex."
>
> ∞ "I still need time alone."
>
> ∞ "I leave lights on all over the house, and I still want decorative hand towels to be just that."
>
> ∞ "Lying on the couch eating bowl after bowl of cereal. My husband looks at me like, "Do you need to be eating that?"

As has been true of every generation in which married people have experienced restlessness, Michelle knew that her dissatisfaction was a springboard for her marriage to succeed or fail. In the end, she made peace with her decisions, mourned her former life, but moved on to make her marriage richer and more fun.

Ultimately, people say, getting over the thrill standard is just a part of growing up. But I think it is more dramatic than that. American society ingrains in all of us an addiction to fast life, quick fixes, and instant gratification so that often marriage becomes a decompression chamber for a diver who has come up too fast. And while marriage can offer very good air, it takes long, deep breaths to inhale its immense healthfulness.

With these three standards weighing you down, how can a bride decompress and start taking in marriage? The best way I know to help is to tell you about the crisis I faced, a crisis that involved all three standards.

You'll remember I wrote my first book the first year Duke and I were married. I had never been as fulfilled, or as challenged, as while I was writing. Most of the time I was working on it, Duke was at sea or otherwise overwhelmed at work. But when he was home, I told him about chapters that rushed out of me as if from a spigot and others that dripped, dripped, a drip so slow that I never thought I'd meet my deadlines.

Then one day, I did. Eventually the first copy of the book arrived and I handed it to Duke, panting for him to read and react. I thought he'd throw a party for me, sharing the book with all our friends. I thought he'd say the book changed his life, or at least that I was the most brilliant author who ever lived.

Weeks later, he hadn't. I picked Duke up at the airport late one night after one of his many business trips. He got in the car and reeled off the travel delays he'd encountered—so many, he told me, he'd bought a paperback, *Devil in a Blue Dress*, in the airport and finished it on the plane.

I was silent the whole drive home, trying not to start an argument at that late hour. And my apologies to Walter Moseley, but I wanted to hurl *Devil in a Blue Dress* out the window and onto a tarmac where it could be run over, its spine broken, its pages sucked into a plane's engine and spit out in a storm of confetti on take-off. I could not believe Duke had not yet finished my book.

We did argue that night, because by then Duke knew that a curt "nothing" meant everything was wrong. And in my mind it was. For weeks, I had nursed disappointment over his lack of reaction to my book, counting up all the navy functions I had been to, all the separations we'd endured, and the two moves I'd made in two years—one from Boston to San Diego, the other from San Diego to San Francisco—for the sake of his naval career. My support of his career seemed to far outweigh his of mine, if one applied the fifty-fifty standard.

Then I succumbed to the standard of comparison. I had, after all, fallen for Duke in a very different way than I had fallen for other men. Because I am a writer, words had usually been my undoing. I was seduced by the way men told a story, by the words they chose, especially by words of mine they fixated on or laughed at. I fell in love with who I was when I was with them.

With Duke, I fell in love with the fact that he adored me, and that he wanted to embrace my whole life, seemingly my whole being. He didn't laugh particularly heartily at my jokes, and he wasn't glib. Once, he read a play I had written and picked a line as his favorite that held absolutely no meaning for me.

Because of this discrepancy, I had a hard time deciding whether or not to marry Duke in the first place. I vacillated wildly between my desire for the constancy and devotion he offered and my desire to be utterly and completely understood. I took married friends for beers and quizzed them, saying, "I know it's okay to marry someone who doesn't fill all your needs. But what if he doesn't fill what you consider to be one of your most

important needs? Is it okay to seek this kind of fulfillment outside of a marriage?"

Months before the wedding, Duke and I were sun-
ning ourselves at a lake in New Hampshire when he said
something so profoundly moving, so perfectly beautiful,
that no writer could match it. He evoked something I
had written months and months before about the fact
that I am adopted, and that being adopted sometimes
makes me feel like an island. My writing, I told him,
was my way of gaining authenticity—a sense of what it
was to have normal beginnings and deeper roots.

On that flat rock just big enough for the two of us,
Duke said, "You know, you aren't an island anymore."
And with those words, I wasn't. I married Duke because
no one had ever tried so hard to understand me. And as
much as other men—less faithful men—had seemed to
understand me right away, Duke wanted an intimacy
with me those men appeared incapable of sustaining.

And yet the bargain I made with myself when I married him had suddenly gone awry. I had given up the
thrill standard, hadn't I? I wasn't expecting to feel "the
rush" that comes with being intimately understood *all
the time*. I just wanted him to *try* harder than all the men
before him had, and in this important test case, he
hadn't.

This was *my* rock bottom. In the middle of our argument, Duke stormed downstairs to the living room to
read the two chapters he had remaining in my book—
you know, in just the state of mind I hoped he'd be in
when he read my masterwork. And for the next week,
I could barely hold my head up about my life. Duke's
not finishing my book, and his not making a fuss over
it, colored everything I thought about our marriage and
about him.

How to Get Out of the Abyss

Eventually, I scrambled out of the abyss. I got over the immense disappointment. And I found a way to love my husband more, not less, as the result of this episode. But it wasn't by denigrating what I felt or what I deserved in marriage. I did it the same way I learned that women and men in happy marriages do, and I share those insights with you:

1. ABOLISH "ALL OR NOTHING" THINKING.
CHOOSE UNCONDITIONAL LOVE INSTEAD.

With our mathematical formulas and our "You can't change me" dares, newlyweds constantly present "test cases" to one another. We don't necessarily tell one another how to succeed in these test cases; we just expect our spouses to know what to do to prove their love to us. When they fail, we often succumb to "all or nothing" thinking: the behavior psychologists call "splitting."

Scientists suggest that splitting buffers us from depression, so that we don't have to believe the "good person" we love is capable of such "bad behavior." Instead, we split the image so that the person doing bad is all bad, incapable of good. In their book *The First Year of Marriage*, Miriam Arond and Samuel L. Pauker, M.D., suggest that splitting is especially common in the first months of marriage, when individuals are merging their lives and their identities into one. In those first months, we are shocked to learn that despite our desperation to overcome separateness—to have someone join us on our island—we ultimately cannot do this, at least not every minute of every day. Nor sometimes even when it is most important to us to do so.

When all this happened with my first book, I was so hurt I couldn't see the good in Duke. I had to lie with the pain for a while, something I would never have done as a single woman. My predilection then was for immediate action, closure, assessing the damage, and moving on. But something stirred in me when I waited out the pain.

Sometimes the most loving thing you can do, the most generous act you can summon, is to wait. To let the hue of life change as, I promise you, it will. I learned this from Duke, who isn't prone to snap decisions. He has a patience with the world I have had to borrow many times.

A friend told me recently about a talk that Holocaust survivor and author Corrie Ten Boom gave on the subject of forgiveness. After her speech, many people came up to shake her hand, among them a man Ten Boom recognized as a Nazi soldier she had encountered in her youth during the torturous years she describes in her book *The Hiding Place*.

The man did not identify himself but outstretched his hand and thanked her for her presentation. Ten Boom did not know what to do. She could not muster words or the wherewithal to put out her hand. Nowhere in her heart could she find even a speck of forgiveness for this man. But she stood there nevertheless.

Then, quite on its own, her arm extended. She felt a wave of forgiveness—something beyond her, something beyond both of them. All she had done was to remain in a posture of reconciliation. But suddenly reconciliation was hers.

Few of us face the hurt, or the unthinkable acts, Corrie Ten Boom had to in this dramatic example of forgiveness, but we can learn a lot from her. Remaining when you'd rather run, and standing when you'd rather crumple, is a position of considerable power—not your own power, but the power of love. And it is the first step in overcoming disappointments that inevitably arise in marriage.

Call it God, call it mystical healing, call it the ebb and flow of life. Whatever you call it, there will be times when nothing else will work, when your mind is racing like a penned-up animal, and the only way to peace is to let go of the worry and wait.

People will tell you that unconditional love is loving someone in spite of their faults. But in my experience, unconditional love is communing with your fears, feeling them as palpably as you ever have, and standing by the man who is at the center of your pain until something new stirs inside. I had experienced nothing like it before I got married. Yet in this new place, in this very painful place, I felt my heart extend, and the wherewithal to love return, stronger than before.

2. FIGURE OUT WHAT *REALLY* PREVENTS YOU FROM FEELING LOVED AND CHERISHED.

Remember in Chapter 2 how my friends and I suggested you hold on to certain identity badges that make you feel safe? Or that you keep a packed suitcase under your bed so you feel free enough to remain forever? These were symbols of the things about yourself you treasured most, the things you most feared losing in your marriage. Yet sometimes in marriage, instead of jumping to the conclusion that your husband is trying to plunder your identity, you should ask yourself, "Is there something about my identity that is preventing me from feeling as loved and cherished as I want to feel?"

In my suitcase was my writing. But in this crisis with

Duke, what was at stake was how I felt about myself as a writer. In part, Duke's not reading the book, cover to cover, echoed the experience I'd had as a child, when my father missed important events in my life. But more so, I still desperately needed other people to affirm that I was a good writer. That's why the buzz of men "getting" my jokes and my stories had been so alluring.

For this reason, I had to learn to love Duke more and need him less, a strategy recommended by Judith Sills, Ph.D., in *Loving Men More, Needing Men Less*. In many cases, what we ask our spouses to give us is something we have not been able to give ourselves. And in these situations, not even the most generous, forthcoming spouse will succeed at satisfying his wife's craving. This is, of course, precisely what single life taught us, but sometimes we need to be reminded of how important self-reliance is in marriage as well.

Needing your husband less does not mean needing less in general, Sills points out. It means you are free to get what you need from other sources. It means I have to cultivate friendships with writers, with people who know what it is like to get thirty rejection letters from magazines before you get one assignment, with people who write their hearts out and live for "show and tell" just like I do.

3. Help him "get you loved."

But why love more? Why not just need less and love the same amount?

Loving your spouse more—trying to see his imperfections with more loving eyes—is a powerful gesture. It does not mean that his flaws will not bother you, or that his mistakes will not hurt you. It does not mean you "settle" for less than you wanted. It means you have greater empathy for your partner and for what prevents him from "getting you loved," as Warren Molton, a marriage and family counselor, puts it. Molton uses this passive terminology on purpose, to avoid the "blame game" we'd otherwise play. He asks couples to consider, "What do I need to 'get me loved'?" and "How can I help you 'get me loved'?"

Loving Duke more meant I had to acknowledge what he *had* done to support and affirm my work. First, he had bankrolled the book. He went on to sit through, and recruit many friends to come to, numerous book readings, not to mention dinner parties in which my book dominated the conversation. And he spoke of me in the most flattering terms at work, to the point where other women told me they were jealous of how much Duke respected and supported my career.

Loving Duke more also meant I had to really listen to him when he said he didn't know the first thing about throwing a book party for me. A kegger for a bunch of his buddies, sure, but he knew I expected more than that. I also had to teach him what I wanted from "show and tell." So that now, before I read him something I've written, I tell him I don't want to know about dangling participles, I just want him to tell me I'm a genius.

We like to think that soul mates are born, as Morgan, the artist from Maine, maintains. But in truth, you have to help your husband become your soul mate, and vice versa. No one can say all the right things to you, and do all the right things for you, ad infinitum. We have to teach each other.

If you aren't sure you know exactly what to ask for or how, take a look at the list of "101 Things a Man Can Do to Make a Woman Feel Loved" that John Gray includes in *Men Are from Mars, Women Are from Venus.*

Then make a "honey, do" list of your own, not about yard work or errands, but about the simple, kind gestures your husband could build into everyday life that would please you.

Women often know more about doing loving things. We are often better at it than men, whose tendencies toward tenderness and expressing themselves get suppressed early on. There are exceptions, of course; several brides I interviewed said their husbands are much more romantic and thoughtful than they are. But the point is, we can't expect our partners to meet us halfway if they don't know how. And sometimes, even when we tell them how, halfway may be too big of a leap. The beauty of marriage lies in how two people with different skills tend to the relationship in complementary ways, not necessarily in equal portions.

4. LOVE FOR THE SAKE OF LOVING.

Love isn't, or shouldn't be, a game of tit for tat. If you give someone something because you want something in return, you haven't truly given in the spirit of love. Or so I've heard Dr. Laura Schlessinger say a dozen times on her radio show. Women callers who have a lot more guts than I do call with my question all the time. They tell "Dr. Laura" about the elaborate birthday celebrations they throw, and the time they put into searching for the perfect gift for their husbands, only to turn around and have their husbands give them only a card for their birthdays. Understandably, the wives want more.

Dr. Laura always squashes them, and me, like a bug. She says, and rightly so, that love doesn't give to get. Loving, not getting, is the point of love. Sure, when we give love to others, we are often rewarded, but not always in the precise ways we want to be rewarded.

Susan Page, the author of *Now That I'm Married, Why Isn't Everything Perfect?*, suggests our reward may come in the form of a good marriage. Because, she says, "couples who thrive tend to be more concerned about whether they are giving their fair share than whether they are getting their fair share."

If you want more, give more, or so says Emerson's law of compensation. You'll remember that is what Tom did for Janice. Newlyweds in Silicon Valley, Janice was reluctant to call Tom her "best friend" because she had closer, longer relationships with the women in her life. Tom wanted more, so he gave more. He asked Janice to teach him to talk "like girlfriends do," so that, as much as possible, he could build the intimacy she associated with "best friends."

> **BRIDE-TO-BRIDE**
>
> *What traits of your husband's have you had to accept?*
>
> ∞ "That he stops at yellow lights, likes Miracle Whip, and doesn't dry off the sink after shaving."
>
> ∞ "That he isn't more detail-oriented like me."
>
> ∞ "That he won't share housework and cooking equally."
>
> ∞ "That his graduate studies come first and we don't have a lot of time together."
>
> ∞ "That he isn't more affectionate."

And if, like Michelle, you are restless and bored with your marriage, and if married life isn't nearly as much fun as single life, you need to create more excitement. You and your husband have to get off the couch and do more, see more, entertain more, and learn more. And as individuals, you have to seek out stimulating activities on your own.

The other pragmatic reason to love for the sake of loving is that getting your fair share won't necessarily make you happy. I found, as many brides have, that when it comes to household work, it often means more to me that Duke acknowledge what I do and how well I do it, than when he actually makes dinner or cleans the house himself. I evidently need to feel cherished for the work I do more than I need Duke to share the work. Interestingly enough, Francine Deutsch, the Mount Holyoke professor who studied household work, found that there was no correlation between an equal division of household labor and marital happiness.

Years ago, I went to a lecture given by theologian/author Anthony Campolo, Jr., in which I remember he said, "In our world, the person who loves least is always in the position of power." Campolo drew a contrast between the way the world aligns love and power and the way people of faith do. On a higher plane, he said, power lies in the hands of the person who loves most.

> ### WHAT NO ONE TELLS THE BRIDE ABOUT . . .
>
> *"Standards" left over from single life:*
> - The Fifty-Fifty Standard: Expecting to Get What You Give
> - The Standard of Comparison: Comparing Your Husband to Other Men
> - The Thrill Standard: Being an Adrenaline Addict
>
> *Our brides' solutions:*
> - Abolish "all or nothing" thinking. Choose unconditional love instead.
> - Figure out what really prevents you from feeling loved and cherished.
> - Help him "get you loved."
> - Love for the sake of loving.

Campolo might have been contrasting single and married life. Because in dating, loving more is often unwise. Not only is it a turn-off in the chase mentality of single life, but consistently doing more in relationships than is done for you degrades and turns you into a martyr. But marriage is not a transaction. It does not, or at least it should not, rise or fall with the balance of the books.

Campolo's message is even more profound. Because

although the point of love is not power, and although a balance of power is no guarantee of happiness in a relationship, the person who loves more than he or she thought possible is often empowered by it.

This is a terrible, wonderful paradox. Only by standing when you want to run, loving when you want to withdraw, can you be empowered to reconcile and love more. Only by looking within can you help someone love you better. Only by loving selflessly, for the sake of loving, will you feel the earth move.

Only the earth won't really have moved. You will have.

Chapter 8

SEX AND THE MARRIED GIRL: DEFYING THE ODDS WITH LUSTY MONOGAMY

It is normal to take sex for granted now that you can have it all the time. It is normal to get distracted and forget how great lovemaking can be. But the key to lustful monogamy is engaging the senses, saying no sparingly, and letting go of anything that keeps love from rocking your world.

A few months before Duke and I were married, when we were living together, I woke up to find my amorous fiancé putting the moves on me. At the time, I had mononucleosis, which meant that every waking moment I had phlegm or mucus to expel from my body, a process usually accompanied by a honking or hacking sound.

I also smelled. My breath was heinous, just short of dog poop. And I had sweat a little in my nightshirt.

So I was flabbergasted at the idea that anybody, much less my fiancé—who knew I could look, smell, and taste much better than this—would want to make love to me just then. And considering that I had been celibate for months and years during my single life, it was also a head trip to discover, for the first time, that I could want nothing to do with sex.

In many ways, although we were not yet married, this was my introduction to married sex and to the mysteries brides encounter in the intimate lives they share with their husbands. It may sound as if there was no mystery left that fateful morning. But in fact, so many things went unsaid and so many surprises were in store for me that I might as well have been a new recruit, standing in the hallway outside our bedroom, afraid to go in.

There is, indeed, a great deal that no one tells the bride about sex in marriage. When Helen Gurley Brown, the longtime editor of *Cosmopolitan*, wrote her book *Sex and the Single Girl* in the sixties, it was scandalous. Today, however, it's almost scandalous to talk about the opposite. Very little ink gets devoted to sex *in* marriage; we think the racy stuff only happens out of wedlock.

As is true with every other aspect of marriage, our expectations often shape the way we approach one of its real benefits—regular, safe, and loving sex. In this chapter, we'll discuss four factors that complicate and diminish the romantic life of modern brides. Then my friends and I will share what we think are the keys to lustful monogamy. And I hope we'll make you laugh, because comfort breeds the best sex of all.

Preconceived Notions

The decline of sex and romance in matrimony is such a tired sitcom joke. And of all the clichés about marriage, this was the one Duke and I were most eager to chain to someone else's bedpost. So, mostly because we've worked at it but also because we dared to think married sex could be fun, our romantic life has not diminished in the two and a half years we have been married.

Of course, there is some truth to the cliché. Researchers tell us couples do have sex less often once they are married. But the more brides I interviewed, and the more fun Duke and I had together, even with rings on our fingers, the more I realized how underrated married sex is in the public domain.

My survey was far from scientific, but the fifty brides I interviewed were evenly split, half saying they had sex less often than before they said "I do," and the other half saying they had the same or more sex than before they told God and everybody they'd be "doing it" to each other for the rest of their lives.

Almost all the brides I interviewed said sex was different and better after they got married. In fact, many of them were surprised by their own levels of happiness with sex, and with the extension of their passions into matrimony. Kathryn, a thirty-year-old attorney in Washington, D.C., remarks, "I had always heard that married couples made love less and it all became rather routine. Happily, that has not been a problem for us." Kathryn said that because she and her husband are religious, there was a degree of guilt to the sex they had before marriage. With that gone, she smiles, their sexual life has only improved.

Janice, the thirty-three-year-old advertising executive from California, says she is amazed that after four years of being involved with Tom—three in which they have been married—she still finds him "devastatingly attractive." She says, "I could have sex with him every day and not tire of it. Now that we're trying to have kids, sex is more about regularity and timing rather than impulse, but it's still okay by me."

So while the amount of sex may taper off a bit when you know you can have it anytime, the probability is that you'll *want* your partner more than before. Miriam and Samuel Pauker, the authors of *The First Year of Mar-*

riage, report that 59 percent of couples report an *increase* in sexual attraction once they are married.

But what no one tells the bride is that even if your desire wanes, there are many things you can do to see stars again—only, they may not be the same stars you saw when you were sixteen and your boyfriend's hands went where no boy's hands had gone before. To tell you the truth, I have never actually seen stars, but I have heard drums; the best thing I have to tell you about married sex is that husbands can be very good percussionists.

So why do brides and grooms succumb to calling one another "the ol' ball and chain"? Why do we so easily adopt the prevailing belief that monogamy equals monotony? Susan Page, the author of *Now That I'm Married, Why Isn't Everything Perfect?*, says, "the prevailing belief about marriage endures because it allows us to feel normal if our marriage is unexciting."

In the days when sex was reserved for marriage, couples expected a honeymoon period. But brides today fully expect their sex lives to slow down, even calcify. We are often encouraged to settle for less passion in marriage, as if marriage is too high brow for high jinx. We are told it's okay if you are too tired to have sex on your wedding night. And the idea of the honeymoon being an initiation of anything new and sensual has been cast aside, as if something new and sensual isn't possible for a couple who has had sex before.

And yet I have had to include an expanded list in this chapter to accommodate all the ideas brides had for creating romance and excitement in marriage (see pages 193–94). Listing these ideas, it became abundantly clear that brides and grooms are working, cleverly and secretly, at their sex lives. They are pursuing their passions in ways we might otherwise never have heard about.

Often, though, the most difficult preconceived notions with which couples battle are those that ask wives to conform and act like, yawn, wives. In this respect, brides get off to a good start, wearing white dresses on their wedding days. Most of us wear white without thinking much about ancient notions of virtue and honor, a cleanliness that made women "worthy" of marriage. But I like to think we snub our ancestors and their stuffy ideas by making their traditional garb our own, showing as much cleavage as we want to, dancing to songs they'd consider blasphemous, and drawing a train of symbolism across a modern threshold.

A guy friend of mine got married in a vineyard in Napa Valley last year, and a few days before the wedding, he told me he'd heard his bride's dress was "sexy." I was struck by the use of the word *sexy* in reference to a bridal gown. No Madonnna/whore complex there. The groom had no trouble integrating the idea that even on this most sacred of days, the woman he was marrying was erotic. To him, this was the best of all possible worlds.

But instead of seeing it this way, instead of imagining that sex within marriage could be the best of all possible worlds, many of us are still hemmed in by inhibitions. One bride I know thinks she shouldn't wear leather pants now that she's married even though her husband encourages her to. Another bride, a folk singer, feels self-conscious about performing in coffeehouses and bars now that she's an investment banker's wife.

Teresa, a thirty-year-old retail manager from Denver, said that when she and her husband, Blaine, were first married, he had trouble having what she calls "raw

sex"—the kind of no-holds-barred sex they enjoyed before marriage. She explains, "He wanted 'loving sex' all
the time, but that was so predictable. When I questioned
him about it, he said it was difficult for him to think of
'his wife'—the woman who would someday be the
'mother' of his children—as a passionate, animal, sex object."

Of course, Teresa was devastated by this, thinking her
husband no longer found her attractive. She quietly con-
sulted a friend of hers who was a counselor, who reassured her that Blaine's perception was not uncommon.
The counselor suggested that Blaine had put Teresa on
a pedestal, as he had his mother, and that Blaine probably
thought that throwing his wife on the bed and going at
it—something Teresa was eager for him to do—would
be disrespectful.

Seeing it this way made it easier for Teresa to talk to
Blaine about it. Blaine was surprised to find she was so
concerned and quickly realized he could have both kinds
of sex, tender and bold, and still express his love and
respect for his wife. Teresa, in turn, felt sexier, knowing
that any hesitancy Blaine demonstrated from that point
on was a sign of his love for her, not his lack of desire.
Today, despite the fact that they now have two young
children, they continue to schedule "dates" and time
alone together for what Teresa says is their "wonderful
sex life."

Like many of the brides I interviewed, Teresa had no
problem seeing herself as both wild lover and good wife/
mother. With friends, she flaunted her sexual side the
same way she flaunted her skill in running a household
by dressing the kids in Gymboree clothing and finding
a beautiful lamp for the living room at an antiques store.
Ultimately, it was her comfort with herself, and Blaine's

love for her, that allowed them to overthrow traditional, and very limiting, notions of how married sex was *supposed* to be, and what married women were *supposed* to enjoy.

A Lack of Comfort and Knowledge

When I was single, my friend Katie told me something I could hardly believe. She said her fiancé often found **her** most attractive the times she thought she looked her worst—when she'd skipped a shower and makeup, put her hair up, and thrown on jeans. And it wasn't that he favored the natural look. It was that he loved and desired her, through and through.

In other words, her fiancé's passions weren't subject to the neurotic chorus that goes on inside most women. He didn't have to think about how much chocolate she'd consumed the night before, or how many days it had been since she worked out, to conclude that she was beautiful. This kind of love was unfathomable to me since I was, at the time, going out with men who thought Kate Moss could stand to lose a few pounds.

Making love to someone who desires you, week after week, year after year, is mind-boggling, especially for women who gauge their attractiveness on a constantly sliding scale. But this constancy breeds comfort after a while. And comfort, if no one filled you in, is the world's most potent aphrodisiac.

Barbara, a twenty-four-year-old teacher from Des Moines and her husband waited until they were married to have sex for the first time. But in marriage, their sex life flourished. Lingerie was flung with wild abandon, innuendoes filled their answering machine messages, and champagne and rose petals populated their bedroom.

Most important, Barbara said they were very comfortable in their sex life.

But then, within a few months of getting married, Barbara got pregnant and watched her waistline disappear. She was already worried, having put on weight since they'd gotten married, but now she was pregnant and vulnerable to morning sickness and hormonal shifts to boot. She couldn't imagine her husband continuing to find her physically attractive.

Barbara's self-esteem and her newly developed sexuality seemed to evaporate overnight. And because she and her husband had yet to face a sexual dry spell— something common to all marriages, when, for one reason or another, sex is less frequent or less appealing than usual—they did not have a confidence in the ebb and flow of marriage. They had not yet experienced the way love can restore what yesterday felt bereft.

In this respect, couples who live together for years before marriage, or had the luxury of regular "nookie," may have an advantage. Because no matter how proficient the rest of us thought we were, there's a lot to learn about sex, especially about making it good when you make it regularly with the same person. Marriage counselor Don Childers says, "Sex really isn't all that easy. Pop culture implies that it is. We think sex happens naturally, especially for males. But a lot of people are not very informed about their physiology. And most of us would rather have our teeth pulled than talk about sex."

A friend of mine who had been married for several years once asked me about orgasms. She thought a woman's orgasm was like a man's and involved an abrupt release of fluid. She knew she had never had one before, but she was all the more amazed to find that an orgasm was something different from what she thought it was.

My friend's experience is not uncommon; experts tell us a fourth of newly married women have difficulty achieving orgasm. Even more problematic, some women are either too embarrassed, shy, or insecure to remedy the situation. So they fake orgasms, diminish the importance of sex, avoid or decline it. Meanwhile, they entertain rich but frustrated fantasy lives.

What else is a woman to do if she's married and has yet to hear drums? Experts tell us that, ultimately, the only way to get what we want is to ask for it, as specifically and descriptively as we can. If you're at a loss for the specifics you're supposed to describe, go to a bookstore, find yourself a plush chair, and read *The Joy of Sex* and any other sex technique books that appeal to the voyeur in you. Or if you've got the mechanics down but could use help in mood-making, try *The Book of Love, Laughter and Romance* by Barbara and Michael Jonas.

Most important, rescue yourself from the fantasy that sex should be instinctive. What *is* instinctive in couples who thrive, says author Page, is their understanding that "they had to take responsibility for getting what they wanted in sex, even if it was difficult." She continues, "They did not expect their partners to be mind readers."

As difficult as it may be, talk about sex with your spouse. Cultivate a relationship in which you can ask for something new and different without implying that there is anything wrong with the old way in which you've done things. Some newlyweds I know keep a "couple's journal"—a book they write in and take turns putting on one another's pillow. The journal feels safe and erotic to them at the same time. Without first having to voice fantasies and requests, as well as other thoughts about the marriage, they nevertheless share them with one another, prompting discussions and giving one another great ideas.

In general, Page says, great sex starts with a spirit of acceptance. We have to accept ourselves, and the dimpled hips our husbands nevertheless love to grope. And then, Page says, we have to stop sabotaging our "sexual happiness by worrying that things ought to be other than what they are." Couples who thrive "waste no time on such thoughts."

After all, different sex lives suit different couples. And there are different kinds of sexual encounters, even in the happiest of marriages, as Page explains:

> Sometimes they are in perfect sync with each other, and they have really passionate, heightened pleasure and feel absolutely wonderful. Other times their moods are mixed or low and they just go through the motions and don't get especially turned on. They go through periods of time when they are making love often, and other periods when they suddenly realize they have gone a month or more without making love . . . But the quality that made all these couples say that they are happy with their sex lives is that they did not worry about these shifts and evolutions.

Abundant Distractions

On the other hand, many couples blame their lackluster love lives on "natural shifts and evolutions," when distractions are, in fact, responsible. Distractions abound in our busy lives, although you'd never know it looking at a Victoria's Secret catalog. Nothing but a lacy thong stands between Claudia Schiffer and her afternoon romp, not job stresses or dirty dishes, not a dog that needs walking or a stomach that's growling.

But somehow, amid enormous stress and lives teeming with distractions, some couples still make their "romps" a priority. Elizabeth, the twenty-nine-year-old account manager for a private health-care system in Boston, is also pursuing her master's in public health. Her husband, Stephen, is a full-time, second-year medical student. The last time they had an entire day to spend alone together was three months ago. And on a daily basis, they have only an hour and a half together, from 10:30 P.M. to midnight, when both of them have finished studying. But despite how tired they are at that hour, Elizabeth says their sex life hasn't languished. "We actually work very hard at it," she says.

Couples *have* to work at it, especially today, when both husbands and wives are pursuing careers. Life is more complicated than ever for newlyweds, with the average couple marrying in their mid-twenties, when the demands of burgeoning careers can overtake even the raging hormones of youth.

These days, it isn't easy for anyone to slow down and let love, not life, distract us. Rachel, the forty-year-old editor in San Francisco, is in the prime of her career. Her business is thriving, and the hours she puts in are, accordingly, rigorous. On the other hand, Rachel's husband, Sam, seventeen years older and semiretired, enjoys a more relaxed phase of life.

In and out of the bedroom, bringing these two lifestyles into sync has been challenging. "I'm a Puritan," Rachel says, "so when I'm up, I'm up, and out of bed. I never used to linger in bed." But loving her husband as much as she does, Rachel has, on weekends anyway, let her Puritan hair down. "Now there is this delicious man in bed. So I've had to *learn* to linger."

Savoring the intimacy that marriage affords us is a monumental task for busy people. Not to mention how many of us are lulled into spending hours on-line or watching nightly TV. Let's face it, the electronics in our lives are often the boudoir's mortal enemy, as Duke will attest since his powers of persuasion are often challenged on Monday nights when I am loathe to miss *Melrose Place*.

Surely, many of the distractions in our lives are within our control. And nothing is as distracting to the libido as built-up resentments and miscommunications—the feeling that your husband didn't really listen to you at dinner, or that he put his feet up while you cleaned the house, or that his pleasure always comes before yours. Sometimes tending to our sex lives means tending to any problems in the relationship first.

Great sex is generous and eager to please. It will not emerge from a sullen heart. So, when the bedroom is piled high with folded laundry and misunderstandings, you have to clear the air and the bed, and make room for a little tenderness.

Laziness

Distractions may keep us out of the bedroom, but boredom is worse because we're in the bedroom *and* wishing we were somewhere else, *doing* anything else. Indeed, all of us experience dull sex in marriage, times when our bodies feel like dead weights, when our lips and limbs are numb to the experience, and our minds are all too cognizant of the time it's taking to finish.

Then sometimes in the midst of predictable sex, you get drawn into it. You stop going through the motions and start wanting the motions to work for you. You find that even though you weren't "into it" a moment before, *Melrose* is now the last thing on your mind.

This is, I think, the body's way of reminding us that boredom is an affliction of the mind. Our erogenous zones aren't checking off items on a clipboard, muttering to themselves "been there, done that." Our bodies are always receptive to surprise. It is the mind that gets lazy and passes over the silky, itchy chemise for the oversized Bulls T-shirt; it is the mind that is too sleepy to remember to bring massage oil or fresh strawberries to bed.

In the end, mechanized lovemaking is only the result of our own laziness. We fail to give it the time and energy it deserves. Teresa, the retail manager from Denver, said her minister gave her very valuable advice about sex before she and Blaine were married. He said to have sex only when they had at least forty-five minutes to enjoy it. He believed that years of "quickies" erode a marriage, creating resentment and sapping passion of its tremendous transforming potential.

So carve out time. And then "prep" the mind. Use "props"—songs, scents, words, foods—that are secretly suggestive to you. Maybe there's a perfume you can put on the minute you get home from work that will get the evening started, not with the usual "How was your day?" but a more declarative "Let me show you how I'm feeling." Perhaps there is a restaurant in town where you could perpetually make reservations, meet at the bar, and never make it to dinner. Go ahead, do something furtive, have fun at the expense of the maître d'.

Suggestive props are especially good for brides who

have yet to master the art of initiating sex. Instead of falling into bed, kissing good night, and playing the "Are we going to or aren't we?" guessing game, try communicating with your husband, choosing subtlety

if it makes you more comfortable. One woman I read about has a system in which she lays a silken nightie across her pillow when she's really in the mood. If she's open to persuasion, she lays the nightie halfway down the bed. And if she'd rather pass on it tonight, the nightie is nowhere in sight. This way, the minute her husband walks into the bedroom, he knows what's on her mind. And they both anticipate making love, giving their *minds* time to fondle the idea and all its possibilities.

We make lots of excuses for ourselves when it comes to sex: we're too tired, we're preoccupied, we tried that last time and it didn't work, I don't want to do what he *really* wants me to do. Some of us are so particular that we don't want to muss clean

> **BRIDE-TO-BRIDE**
>
> *What has been the biggest surprise for you about your secual relationship with your husband?*
>
> ∞ "That after five years, it is still so great."
>
> ∞ "That I don't really want sex as much as he does. After eleven years single, with only occasional sex, I thought I would be incredibly horny, but after a few years, I've calmed down."
>
> ∞ "That he is a lot more revealing about his fantasies. We once talked about having phone sex, and we both got very excited. Then we never did it, but the idea that we can is exiciting."
>
> ∞ "That we are extremely comfortable and compatible with each other."
>
> ∞ "That there is less of it."

sheets, as was the case with a woman I know who went into conniptions on a rendezvous at the Four Seasons because there was blood on the sheets after she and her companion made love. As she washed the sheets in the sink and called housekeeping to report a terrible accident that necessitated a linen change, her beau sat in their suite, stunned and amazed—in something less than afterglow, I can assure you.

Just as is true of so many aspects in marriage, it is crucial in sex to "refocus," to choose different ways of looking at the same situation. This is creativity, the impetus for making love right after dinner rather than waiting till after Jay Leno, for doing something he likes simply because he likes it, and for using chocolate syrup in ways you never have before—clean sheets be damned!

Creative Initiatives

The point is, the only thing that really stands between us and lively, interesting sex is our own lack of initiative. And what follows are the creative initiatives that helped me, and the women I know, find great joy and intimacy in our marriages:

1. ENGAGE THE SENSES.

A 1994 *Newsweek* study on spirituality found that people often "sense the sacred" while making love. It was also common for people to "sense the sacred" during the birth of a child. And yet both of these experiences are utterly visceral. What is it about the bodily experience of sex that can, at its best, transport us to an out-of-body experience?

Marriage counselor Warren Molton says that our five senses, the basic arbiters of our reactions to life, are the key to our sensuality. If our experience of sex is less than we want it to be, we should start by engaging our sense of smell, taste, touch, sight, and hearing. Molton encourages us to think of lovemaking the same way we would a great meal, with its elements of preparation, enjoyment, leisure, and compliments.

Again, use suggestive props to captivate the senses. Food and wine are so often the prelude to romantic evenings. Duke has cultivated an indoor herb garden and often slips up behind me when I'm cooking to give me a taste of peppermint or a whiff of basil. For us, and other couples we know, the simple act of cooking together—tasting as we go, pouring wine, and lighting candles—is sensual. We didn't need *Like Water for Chocolate* to tell us that everything about the kitchen, from its aromas to its countertops, is meant to delight.

One couple I know has a picnic fetish. If they aren't renting classic automobiles for a drive into the country, they are setting up meals on the rooftop of their apartment building. And they specialize in finger foods, delectables they have to feed to each other, no utensils allowed.

BRIDE-TO-BRIDE

What do you do to add excitement and romance to your marriage?

∞ "Surprise him by making dinner in lingerie."

∞ "Go on vacation!"

∞ "Talk dirty on the phone, if it's possible."

∞ "Take advantage of hotel rooms, if only for one night."

∞ "Give massages."

∞ "Go out on a date night."

∞ "Appreciate each other's bodies by showing and talking about them."

∞ "Speak French, light candles."

∞ "Cook a really nice meal."

∞ "Kidnap him; take him out somewhere."

∞ "Have 'intimate time' in bed; close conversation with the TV and the lights off when we can reconnect with each other and talk about hopes and dreams, not necessarily sexual talk but intimate talk."

∞ "Discuss what pleases each of us."

∞ "Light candles and wear the uncomfortable nightgown."

(continued)

∞ "Now that we have a baby, just stay awake!"

∞ "Exercise together."

∞ "Jump into the shower with him."

∞ "Surprise him with something special for no reason!"

∞ "Buy some 'dirty dice.' Roll them on the sheets of your bed and then do what they say to do."

∞ "Leave notes for each other around the apartment."

∞ "Wear the thong even though it's lace and really scratches."

∞ "Be spontaneous!"

∞ "Drink good wine."

∞ "Watch sexy movies together."

∞ "Get a book called *101 Nights of Grrreat Sex*. Each page is sealed so you can't look ahead. But each page has something cool and fun to try."

∞ "Have sex in the middle of the afternoon."

Obviously, much of our pleasure in sex requires us to experiment with touch, to help our partners find where we want to be touched and how. But touch is also the sense that gets saturated in sex. So to create electricity again, you have to be creative. Massages are a natural, not just back massages, but foot, hand, and facial massages, too. One bride I know cuts her husband's hair. Each time she does, they pretend they don't know each other and that they are meeting for the first time. Of course nothing sends shivers down the spine like a stranger's fingers on your scalp. So, she reports, "Things usually get raunchy from there. . . ."

You get the idea. To get out of the brain, you have to focus on the body. And having something as simple as the senses to focus on takes away some of our self-consciousness about sex. The focus is very specific, so the less romantically inclined partner gets a lot of direction, not nebulous suggestions about what lovemaking is supposed to be like. Also, approaching lovemaking as an experiment of the senses takes the blame off either partner, freeing both of you to have fun, without necessarily having to be direct about what has been missing in your previous encounters.

2. SAY NO SPARINGLY AND CARINGLY.

Go ahead, have sex sometimes, perhaps even frequently, when you aren't in the mood. Establish a "mood/schmood" policy—the brainstorm of a two-career couple with a new baby in Page's book, who try to make love no matter how exhausted or unmotivated they are.

I know this advice goes against the grain. And it probably sounds as if I'm suggesting that "nice wives" go along with sex just to keep the peace. After all, what possible reason is there to go along when you don't feel like it?

Page offers three reasons why women in successful marriages "ignore the initial urge to withdraw." She writes: "(a) they have enough experience to know that if they give themselves a chance, they will get turned on and enjoy themselves; (b) they want an active sex life because they believe it is an important component in their relationship; and (c) they want to make their husbands happy and to accommodate their desires."

Let me take you back to the incident I mentioned earlier—in which "mono" and my not being a morning person combined to make intercourse unimaginable to me—because, before breakfast that day, I learned something very important about giving and receiving. I had been warned all my life that men only want one thing: All they really care about is getting their rocks off. On face value, the man with the razor stubble and the equally bad breath who was kissing me seemed to fall into that category.

Yet *this man*, the night before, and for many nights before that, had confounded me with his patience and compassion. My incessant coughing had kept us awake for more nights than I could count. And each time I got into a coughing spell, a barking so deep my whole rib cage hurt, I expected Duke to punch his pillow, sigh loudly, and whip himself over in bed.

What he did instead was put his arms around me and pull me closer until he was sure I was all right. A couple of times, I gathered a pillow and a blanket to go sleep on the couch, only to have him awaken and pull me right back into bed. He said he'd rather be awake and close to me than sleep and be apart.

I was sure he was delirious. But come daybreak, his tenderness continued. He wasn't mad that there was no end in sight to my sickness. He wasn't repulsed by my less-than-dewy appearance. He just wanted to be close to me.

This generosity is the mark of a great lover. And after many years of thinking of men as greedy and self-absorbed, it knocked more than my socks off to find someone so concerned with my pleasure. I came to think of sex and lust entirely differently.

That is why I say no rarely and only in the gentlest of terms. Not because my husband's ego is so intimately tied to his sexual performance but because I am now keenly aware that sex is one of his favorite ways of making me happy.

As has been said before, giving for the sake of giving is often its own reward. What I learned that particular morning by accommodating my husband's wishes was that sex, and its wonder, can sneak up on the least motivated soul. More than once, I have grudgingly gone along with Duke's advances and found myself taken up by them, by the relaxation there is in this grown-up kind of play, by a tide that carries me far from where I was previously grounded.

I've learned that I often need to be reminded how great it is to make love. Both men and women need reminding. But like most women I know, I am often preoccupied with lists of things I should be doing, with books I should be reading, or sleep I should be getting. All of this interferes with great sex, which requires us to surrender the mind to the body's whims.

Surrendering to the whims of the body may not seem urgent to you, but experts tell us all our infinitesimally small choices add up in marriage. Remember this when you decide whether to drop what you are doing to greet your husband when he walks in the door, whether to brush your hand across his back when he walks by, or whether to surprise him in the shower before work. Ultimately, these small decisions are a matter of tremendous urgency, the happiness of marriage. It is essential to thriving marriages, Page says, that couples "experience sex as an integral part of their love."

Of course, there are healthy marriages in which sexual passion is not a top priority. Nevertheless, many of us still want sex to be an important component of marriage. For us, the difficulty often lies in remembering not to pass up the great opportunities we have to indulge our senses. Sure, there are times when a lapse in sex will reawaken our senses, and when abstaining can be stimulating. But most of the time, cultivate your will to say yes. I promise you, there is no more enjoyable refresher course.

3. LET GO.

Women are socialized to believe that if we are good, good things will happen to us. If we don't sleep around, someone will want to marry us. If we are good wives, and make everything beautiful and don't nag our husbands too much, our marriages will last. Sure, this is archaic propaganda, but no bride I know is truly immune to it.

It is legend in my family that the summer I met Duke, when I tried to make our relationship nothing more than a summer romance, my mother and sister swooned over him. They were visiting me in Newport, Rhode Island, where I had a summer place with friends and where Duke was in a U.S. Navy school. We happened to be out shopping when Duke was driving home from school in his uniform.

I should add that my mother and sister are both married, and are anti-military-spending, die-hard liberals. But at the sight of this man in uniform, they were swept up like Debra Winger in *An Officer and a Gentleman*. For the sake of their vicarious thrills, they beseeched me to keep going out with Duke.

I was mortified by the fuss they made over him, but deep down, I was swooning, too. I made grand pronouncements about how little the relationship mattered to me, but all the while my surrender was imminent. I did, in fact, go ahead and sleep with him—something that was totally out of character for me.

You see, I'm a minister's daughter, and while my family isn't prudish about these matters, I had, for the first twenty-eight years of my life, abided by a sexual code that set me apart from many of my peers. I never wanted to have a long scroll—names of all the men I'd slept with—to unroll in front of a fiancé. I couldn't conceive of keeping this information from a husband any more than I could conceive of a man who wouldn't care how many had preceded him. Maybe it was growing up with so much religious teaching. Maybe it was growing up with parents who had saved themselves for marriage and who adored one another thirty-nine years later. But I always thought sex was a treasure. I tried to reserve it for a love that would prove important. Granted, I didn't save myself for marriage as I was devoted to doing throughout college. But I saved myself for men I thought I'd marry—for a very short list of men I loved.

I decided early on that Duke was *not* going to make the short list. He was moving cross-country and I was not about to add another doomed long-distance romance to my scroll. Besides, he didn't give me the "buzz" that other men had.

Nevertheless, I wanted him. I wanted him big time. And so, a couple of months after I met him, I made him an exception to my lifelong rule. I let myself go, and not for any rational reason except that I could live with this deviation, and Duke knew where things stood between us.

And yet, in many ways, I regressed that summer and became the nightmarish, hormonally possessed teenager I had never been. Duke wanted to spend as much time as he could with me before he had to move cross-country, but I was skittish about my motives, doling out only small portions of time to him. Once, after telling Duke I'd be writing all weekend in Boston, I went to Newport and hung out with my friends in a bar, hoping to meet up with another guy. And when the guy hadn't shown up, I called Duke at two A.M. and asked him if I could come over.

This was classic bad girl behavior. For me, a supposedly "together" twenty-eight-year-old career woman, it was outrageous. I thought I deserved to rot in hell.

But do you know what Duke said to me when I came over to his apartment at two A.M., albeit without telling him that I'd spent the rest of the night chasing another guy? He invited me, the bad girl, into his apartment and

into his arms, and he said, "This is the nicest thing anyone has ever done for me." Surprising him in the middle
of the night, sullied motives and all, was, I repeat, the
nicest thing anyone had ever done for him.

I have said that loving Duke was like going back to
Sunday school. He reintroduced me to virtues like kindness and goodness that years of dating and protective
game-playing had made convoluted. Standing there in
the porch light that night, as exposed as I have ever been,
I felt about Duke the way the disciples must have felt
about Jesus, being welcomed into the fold.

If truth be told, Duke had just gotten home from a
night on the prowl himself. But the point is, he was a
good person with kind intentions. There was none of
this "he-was-getting-the-milk-for-free-so-why-should-
he-buy-the-cow" stuff. He just loved me. And he
wanted the chance to prove it to me, which I was stingy
with and scared to provide.

Now, I'm not suggesting there are any easy answers
to the matter of sex between adults before marriage. The
truth is, I don't regret my choices. And although Duke
does not harbor a Madonna/whore complex, he does
respect the judgment I exercised to keep my scroll so
short.

What I am saying is that the presence of unconditional
love changes the rules, turning love stories like this one
into topsy-turvy parables. All my life I'd reserved sex for
a love that would prove important when, ironically, in
this case, it took surrendering my mind—something I
was loathe to do—to get me to fall in love with him.
Only by letting go of my carefully maintained morality
and my precious reasoning, only by letting go of all the
things that held me back from loving Duke, did I find
real happiness and fulfillment.

To feel love's force in marriage, we have to "let go." We have to accept ourselves and trust our partners to love us and the tangle of scruples and desires that define us. We have to let go of the prim Laura Ashley picture we have of wives and mothers, or at least come to enjoy the idea that the same scruples and desires make their homes in floral dresses and empire waistlines. We must let go of the notion that our husbands love us because of what we "do" instead of who we are. And we must vanquish the notion that our desire for pleasure is any less valid or urgent than our husbands'.

The second-guessing brides so often do, about how they *should act*, how they *should look*, and how they *should feel* about their own complicated desires, undermines the real joy there is in marriage. It is often far better to let our instincts guide us, particularly when it comes to reveling in the safe, sanctioned freedom of making love in marriage.

After all, true love wants to accept and celebrate the totality of who we are. When we let it, true love rocks our world, rocks the bed, rocks the house, rocks the very foundation on which we so meticulously build our lives. And this is the source of stupendous lovemaking.

Of course, sex within marriage is what it is. The fire you build in marriage is not the fire you once felt in first kisses, nor the fire you felt being touched for the first time by someone you really wanted to touch you. For married couples, the temptation to have an affair, to feel again the sensations of a new relationship, is ever-present. What we forfeit by choosing fidelity is never far from our minds.

The real drawback of writing a book from the perspective of two and a half years of marriage, and of interviewing brides married five years or less, is that we cannot claim, or probably even imagine, the depth of feeling that accumulates in marriages that celebrate silver and gold anniversaries. We cannot truly know what it feels like to make love to one person for the rest of our lives. And I know it is not enough just to say that married sex is "different" and "better."

But sometimes, I have flashes of what makes it so different, and so much better. Sometimes, I am so happy making love to my husband that I cry. And in those moments, when I hide nothing from him, when I hide nothing from myself, the honesty of us is so piercing that it feels as if we have struck upon life's very core. We have fused utter vulnerability and its sweetest reward. And those two competing truths are embodied in us, not in one kiss, but in thousands of kisses, not for one night, but for what often seems an impossible amount of time to sustain such a fusion—for a lifetime.

> **WHAT NO ONE TELLS THE BRIDE ABOUT . . .**
>
> *Four factors that inhibit great, married sex:*
> ∞ Preconceived notions
> ∞ A lock of comfort and education about sex
> ∞ Abundant distractions
> ∞ Laziness
>
> *Our brides' solutions:*
> ∞ Engage the senses.
> ∞ Say no sparingly and caringly.
> ∞ Let go.

Ours, in marriage, is a very brave undertaking. There are a million stumbling blocks that would keep us from sustaining love and desire. But if you can conceive of such a fusion for yourselves, these pleasures will be yours—sometimes waning and calling upon your creativity, sometimes so dear you cannot fathom them dearer—for a lifetime.

Chapter 9

DON'T "START A FAMILY,"
DON'T BUY A DOG,
NOT EVEN A GOLDFISH . . .
UNTIL YOU READ THIS!

It's normal to think that now that you're married, you ought to "catch up" with everybody else and start a family. But it is important to wait. Indulge yourselves and your marriage first. Build a foundation before you build a family.

Like many women I know, I pride myself on keeping my fists close to my face and approaching life with a "C'mon-world-give-me-your-best-shot" attitude. So I didn't flinch when my engagement and marriage brought two long separations from Duke while he was in the Persian Gulf, a jolting introduction to the protocols of the U.S. Navy, a long battle with mononucleosis, a challenging book contract, and three household moves in three years—from Boston to San Diego to San Francisco to Washington state.

Instead, I heaped another complication onto my life. Eight months into our marriage, in my eagerness to please my husband the dog lover, I initiated a search for a puppy we could call our own.

Our dog was born on Friday the thirteenth, and this should have been a sign to us. But we named her "Lucky" and brought her home for Christmas—you know, the most frantic time of year, the time when veterinarians and humane societies everywhere discourage people from trying to introduce a new dog into a household.

In addition to Duke, I was eager to please my dog-fanatic sister who, along with the rest of my family, was coming to San Francisco for Christmas. This was the first time Duke and I were playing host for the holidays, and perhaps I also wanted the dog to fill out some idyllic photo of us in front of the fireplace. Only we didn't have a fireplace, and Lucky was teething—biting us non-stop from the day we brought her home—so that we only took pictures of her from a safe distance.

The dog turned out to be a much greater infringement on my independence than marriage had ever been. Any trip I made into the city for meetings, errands, or Christmas shopping had to be completed within four hours, the maximum time one should leave a young dog without a bathroom break. When I was home and trying to work, Lucky whined to be near me. Then when I let her into my office, she chewed holes in my rug, she chewed holes in me, and all fifteen pounds of her barked at St. Bernard decibels when my editor would call.

Within three weeks of Lucky's arrival, indefatigable me cried "uncle." Duke and I agreed that if things did not improve within the following month, we would have to find Lucky another home.

Obedience classes ended up being Lucky's saving grace, teaching us to be dog owners more than they taught the dog to behave. And I got addicted to being greeted by the sight of Lucky's tail, whipping back and forth like a metronome on speed. Love made me keep working at it, even though I felt as if I was down for the count.

How do newlyweds gauge when they are truly ready to "start a family"—to add kids, dogs, cats, goldfish, Venus's-flytraps, or other animated complications to a marriage that is still in its formative stages? I got a lot of input on this matter since fifteen of the fifty women I interviewed were either pregnant or new moms within four years of getting married.

We'll talk about timing in this chapter and about the foundation on which "families" are built, whether they be families with children, 101 dalmatians, or one over-indulged cat. We'll also talk about the double whammy, the shock women experience when they become mothers as they are still shadowboxing all the expectations that come with being wives. And although we could devote a whole other book to this aspect, my friends and I will try to prepare your marriage for the onslaught of change parenthood brings.

The average American married couple waits four years before they have children, according to Dr. John Gottman, professor of psychology at the University of Washington. Fifteen years ago, he says, the average couple waited only two years. There are no statistics, he says, that pertain to women over thirty, but my interviews suggest that brides circling the thirty-to-thirty-five age range start trying to have a baby sooner than their younger counterparts.

There's Pressure to Marry, Then Multiply

At every age, the question of parenthood is thrust upon couples before they are even married. Once you have the ring, people seem to think they have carte blanche to ask you *if*—or, more often, *when*—you want children, as if marriage and children are synonymous. Again, there is considerable pressure on brides and grooms to feel that their decision to spend eternity together is *not enough*.

As I write this, the tabloids are speculating that Carolyn Bessette Kennedy is pregnant. They have scarcely stopped fawning over her bridal gown, and now they want her to traipse off to Paris for the latest in maternity fashions. The pressure on her, and on us, is immense. The world seems to want only two things from us: a big, fancy wedding and, on the heels of that, our progeny. One couple I know got a camcorder from the groom's parents as a Christmas gift six months into their marriage. They didn't see it this way, but to me it was an obvious nudge, the grandparent-wannabe's outfitting the couple for parenthood before the newlyweds even had enough china place settings for a dinner party.

The church gets a hand in, too. Religious and premarital counselors play an important role in preparing couples for marriage by asking them to think about whether they want children, and to approach this matter thoughtfully. Nevertheless, marriage vows that include the admonition that couples should "accept the gift of children from God" feel, to some, abrupt and intimidating. No one, including God, seems to be satisfied with a couple just being a couple. And seemingly, just ten minutes ago, no one, including God, was satisfied with you being a well-adjusted, productive, single person either.

Couples Put Pressure on Themselves

Ultimately, many newly married couples are not satisfied with themselves either. "The baby urge" often conveniently appears just when a couple's lives are steadying and when their new marriage is becoming routine.

Of course, there are other considerations that bring on the baby urge. Couples want to have children while they are still young, or while their parents are still robust enough to enjoy grandchildren. Or they feel they are ready to "settle down," having already whooped it up in single life or having lived together before marriage. Newlyweds also cite their fear of the unknown—that they may not be able to have children or that it will take them a long time. And they wrangle with the logistics, with reaching certain financial, educational, or career landmarks before children are born.

A Baby Changes Everything

What no one tells the bride, however, is that parenthood—in my case, even puppy parenthood—is a gigantic adjustment to impose upon two people who are still getting used to marriage. "Triangulation" is the term that psychologists use to describe the dynamic that occurs in "threesomes." You'll notice triangulation rhymes with strangulation, which I assume is unintentional. And yet a third party can create considerable tension.

Emily, a thirty-seven-year-old director of operations at a company in Salt Lake City, got pregnant within months of getting married to Jonathan. Though parents now, they are also still newlyweds, and subject to the adjustments therein. Emily is a talker while Jonathan, when he is upset, is the proverbial silent type. He comes home from a bad day at work and doesn't want to talk about it—a habit that frustrates Emily.

These days, when Jonathan comes home in a bad mood, he makes a special effort to cuddle and coo to the baby. But once the baby's asleep, he shuts down completely around his wife. "So then we're mad at each other and not being nice to each other at the same time as both of us are being nice to the baby," Emily says.

Babies, in particular, bring forth a host of new irritations, insecurities, and jealousies as a couple grapples with the inevitable shift in the focus of the relationship. Or, sometimes, babies alleviate problems in relationships, diverting a couple's attention from boredom, or from a lapse in their love life. Then, years later, when their children are grown, the couple may discover they have few skills for loving each other, for overcoming boredom, and for generating intimacy.

Seventy-five percent of couples will, in fact, experience a precipitous drop in marital satisfaction with the birth of a child. And while reports of the death of romance with marriage are highly exaggerated, there is no denying that romance and intimacy are dramatically curtailed with the arrival of a newborn.

The Effect on Women Is Profound

The upheaval that accompanies the arrival of a new baby profoundly affects both partners, but women bear the brunt of it, physically and psychologically. Every woman experiences a kind of emotional pandemonium when she becomes a mother, so powerful are the pulls of love and maternal responsibility and so dramatic is the change in a woman's perspective and routine.

Not to mention that pregnancy and motherhood quadruple the emotional tumult already experienced by recently married women. If it felt to you as if a cool breeze came over your relationship with single friends when your engagement ring and new husband came on the scene, news of your pregnancy will bring on the next ice age. Hormones and a host of pregnancy side effects will ensure that, this time, you will *feel* dramatically different from how you felt when you simply added a ring to your finger or a hyphen to your name; now the gulf that divides you from your former life will grow much, much wider. Whereas it was possible for you and your friends to relate to the idea of marriage and male companionship, motherhood seems to seal your fate, your utter acquiescence to conventional life.

In her book *Surviving a Writer's Life*, Suzanne Lipsett relays the confusion she felt upon realizing this:

> I saw in the eyes of some of my single friends that my own pregnancy was inspiring emotional dust devils similar to those I had once experienced on seeing [a pregnant friend]. What on earth was I *do*ing? I was no sort of mother—held housework in the highest contempt, read rather than cleaned, wrote rather than cooked. . . . The joy of my life was finding myself living with a man pursuing his work in the darkroom as passionately and for as many hours as I pursued my own in the bedroom, hunched over the typewriter or poring over a book.

As we've seen, it takes brides and grooms a while to realize that choosing the convention of marriage does not doom them to conventional lives, unless they allow themselves to be drawn into the cult of low expectations, stereotypical assumptions, and lack of creativity. The onset of parenthood often causes another crisis in confidence, particularly because the needs of a newborn are overwhelming and undeniable. Yet once new parents settle into their roles, they find that their individual preferences and styles play as large a role in forging a unique and satisfying family life as they did in customizing marriage.

In many cases, the delight of having a child sneaks up on them in much the same way the marvel of marital friendship did. Lipsett describes it this way:

> I believe that the very feel of our baby's skin, the sound of his cry in the night, the depth of his gaze as he stared mildly up at us with infancy's utter lack of self-awareness—these flesh-and-blood experiences worked on us, seeping in under and around our creative concerns like healing vapors. . . . Within my soul, ripped places began to knit together, and the feminist in me was shaken to feel moments of unexpected, unimagined joy.

Marriage and motherhood are two of the three biggest transitions women experience in life (puberty being the third). These transitions have much in common; in many cases, they bring on both unexpected, unimagined depths of joy and unexpected, unimagined depths of isolation and despair. For women, who layer these transitions onto their souls simultaneously, the effects can take years to absorb and sort out. They may overwhelm a woman's, or a young couple's, ability to cope.

Just as a change in your eating or living habits threw you in early marriage, sleep deprivation and the constancy of an infant's dependence have an impact that should not be underestimated. However, when postpartum hormones try to play tricks with your mind, remind yourself that marriage need not obliterate individuality any more than motherhood need silence your intellect or eccentricities. Just as your baby squints to take in an unfathomable new world, you have to imagine for yourself a world in which love and family life work for you.

Pointers for Future Parents

If you believe children are in your future, perhaps it will help you to mull over the following points. Maybe then you can conceive of and construct a future of love and family life as expansive as it is resilient and steadfast.

1. ADD TO YOUR FAMILY ONLY FOR THE RIGHT REASONS.

No first-time parent is ever fully cognizant of, or prepared for, all the sacrifices that come with having children. But it is critical to the health of your marriage, and to the health and happiness of your child, that you be honest with yourself about your motivations for having a child.

In *John Rosemond's Six-Point Plan for Raising Happy, Healthy Children*, the author suggests you and your husband ask the following key questions to gauge your readiness to be parents:

- "Are we both in favor of having children, or does one of us harbor reservations?"
- "Do we feel emotionally up to dealing with the loss of freedom and with the long-term obligations, financial and otherwise, that come with having children?"
- "Do we enjoy being around other people's children or do they tend to annoy us?"
- "Did we have happy childhoods?"

Certainly, people who didn't grow up under the happiest of circumstances can go on to be good parents. But Rosemond believes that people who enjoyed being children are most likely to enjoy raising them.

These questions may seem rudimentary if you know you want children. But even so, I suggest you pay special attention to the second question, the one that asks if you are emotionally prepared for the long-term sacrifices and obligations of parenthood. I also urge you to disqualify two reasons that compelled many brides I interviewed and many women I know to start trying to have children. (Notice I say "start trying" because according to the 1995 National Family Growth Survey, only 12½ percent of married women between the ages of twenty-five and thirty-four, and only 14 percent of those between thirty-five and forty-four, report that they are experiencing infertility or difficulty getting pregnant after a year of sex without using contraception.

My rationale for launching a baby-making venture differs from that of my peers, probably for two reasons. First, I am adopted, and thus, I am not that impressed with the biologic imperative, or the simple desire to reproduce. I have learned that wanting a baby, or a pet, is not a good enough reason for having one. The fact that we are biologically equipped to have babies does not make us good parents. What makes us good parents—and what made my adopted parents great parents—is a remarkable reserve of love and selflessness, patience and faith.

Embark on this act of love because of what you have to give, not because of what you expect the experience to do for you. In other words, don't have a baby because you think it will cement or improve your marriage. Don't have a baby because you are eager to please your husband or your families. And don't have a baby because you think doing so will be your ultimate source of fulfillment. It may very well be, but as dangerous as it is to expect marriage to fill a hole inside you, it is criminal to ask a child to meet needs you have not learned to meet yourself.

When I was twenty-one, I also learned that I had less than a 30 percent chance of conceiving a child, due to a severe case of endometriosis. So I have spent the last decade pursuing specialists, the latest research, and cutting-edge treatments, hoping to preserve my fertility. In the end, the doctors I came to respect most were the ones who helped me appreciate that the most important thing I could do to improve my odds was to go on with my life, to fill it with love, and to let them worry about my medical condition.

This is the second reason I differ from women I know, many of whom stayed single longer and are, as Bonnie Raitt sings, "scared to run out of time." I do not believe that the fear of infertility is reason enough to start trying to make babies. Because if, up until now, neither you nor your spouse has had health problems that cast doubt on your fertility, the best thing you can do for your future family is to slow down, buttress your love, and approach major life decisions with calm and optimism. Because not only do fear and anxiety contribute to infertility, they are also a lousy emotional platform on which to approach the whole matter of making love, conception, and bringing a child into the world.

2. Wait a little longer. Grow up a little more.

If you and your groom are under the age of twenty-five, wait four years after getting married before you start trying to have a baby. If you and your groom are over twenty-five, wait two years. And if you are over thirty-five or have had health problems that would lead you to believe you will have difficulty conceiving, wait a year.

Remember that marriages are most vulnerable to divorce during the first five years, and that you need to shore up the foundation to your house before you start decorating a baby's room.

Several brides I interviewed got pregnant on their honeymoons or shortly thereafter. And while all of them loved their babies and rose to the challenge of parenthood, they cited the hazards of taking on too much responsibility too fast. Karla, a thirty-year-old Baltimore bride, was married in June and pregnant in July—the repercussions of which were overwhelming. She remembers, "I was so hurt, because it was such a big adjustment for [my husband, Charles], the whole idea of the pregnancy. He was so nervous about whether he could be someone's father."

Charles had not had Karla's happy childhood, nor had he witnessed a marriage that worked the way Karla's parents' had, now married more than thirty-five years. "He expected all of the hard stuff and none of the good stuff" in both marriage and parenthood. It took time for him to collect himself, to become enchanted with family life and its potential happiness, to enjoy putting a home together, and to adjust to "a six-foot Christmas tree instead of a three-footer," Karla explains.

The truth is, *all of us* need time to collect ourselves before we take on responsibility for the health and happiness of another living, breathing being, whether it be a baby or a strong-willed, hyperactive Chesapeake Bay retriever like my dog, Lucky. We need time to get used to what marriage *really* is before we start tackling the real-life drama of raising children.

I know how hard it is to wait. After all, doctors who diagnosed me with endometriosis twelve years ago urged me to get pregnant right away. For a long time, I lived my life under the specter of infertility and looked for a love that merited a life commitment. So it was momentous to start actually trying to have a baby, as Duke and I did a year ago, when we had been married a year and a couple of months. It was also damning to find that month after month, what the percentage-wielding doctors had predicted seemed to be true.

But then, seven months ago—by love and faith, and not by medicine—Duke and I conceived. And as I write this, there is considerably less room between me and my keyboard than there used to be. The baby kicks most when I write unfavorable things about his/her father-to-be. And I am quieted, humbled really, by the way life works out and by the way time heals, even though we think of time as our enemy.

Time to grow up and become a whole person may be the best gift you can give your heirs, because research shows that mature parents are better parents, according to author and University of Washington professor Dr. John Gottman. Good parenting requires you to trust your instincts, which you are more likely to do, Gottman says, if you have five to six years of decision making under your belt, and a confidence that comes with having tested your mettle. Besides, young people face enormous economic and job market challenges today. Because of these challenges, couples who marry at an early age typically work very long hours, or they are trying to finish their educations, incurring hefty school loans in the process.

But even if you were married at thirty-five, chances are that the expectations everyone has of brides did take their toll. It's likely you won't feel like yourself again, or make peace with this strange new married life, until you've been at it a year. And if you thought the pressures on you then were intense, just wait till you're pregnant, hormonally deranged, and every woman who's given birth on the planet starts telling you how best to raise your child. That's when you'll need to know your own mind, and your husband's, to separate the truth from that which is only meant to sow guilt and martyrdom into motherhood and parenthood.

3. BUILD THE FOUNDATION.

A whole marriage is much more than a gift to your off-spring. Child-raising expert and author John Rosemond says that to be good parents we must make the marriage, not the children, the center of the family. His message flies in the face of much of what we have been taught.

Rosemond contends that so much of what is wrong with children today is that they have been given too much attention and not enough limits. Obviously, in the first eighteen months, parents must attend to an infant's needs. But after that, it is unwise to play into a child's egocentric, self-centered view of life. Rosemond suggests couples right this wrong with certain marriage-protecting strategies, by planning a weekly couple's "night out," by not allowing children to interrupt adults when they are talking, and by establishing early bedtimes for children so that a couple may enjoy a few hours alone each night.

Obviously, it is in a child's best interest that couples prevent divorce by nurturing marriage, even during the intense child-rearing years. And couples who, from the very start, appreciate the importance of safeguarding the marriage will be better equipped to do so once children, hamsters, and goldfish come along.

Rosemond cautions couples with children about a

dangerous game he's observed in relationships called "Who's had the worst day?" In this game, a stay-at-home mom and a breadwinner dad, for example, act out their resentments and compete for the prize of who has it "worse."

Something I call "competitive neediness" is usually the catalyst for these resentments. Duke and I struggled with "competitive neediness" in that early period of our marriage, when he was stressed out and working all the time, I was desperate for attention and excitement. Duke resented his job for taking him away so much. Living on the blond coast, far from my family and friends, I resented life in general, and didn't recognize the person I had become. So Duke and I greeted one another at the end of a workday with this litany of woes and this put-upon body language, starting off what little time we had together with a competition instead of empathy and support.

The stakes in this game get only higher from pregnancy on. You see, two years into my marriage, and seventeen weeks into my pregnancy, Duke and I got a scare that our baby might have Down's syndrome. Doctors later informed us that the alpha-fetal protein test that gave us the scare has a 40-to-1 false-to-true-positive rate, and that the chances of a birth defect were actually about 5 percent. But the week we waited to have the ultrasound and counseling that would ease our fears was torturous. Thus far in our marriage, we had confronted nothing as daunting as this.

Then, almost simultaneously, Duke learned that the radical downsizing of the navy would extinguish his life-long dream of commanding a ship someday. No one was prepared for how drastic the cuts would be, particularly among officers his age who came up during the Reagan era of navy expansion. The two of us felt as though we were lost at sea, as two major blows left us sleepless and preoccupied with worry.

Of course, Duke said again and again that the health of the baby was far more important than the health of his career. And I felt his unequivocal support. But the "competitive neediness" we fostered early in our marriage seemed like child's play to us as we lay in bed, his apprehensive hand on my swollen belly, my eyes a fountain of tears.

Having weathered smaller problems, we had learned by then that sometimes both of our needs would be so great, and our abilities to offer support to one another so taxed, that at least in part we would have to bolster ourselves through hard times. And ultimately, we had to put our fears in what Anne Lamott calls "God's in-box," relying on faith and a healing source bigger than ourselves to carry us through.

This is another crucial preparation to make before having children. Understand that you cannot do it alone. You must line up help from outside the marriage, from other mothers and fathers, from play groups and church groups, and from whatever faith you can muster in something bigger and more powerful than yourself. Because it may take "God" with a capital G to help you endure a colicky baby, night after screaming night. And it may take Mary, Muhammad, Buddha, and a couple of saints for you to cope with a hostile stepson or -daughter.

Marriage expert Gottman says two traits made the difference among the 25 percent of couples who remained satisfied with their marriages after the arrival of the first child. First, a husband must be able to empathize with his wife. "It is particularly important for a husband to know about his wife's psychological world, for him to know about her worries, stresses, fears, and dreams," Gottman says.

In his marriage workshops, Gottman uses a "love map" board game, in which players cannot advance without knowing certain things about their partners. (The game will be included in his upcoming book, *The Marriage Survival Kit.*) The game helps men, in particular, by showing them how much it pleases their wives when they ask questions and gain insights into their wives' thoughts and feelings.

Along those same lines, I asked brides I interviewed to suggest conversation-starting questions. Perhaps the questions will help you access one another's innermost, or zaniest, thoughts. Because the more you know, the more you empathize, the greater your chances for happiness in a complicated marriage.

The second key trait found in the 25 percent of couples who remained satisfied in marriage after the birth of a child was that of "fondness and admiration." Largely,

---

BRIDE-TO-BRIDE

How has having a baby affected the fun you and your husband have together?

∞ "We definitely had the most fun before our son was born. Back then, we would easily whip out Boggle at 11:30 P.M. on a weeknight and play a couple of rounds before we went to sleep. Now, after putting our son to bed, my husband will say, "Let's play Boggle,' and my reaction is, 'Are you out of your mind? I live three lives in one day and you want me to play Boggle?'"

∞ "Time alone now is a rarity, and intimacy is a joke with two kids."

∞ "Now we have fun going camping and going to Disneyworld."

∞ "It is fun watching him become a father."

∞ "My husband has a great sense of humor. He makes me laugh at everything, including myself."

Gottman says, this fondness is derived from everyday interactions, from the millions of little choices couples have to "turn toward or turn away" from one another.

Gottman believes that mature couples have the upper hand in this. After all, they have more experience balancing work and other aspects of their lives, and are more apt to have their priorities straight. "They know that moments of intimacy are rare and special in life," he says.

4. HAVE FUN. GET FUNNY.

Overlooked so far in this master plan is perhaps the most important newlywed "task"—that of having fun. Because, I am told, you cannot imagine how much fun is siphoned off a night on the town when you have to hire a baby-sitter. Or how you will worry during a vacation about having left your puppy at a kennel—an anxiety I swore I would not succumb to but promptly did.

Starting a family, as I've intimated, can quickly draw you into much more serious life matters. Thirty-one-year-old Maureen, an actuary from Connecticut, and her husband, Chris, started trying to have a child several months after they were married, having lived together for four years before that. It wasn't long before they were experiencing the frustrations of infertility, the usual feelings of "what's wrong with me?" and "a nervousness about how far into the process" of medical interventions they would have to go, Maureen explains.

Then, with the help of fertility drugs, Maureen became pregnant with twins. In her final trimester, at the time I interviewed her, Maureen and Chris were abruptly dealing not with perplexing and painful infertility issues but with the logistics of expecting two babies, figuring out how they could take leave from their jobs, and bracing themselves for an overwhelming bundle of joy.

Angie, a twenty-seven-year-old bride from Philadelphia, is on a different kind of emotional roller coaster. She has a history of Huntington's disease in her family, a degenerative disease of the nervous system that strikes middle-aged adults and has already claimed the life of Angie's uncle.

Angie and her husband of two years, Michael, would love to have children, but they do not yet know whether Angie has the gene for Huntington's, a condition for which there is, as yet, no cure. They have decided to put off Angie's being tested, as they do not yet feel ready for the news. And knowing all too well what the future might bring, they are living for the moment and enjoying one another right now.

I hope that if and when you decide to expand your family, you have nothing more challenging to consider than which mobile to hang over the crib. But until then, accept that the early years of marriage are challenging enough, and reap as much fun and freedom as you can from them. Travel, spend money on each other, go out to eat. You will not regret having done so when you stagger to the nursery for the two A.M. feeding.

In the three-and-a-half years they were married before their son came along, Natasha and Israel, newlyweds in Portland, Oregon, made a point of having sex wherever they wanted to and going on a lot of carnival rides. (When asked if they had combined the two activities, Natasha was smilingly evasive.) Having married five-and-a-half months after they first met, Natasha says, "We spent every bit of time together that we could, just getting to know one another. And we lavished each other with gifts, not material things but gifts of love, of fun, of ourselves."

Seriously, folks, fun is good for marriage. Indeed, a 1994 *New Woman* magazine survey of five thousand women revealed that those who chose "having fun" as the primary purpose of their marriage were most likely to say their marriages were "great." Other than having fun, the other choices offered to the survey respondents were: "to raise a family," "to foster spiritual growth," "to build character," and "to be financially stable." In the end, the fun-lovers enjoyed the best sex, thought least about divorcing, got the most respect and appreciation from their spouses, and said they'd marry their spouses all over again more often than those who picked other "primary purposes."

In addition, marriage expert John Gottman tells us that humor is an excellent buffer against divorce. But he says the admonition to "be funny" falls as flat as that which tells people to "be spontaneous." Couples don't have shared humor, he says, unless they feel accepted and know each other well.

Ultimately, acceptance and security make us funny;

> **BRIDE-TO-BRIDE**
>
> *Suggest one conversation-starting question that has helped you and your husband get to know one another better?*
>
> ∞ "When did you first learn that life wasn't fair?"
>
> ∞ "What five people, living or dead, would you invite to a fantasy dinner party?"
>
> ∞ "Why don't we turn off the television?"
>
> ∞ "If you hadn't met me, where do you think you'd be right now and how would it be different from what we have?"
>
> ∞ "Tell me your dreams and fantasies."
>
> ∞ "Tell me about your childhood."
>
> ∞ "How about those Yankees?!"
>
> ∞ "Tell me a secret you've never told anyone else."
>
> ∞ "What was the best and worst thing that happened to you today?"

this is a foreign concept for most of us, so conditioned are we to believe a person either is or is not funny. To be perfectly honest, I married Duke thinking his humor was pretty lame. He never rolled in the aisles at my jokes when we were dating either. And it used to really bother me when friends told me they knew they'd found Mr. Right because he made them laugh.

I once told my mom and my younger sister Catherine—married five years by the time I contemplated it—that I wasn't sure I should marry Duke because he didn't make me laugh. My mother, still starry-eyed over the man in uniform, said, "For God's sake, I'll get you a joke book. Or call me long distance and I'll tell you some jokes."

Catherine, the seasoned marriage veteran, was silent and seemingly contemplative during all of this. She waited, she cleared her throat, and then she came out with it. "Marg," she said, "the truth is, you know absolutely nothing about marriage."

I knew then how Charlie Brown felt when, in the midst of kick after glorious kick, Lucy snagged the football away from him. And particularly in print, it pains me to have to admit this, but in this isolated instance, my sister was right. I knew next to nothing about marriage.

Nevertheless, I did learn, and for all of us in marriage, that is the point. You can *learn* to be funny, and not necessarily by enrolling in an adult education class for stand-up comedians, as I once suggested to Duke that we do. In fact, the funniest Duke and I have ever been, and the hardest we've ever laughed, has been in a thicket of stress.

We were sitting in a pothole-filled parking lot on a navy base, having just toured the military housing I would soon be moving us into in the Bay area while

Duke was in the Persian Gulf. The apartments we'd seen were old, run-down, and considerably smaller than the one in which we were then living in San Diego. We nursed our disappointment silently in the car, overlooking a dilapidated miniature golf course and wolfing down crackers and American cheese from a Lunchables tray we'd bought inside an equally dilapidated military minimart.

Not two weeks before, we had been on our belated honeymoon, gluttons for rich food and four-star restaurants. And not a year before, I had lived in Boston in a large, charming, exposed-brick-and-beam studio. Back then, I thought to myself, I'd never resorted to miniature golf for entertainment. Nor had I considered how "khaki" and institutional my life as a navy wife might become.

> ## WHAT NO ONE TELLS THE BRIDE ABOUT . . .
>
> *"Starting a family":*
> ∞ There's pressure to marry, then multiply.
> ∞ Couples then put pressure on themselves.
> ∞ A baby changes everything.
> ∞ The effect on women is profound.
>
> *Our brides' suggestions:*
> ∞ Add to your family only for the right reasons.
> ∞ Wait a little longer. Grow up a little more.
> ∞ Build a foundation.
> ∞ Have fun. Get funny.

Neither Duke nor I really knew what to say to one another about the change in the quality of life we were about to make. But just then, when my mouth was still crammed with Lunchables, Duke ripped into a bag of M&M's, handed me a can of diet Coke, and said, in a pathetic French waiter accent, "Cleanse your palette, madame?"

I can tell you that nothing cleanses the palette quite like convulsing laughter. Because so often in the briar of early marriage, when you are afraid of so many things, the only way out is to *get funny*, and to choose to see life as a splendid comedy that only the two of you appreciate. There is, in the end, no one funnier than the man with whom you share these seemingly insurmountable predicaments, no one funnier than the man whose hand you hold when you conquer your fears.

This is what I didn't know about marriage: that you have to groom it for challenges as wonderful as puppies and babies, that you have to be patient and wait for time to work its magic in your marriage, and that you have to be a fun seeker, especially when you feel your least hopeful, and your least confident. These are the things we must conceive for ourselves, before we add to our families and before a baby takes hold of our hearts.

Chapter 10

THE HEART GROWS FONDER:
THE ALL-IMPORTANT BALANCE BETWEEN
TIME APART AND TIME TOGETHER

It's normal to expect and want to spend all your free time together, but time apart is as critical to your growth as time together. A shuttle between individual and shared experience nourishes marriage.

Four months after we were married, Duke left San Diego for a four-month stint aboard a ship in the Persian Gulf. I was alone—master of my destiny—as I had been for ten years prior to the ten months I had lived with Duke.

Once again, I could write well into the night, eat dinner in bed, leave magazines and mail-order catalogs everywhere, and sleep well past the ungodly hour Duke's job usually mandated we rise. Except that for the first two weeks Duke was gone, I was incapacitated with heartache. I went through a withdrawal, a deprivation that felt as potent to me as that experienced by people addicted to nicotine or drugs.

I consoled myself by going shopping. I shopped for two solid weeks so I would not have to go home—to the apartment *I* found for us, *I* moved us into, and *I* would move us out of, on my own. That same apartment was now unbearably lonely.

Before we were married, I cherished the notion that I would be a hybrid, that Duke's being away at sea for months at a time would allow me to straddle two worlds I was torn between. After all, the productivity of my writing career depended on the solitude I'd enjoyed in single life. And my happiness largely depended on sharing a life with this man I loved.

Still, I never anticipated how hard it would be to be a hybrid—how schizophrenic I'd sometimes feel, pining for my independence and pining for my husband at the same time. I struggled, as I've learned all brides do, with the mix of independence and dependence in marriage.

In this chapter, we'll talk about that mix, about time spent apart and time together, and about how these allotments of time can strengthen or undermine a partnership. Between us, my friends and I represent every conceivable model of marital time allotment. And it is from this spectrum of experience that we have plucked a few important lessons about a full and balanced life to share with you.

The Misnomer of More Time

It often seems that the biggest farce about marriage is that it gives couples more time together. We expect that when we live together and share a life commitment, we'll also share a life. That, I think, is why many newlyweds become more possessive of their husbands or wives in marriage, because we expect time and intimacy to simply materialize once we cross the threshold. Then we learn that intimacy is easily postponed or rescheduled, and that it takes a lot of work to find "quality time" amid the demands of a career, family, and household.

Judy, a thirty-three-year-old public relations professional in St. Louis, expected that she and her husband, Travis, would spend a lot of time together when they were married. But she's had to let go of this expectation because Travis is in school, pursuing his Ph.D. His studies have to come first. Meanwhile, Judy works full-time, and a year into their marriage, she gave birth to their first child. So you can imagine the difficulty they have apportioning the one night of the week they are determined to spend together, and the unspoken pressure there is on them to make that hallowed time very special.

More difficult than accepting the clash of their schedules, however, is that Judy believes she is working harder at the marriage than Travis is right now. Even with a new baby, she says, "I have fewer distractions at present. He is consumed with school and doesn't have time to concentrate very hard on our marriage."

The potential for resentment is substantial. After all, Judy and Travis have been married only two years. Aren't they setting dangerous patterns in which Judy will continue to work harder at the marriage than Travis?

This is the devastating conclusion many brides jump to, and that I jumped to before I came to appreciate the ways that marriages can be renegotiated, the ways that circumstances can change, and the ways that couples are different from one another, incapable of being branded with cure-all solutions or formulas. Right off the bat, most brides and grooms do not appreciate that marriages come with, to use legal terminology, individual sets of aggravating and mitigating factors.

For example, part of the reason Judy does more in the relationship is because she wants to, or feels compelled to. She is obsessive about the house being clean, just like her mother was, and she acknowledges she is too much of a caregiver, taking on more responsibility than she needs to.

Travis, on the other hand, is laid back and less apt to "concentrate" on the relationship in the same ways Judy does. Certainly, he comes through in a pinch. Recently, for example, he took charge of all the baby's nighttime feedings and diaper changes to let his wife sleep.

Travis is also a golfer. And because he is so afflicted, his ultimate relaxation comes on the golf course. As much as golf has slipped in the list of priorities, both Judy and Travis appreciate that his happiness depends, to a certain extent, on his getting in at least nine holes every once in a while.

The Hungers of Our Hearts

All married couples have sets of aggravating and mitigating factors, their own particular expectations, desires, compulsions, and fears to weigh and consider. And it is *these* factors that make time a loaded question in marriage. Time may be money in the work world, but in marriage, we equate time with heart. Thus, the question all newlyweds grapple with is "How do we allocate our time so that we meet the hungers of our hearts?"

When I fell in love with Duke, many of my friends questioned what kind of life I could have with someone whose career took him away so much. They expected me to be jealous of the time the navy demanded of him. Even Duke's father, a retired navy captain, worried I would be a stereotypical wife, putting pressure on his son to abandon his naval career for work that would keep him closer to home.

These assumptions made me nuts. Very few people could envision a marriage that thrived on a healthy mix of independence and shared life. Fewer still could fathom a woman wanting her own space and time. Yet my mother had always attributed the happiness of her marriage to the fact that she and my dad spent enough, but not *too* much, time together.

I was surprised to find that some people considered this an "inauthentic" kind of marriage. And I was aghast to learn how much I wanted Duke around once we were married and how against the grain it felt at first to leave him for travels and adventures of my own.

The Misnomer That Togetherness Equals Happiness

I've since learned that like most brides, two important strains were working in me at the time. First, I was under a lot of pressure to believe that togetherness equals marital happiness. Second, I was clinging to Duke, as newlyweds tend to do, in ways that felt unnatural to me then, and that feel somewhat unnatural to me now. Not only was I experiencing the magnetism of love for the first time, but Duke was my mainstay in what was otherwise a strange, new environment.

First things first. The amount of time a couple spends together is not a yardstick by which to measure marital happiness. Our images of soul mates and lovers are of them spending endless hours together, lying around sun-dappled villas, feeding one another, painting one another, making love, and reciting poetry. But outside the movies, I have never actually met people like this, nor any couple who can sustain this kind of domestic intrigue for more than a few days. Eventually, you have to go out for Häagan-Daz, and when you do, the quirk-iest person waits on you, or some louse cuts you off when you're trying to park, or you notice the hardware store has changed its dusty window display for the first time in three years. These tidbits of life awaken your taste buds—your sense of who you are in relation to the world. And this is healthy.

In my interviews for this book, I've learned that couples vary immensely in how much togetherness they need to be happy. Dede and Michael are together in their Montana art studio all day long. When Dede talks about the marriage, she intermingles talk about the studio as if they are one and the same. She refers to their business as "their child." And yet, she says, the time she and Michael spend "together" at work isn't true togetherness. They devote additional time each night to being together, to taking a walk, giving one another massages, or having a spiritual discussion.

At the other extreme, several brides I interviewed do not live in the same time zone as their grooms. My friend Allison is a JAG, an attorney in the U.S. Navy, and her fiancé, Jay, is a fighter pilot. At present, Allison is stationed in Norfolk, Virginia, and Jay is in Okinawa. They see each other for a weekend or a few days every three months, with no indication that this will change for almost a year after they are married this fall.

The up side of this situation is that their relationship is incredibly romantic. The sex is wonderful; the times they do see each other are a whirlwind of activity and excitement—the phone calls, letters, and gestures in between as heart-wrenching and spine-tingling as it gets. Recently, when Allison was alone in Hawaii on business/pleasure, Jay arranged for her to get room service, timed perfectly to arrive after her morning run.

The table the busboy wheeled in was set for two, cascading with roses and all her favorite things for breakfast and a card that read, "Pretend I am here with you for breakfast."

BRIDE-TO-BRIDE

What is fun about marriage?

∞ "We are both bargain shoppers. We love antiqueing and tag sales, buying beat-up furniture we can fix. The best part is sharing the tale of the purchase and how much money we saved."

∞ "We built a deck together. Getting dirty and building something together was great. Since my husband works in construction, it helped me understand his work better."

∞ "We don't have a television, we just order a pizza and sit on the couch and joke around. We get totally caught up in our own laughter."

∞ "At bedtime we have our books and our cats around us. It is a very positive space."

∞ "We can spend the whole day together, just walking around the city."

But the down side is that they go through miniature versions of the adjustments we talk about in this book every time they see each other. Living out of suitcases for their weekends together, they feel the considerable tugs of their independence and love for one another, a profound kind of schizophrenia between their two totally separate, and minimally yet meaningfully joined lives. The hardest part, Allison says, is not being able to share one another's burdens. Going through physical therapy, between a third and fourth surgery on her knee, Allison needed Jay's emotional not to mention physical support. Having to do without it so much makes her wary of relying on it as marriage ultimately will require her to do.

But brides and grooms need not pursue an intercontinental romance to identify with the notion of being a hybrid, and of straddling two worlds—one of their own making and one they shared with their husbands. All the brides I interviewed said they regularly called upon the skills they acquired as independent-minded women even though they were married.

Clinging Is Normal

Nevertheless, brides also had an intense desire to share their thoughts, experiences, and lives with their husbands. This was the driving force in the first place behind their decision to marry. Yet they feel, or are made to feel, self-conscious about this desire.

It is very common for newlyweds to "cling" to one another. We bring our spouses to work and other social functions where it would have been awkward or cumbersome to bring a boyfriend. And we think twice about going somewhere alone, whereas before we would have thought twice about going places *with* someone.

The main reason we become, as they say, "joined at the hip" is because we genuinely like one another and have fun together. Even mindless, ordinary things, like picking up a gallon of milk or working out, are more appealing when you share them with someone whose company you enjoy.

The words *fun, goofiness,* and *play* came up again and again in my interviews. Couples seemed to approach ordinary life with a degree of playfulness they wouldn't have exercised alone. One bride told me about a long drive she and her husband took without the radio on, in which her husband put a wrapping paper tube up to his mouth and played it like an instrument to keep her awake and amused.

As newlyweds, we work very hard at soldering our relationships, because we want our relationships to work or because we have unrealistic expectations to begin with, believing that marriage will banish our sense of aloneness. It is often difficult at first to tell the difference between the two motivations. So when we start modifying our schedules or our previous tendencies for the sake of the union, we cannot be sure whether we are doing something noble or something that truly endangers our sense of self.

My friend Sarah, a lobbyist now living in Jacksonville, Florida, left a prestigious job, her family, and friends in New England to join her fiancé, Matt, in Monterey, California, where he was in graduate school. Having lost the identity she'd built in her professional and personal life back home, she was astonished at how immediately dependent she became upon Matt.

In Sarah's former life, she'd lived alone, traveled alone on business, and was largely a self-starter. But in Monterey, she found herself utterly reliant on Matt for social connections, for entertainment, even for motivation to go to the grocery store. "I didn't want to go anywhere without him," she marveled. "I wouldn't even go shopping without him."

A year later, Sarah found a job that challenged and demanded more independence from her, and she got comfortable with her new surroundings, marriage, and social life. She seemed to be "herself" again, and yet she was also decidedly different—a self-assured woman who nevertheless continued to enjoy her husband's company.

Holding on to Ourselves

Any step to the side of your usual path feels like a failure to a new bride. But once you grow more assured in your partnership, missteps seem less grievous and become something you just need to work on in the on-going balancing act of marriage. If more brides knew this, I am convinced that women would not be so afraid of marriage and of the turmoil prevalent in young mar-riages.

Of course, it made me shudder to read in the 1996 *Redbook* survey that if asked to by their husbands, 39 percent of new wives said they would change their hair, 35 percent would change the clothes they wear, and 30 percent would try to lose or gain weight even if the women themselves thought they looked fine. However, after interviewing many newly married women, and after coming through this tsunami of change myself, I know that women *can* find their way, *can* throw off ridiculous expectations, and *can*, in the individual pacts they make and constantly reassess with their husbands, hold on to more of their souls in their marriages than this survey portends.

How do women do it? How do they protect the var-ious yearnings of the heart that time represents? Here are some clues:

1. Cultivate a relationship with the world.

Indeed, marriage is about having a companion and about having fun together, and the temptation to "nest" and create an insular world is very strong, especially in the midst of all the change that bombards newlyweds. But be careful not to let your mate become an intravenous line on which you depend for your nourishment.

In *The Good Marriage*, authors Judith Wallerstein and Sandra Blakeslee tell us that one of the keys to happiness among "companionate" marriages—those that try to be different from the marriages of previous generations by emphasizing the equal contributions of husbands and wives—is being involved in the world outside the home. They write:

Finally, the people in [companionate] marriages were engaged in worlds outside their families. They pursued professional and personal activities individually and together. A good number enjoyed the out-of-doors, hiking and camping as a couple and as a family. Some were involved in politics, others in the arts. A few belonged to religious organizations. None led isolated lives. In my experience, couples who divorce tend to lead more isolated lives and to have fewer friends and community contacts. In some cases one person remains engaged in the world while the other shuts down, and the marriage suffers. It takes two to carry on a conversation, and both must be open to ideas. Couples in companionate marriages, where husband and wife straddle two worlds, may find it easiest to avoid boredom.

As my friends and I recommended before, you have to create soul to have a lifelong soul mate. Marriage counselor Warren Molton says that to cultivate soul, or a deeper sense of the world's meaning, couples have to seek out and develop connections with the world.

Look for soul everywhere, Molton says. "Believe you can find it in many places—in your church or synagogue, in music, art, nature, and of course in sex as well. Talk about the sources from which each of you derives soul, and then take turns pursuing those different connections." When we have more of these connections, Molton explains, we don't expect or need our partners to give us all the soul we crave.

Molton says he gets very concerned about couples he counsels who have no experience of nature. Nature delivers us, he says, in ways that computers and televisions cannot. He believes the simple act of taking a walk can be transforming.

I learned this from Duke, who craves the outdoors the way I crave interactions with people. Living in San Francisco the second year we were married, we started hiking together in places as majestic as Yellowstone National Park and Muir Woods. But more often, we walked around the wooded island where we lived, kicking pinecones for our dog, Lucky. No matter how foul a mood either one of us was in, kicking pinecones for Lucky was a miracle elixir. We faked the dog out, we chased pinecones down hills, and we laughed at Lucky when she'd cram six of them into her mouth at one time.

Sometimes we became so consumed with our game that we were oblivious of cars waiting to pass, and of the stress of the day now left behind. And we learned that twenty minutes outdoors—even if the weather was lousy, even if we hardly talked to one another—was time better spent than a half hour of a TV sitcom.

When you defy the couch potato within, when you go for a walk, or to a lecture, a subtle change occurs in your attitude toward life and your relationship whether or not you're accompanied by your spouse. Every marriage needs the "rush" that comes with new ideas and fresh perspectives.

Annette, twenty-nine, a college administrator in Providence, Rhode Island, says a spiritual life makes her open to receiving what her husband, Marcus, has to contribute to their relationship. Church also gives them role models and mentors. "At our church we have a couples' club where we have dinner parties and socialize," she says. "You have another woman to call if you have a challenge in your relationship. It gives you a way to connect with people."

Marcus, Annette explains, is good friends with their former pastor. "[The pastor] has four kids and has been a great mentor to Marcus. He gave Marcus all these books, Bill Cosby's book, for instance, and they go out to lunch. I think that's important—being open to the fact that you don't know everything."

Mentors and a spiritual life bolster Annette and her husband while my happiness in marriage relies on my remaining close to other women. Girlfriends are my backbone, they always have been. And like clockwork, I grow restless with my marriage when I don't get my fix of time with vibrant, interesting women. Their irreverence, their searing honesty, and their willingness to share secrets revitalize me, the same way a dose of Bonnie Raitt or Aretha Franklin does. I am feistier, I am sexier, and I am a lot more fun to be married to when my forays into the world include meaningful relationships with other women.

2. SPEND SOME TIME APART.

During the engagement and the first years of marriage, there are an inordinate number of appearances to make as a couple. There are so many "firsts"—family outings, college reunions, trips, and get-togethers with your spouse's cousins or friends whom you haven't met before. And I think that eventually we internalize these expectations, and begin to think there is something wrong with our relationships if we don't want to accompany one another on every outing, errand, or chore.

Duke and I were at a mall the other day when it

dawned on me that, a year ago, I would have gotten angry that I went off to choose glasses for myself at Pearle Vision while he went off to an arcade. A year ago, this choked-up Mary Tyler Moore voice would have come out of nowhere and said, "Why doesn't Duke know that I would really like his opinion on which glasses look good on me? Why would he rather spend a roll of quarters to dominate the universe than be with me?"

Part of the reason I would've been upset a year ago was because Duke and I saw so little of each other that I treasured every millisecond he was with me and holding my hand. But there is also a freedom, a confidence in the relationship, two-and-a-half years into marriage, that wasn't there before.

I know now that Duke doesn't read minds and that if I wanted him to come with me, I should have told him. But this time it wasn't all that important to me. If he didn't like the glasses I picked, I wouldn't sweat it. He had an hour to be a ten-year-old boy again in an arcade, and I was my own fashion consultant. And we both went home happy.

Isabelle, twenty-eight, who works at a money management firm in San Francisco, seems never to have sweated the issue of how much time she and her husband, Peter, spent apart from one another. The independence they enjoyed in their courtship naturally flowed into her now one-year-old marriage.

They were separated for several months before the wedding when Peter was in Atlanta for the U.S. Olympic trials in sailing. And at home in San Francisco, Isabelle says, "[Peter] travels on business about once a week, and during the winter, he goes duck hunting two nights out of the week. And I have been studying for the CFA exam four nights a week."

Recently, Isabelle says, friends marveled at her independence, just because she volunteered at the Special Olympics by herself. "It's what I want," Isabelle says. "As long as that's the kind of relationship you want, then it's great. Being involved in different things gives you something to talk about. It keeps the relationship exciting. What would you talk about if you knew how the other person spent all of his time?"

Wallerstein and Blakeslee recommend that couples take vacations both as a couple and separately, and that if there are children, you add a third type of vacation, one with the kids. Obviously, not all of us have three weeks of vacation to divide evenly. Nevertheless, a weekend away with your girlfriends can be as important to the health of a marriage as a romantic weekend away.

Some couples, particularly younger couples, don't come at "independence" naturally and really have to work at building time apart into their lives. For others, work obligations ensure that they spend time apart. Elizabeth, the twenty-nine-year-old Boston health-care systems administrator, is getting her masters in public health while her husband, Stephen, is in medical school. But last summer, Stephen had to go to San Antonio to fulfill his obligation to the U.S. Army, which is paying for his schooling. Married but apart for the entire summer, Elizabeth laughs about how she called her husband in San Antonio last summer to say, "Hey, I just got a new job."

This degree of independence may strike some couples as extreme. It depends on what you want from your relationship, as Isabelle suggested. But in every marriage, there are times when husbands and wives must act independently of one another, perhaps even in crises or major decisions. Sometimes, as in the case of my friend who changed a tire on the side of a highway in the middle of winter with a baby on her back, these experiences are downright harrowing. And sometimes these experiences are liberating, particularly for women. But whatever the circumstances, you are guaranteed to feel a bit schizophrenic, drawing upon your own resources, as you always have when, in everyday life, you have also come to depend on a partner.

I learned this most poignantly during the four months Duke and I were separated the first year we were married. After those first two weeks of heartache, I did find my stride again. I finished the book I was working on, celebrating with friends each time I completed a chapter. And I oversaw movers as they packed our belongings before I drove to San Francisco, the place Duke and I would be "stationed" upon his return.

BRIDE-TO-BRIDE

What do you like best about spending time away from your husband?

∞ "I'm an introvert and need time alone to rejuvenate."

∞ "I get a lot more accomplished."

∞ "I don't have to watch or worry about whether or not he is having a good time."

∞ "With my girlfriends, I have license to be catty."

∞ "I see myself without him and I like the picture of myself when I'm not depending on him."

∞ "Having time away makes me realize how much I miss him."

But as a hybrid, I was not entirely in control of my own destiny. I was at the mercy of navy-contracted movers, in this case an unscrupulous company. When I advised the owner of the moving company that I would inform the navy of the problems I encountered, he threatened to "burn, lose, or destroy" our furniture and belongings.

In San Francisco, I was staying in a kind of navy hotel, something called the bachelor officers' quarters. There were no phones in the rooms so I had to call from one of twenty phone booths in the lobby, most of them filled with men in uniform. It was under these circumstances that I placed a satellite call to Duke while he was in the middle of a gas-mask drill on an aircraft carrier somewhere off the coast of Saudi Arabia. It was a miracle I even got through to him, especially again and again, when we were cut off three times during a five-minute call. Between these interruptions, the echo of the international call, the muffle of his gas mask, and the sobs I broke into the minute I heard a semblance of his voice, I can tell you that very little quality, much less soul-quenching communication ensued.

When I hung up from this entirely unsatisfying phone call, I felt utterly alone—a new bride, a civilian woman without my husband in a strange military world, indeed a sorry example of the hybrid I'd aspired to be. Even with all my faculties about me, I stood little chance of tackling the enormous bureaucracy that stood between me and the safe arrival of our furniture in navy housing. And as much as he wanted to, Duke was not in a position to help me.

But I lived through it. I set up my laptop in my room in the bachelor officers' quarters. I nuked my dinner in the microwave. I got a speeding ticket from the base police trying to meet a Federal Express deadline, sending edits to my publisher in New York. Ten days later, our household belongings arrived, some of them destroyed, some of them missing.

By the time I moved out of the bachelor officers' quarters, I strode through the lobby barefoot amid the patent leather and steel-toed shoes around me. I had learned to appreciate the pleasure and pain that comes with being a hybrid, that comes with being someone's wife while at the same time you're your own person. I learned that even in marriage, in which I derive so much comfort from my husband, I must continue to know how to comfort myself, and how to live through it when the relationship does not, or cannot, give me what I want it to.

3. PAY ATTENTION TO LITTLE THINGS. BUILD IN SOME RESTRAINTS.

There are hazards, however, to becoming *too* involved with the world and with spending *too* much time apart from your spouse. Particularly for couples who are in school or just starting out in their careers, it is easy to lose a sense of the centrality of love and marriage.

Twenty-seven-year-old Angie of Philadelphia worries that, just a year into her new marriage, she has stopped trying to impress her husband. "Not that I expected to parade around the house in a ballgown every day," she says, "but I thought I would attempt to keep myself up—wear nice clothes, do my hair, etc. I think the main reason for this is that I've changed my focus. Before I got married, my focus was on getting married. Now that I'm married, my focus is on my career. I work long hours, don't exercise anymore, and eat on the run. What I can't understand is that before I was married, I worked full-time, went to college full-time, worked out, read, etc. . . . Now all I do is work and I'm exhausted."

Perhaps Angie is being too hard on herself; after all, it's wonderful that she feels comfortable in her new life and doesn't worry excessively about the way she looks. Having put herself through college and worked full-time to boot, Angie never focused exclusively on the relationship with the man she eventually married, so the shift she described may not have felt as dramatic to her husband as she fears.

But once again, the potential for resentment and disillusionment is there. What does it mean, now that you're married, that you no longer pursue intimacy and time alone as eagerly as you did when you were dating? It may simply mean that you are in the middle of a big project at work, that you are putting in sixty- and seventy-hour workweeks just to pay the bills, or that you are just trying to survive the first months with a newborn baby. Or it may mean that you have trusted your husband and your relationship so much that you've forgotten to articulate and demonstrate what they really mean to you.

My friend Eliza, thirty, is an American living in Shanghai. Her husband, Brett, is starting a business there. She flew to China, moved in with him, and got a job with an airline while they were still engaged. But the rigors of starting a business and of seizing upon unprecedented business opportunities in China have kept them from spending much time together over the past two years. For a long time, they lived outside Shanghai and had a long commute to and from work. They had to shower at their health club because they didn't have clean water in their home. They'd work all day, meet at a restaurant for dinner, and then Brett would go back to work for several more hours. Often Eliza went back to his office with him and worked on wedding plans.

The problem was that Eliza expected these early years together to be fun, to be selfish and less complicated than those in the future, when they'd have children and the responsibilities of a family. Missing her family and the States, the ten-year time frame they had agreed to stay in China suddenly seemed unbearably long.

So the couple was forced to reassess their situation, and Eliza had to come to terms with her own expectations. After all, she loved the people they were meeting and the adventures they were having in China. And she loved Brett and was committed to his dream.

In the end, Brett and Eliza made a lot of small changes in their everyday life to improve the situation. They shortened the time frame, committing to China for six years as opposed to ten. They moved into an apartment in the city, a place Eliza could fix up and personalize as she wanted, retrieving all their wedding presents from storage in the States. They also set up a computer at home so Brett could work there rather than at the office in the evenings and on weekends. And while they still don't have potable water, they have organic produce shipped to them so that, for the first time, they are eating dinner together at home.

Eliza and Brett have learned the value of the "little things" in marriage. We can withstand more of what life demands from the marriage if we feel respected and cherished. Little things contribute in a major way to our sense of being respected and cherished.

We also have to accept healthy restraints in marriage. A long time ago, my mother told me about a woman parishioner my dad met at church, not long after my mom had given birth to my younger sister. The woman was very attractive and interesting.

As her minister, my dad had nothing but a friendly, professional rapport with this parishioner. Nevertheless, my mom felt very threatened by her, having just had a baby and being harried at home with my sister and me, just fourteen months apart. And my dad and this woman had a certain chemistry that made my mother nervous.

So she and my dad talked about it, and even though

my mom was in many respects reacting out of a sense of vulnerability, they agreed my dad would keep a healthy distance between himself and this parishioner from that point on. I've always respected the pact they made, and the fact that my mom shared it with me years later. I learned from them how important it is to feel safe in a relationship, even though our fears are sometimes unfounded.

Abiding by restraints in marriage may make you kind of crazy. Duke hates that in his rush to catch flights home to me, I demand he stop somewhere in the airport, stand in line for a phone, and call me to say when to expect him. He does this only after several episodes in which I've awaited his homecoming for hours and in my fatalism, worked myself into a panic that something had happened to his plane—when, in reality, he didn't make a flight or got stuck in traffic.

But I, too, have to abide by a restraint. Even though Duke's job takes him away for six months, he can't bear for me to leave him alone at home for more than a week. He gets very sad, or so I am told for weeks afterward by friends who take pity and have him over for dinner while I'm gone. So as much as I can, I limit the time I spend away. And save the longer trips for when he's gone.

Any kind of "leash" would have seemed blasphemous to me as a single person, but these are the understandings marriage seems to require. You and your husband have to decide what rules of restraint make the two of you feel safe. Several brides with whom I spoke believe they are more susceptible to intellectual affairs than physical ones. Thus, they may have to monitor themselves in circumstances other than business travel and hotel bars. In other cases, it may be wise to limit the overtime you put in with a colleague you consider "just a friend," to limit the hours you spend in on-line chat sessions, or the number of romance novels you read. To use marriage expert Dr. John Gottman's terminology, make conscious choices to "turn toward" the marriage rather than "turning away" from it.

4. MAKE INTIMACY "PRIVACY YOU SHARE."

Make the time you do spend with your husband sacrosanct. Dedicate time in which you have one another's full attention. Have a private world you can't wait to share with your spouse.

Several brides I interviewed talked about spending time in bed with their spouses, not just to sleep or make love. It was there that they cuddled and read; it was there they prayed, talked about the day or about their dreams. It was there they gave one another massages, played cards, and watched movies.

Marriage counselor Warren Molton defines intimacy as "privacy you share." To make a private world you share, you have to make the marriage the same haven your bed has become. This haven of yours is ripe with inside jokes and secrets, with a language of love that includes your pet names for each other and the cache of "right things" you have said to each other at just the "right times."

But remember, marriages only amass "secret codes" over time. The first year Duke and I were married, I grilled him about his days at work and about his co-workers. Let's face it, I wanted the dirt. Yet he wasn't used to talking about work with anyone, much less the angles I was interested in.

But that didn't deter me from *my* monologue. I would dominate dinner with what I thought was my very colorful rendering of the guy with the stud in his tongue trying to set up job interviews on the complimentary phone at Kinko's. Or with my report on the couple next door's latest screaming fight, or screaming orgasm. Or with my ranting about the maintenance people who spent hours outside my office window, blowing a blade of grass around with their interminable leaf blowers.

Eventually Duke got the hang of it. He still doesn't give me all the details I want, but he does collect stories that become part of our running commentary on life. The time we spend apart has become fodder for the time we spend together. We know that when we run out of material, we need to get out and spy on the world again.

Besides devoting time and attention exclusively to one another, and developing a language and symbolism of your own, the other ingredient for creating a secret world in your marriage is saying out loud how you feel about each other. When your spouse is sick in bed, and you're stuck attending to him, tell him there is no place you'd rather be. When your husband is considering relocating to cities that sound as appealing to you as a penitentiary, tell him that as long as you are together, everything will be okay.

Often Duke and I say these magnanimous things to

WHAT NO ONE TELLS THE BRIDE ABOUT . . .

Time demands in marriage:
- You won't necessarily have more time with your beloved once you are married.
- The amount of time a couple spends together is not a yardstick by which to measure their happiness.
- What society calls "clinging" is normal among newlyweds.

Our brides' solutions:
- Cultivate a relationship with the world.
- Spend some time alone.
- Pay attention to the little things. Build in some restraints.
- Make intimacy "privacy you share."

one another, with hearts that are lagging behind. It would be much more comfortable to qualify these statements. I'll follow you to the ends of the earth, I'd like to say, as long as there's a Nordstrom's nearby. You are the sexiest woman on the planet, he'd like to say, when you don't have spinach lodged in your teeth.

But unconditional love means you can't attach conditions. And intimacy is fostered only when you offer up more of yourself than you thought you could, when you set aside time for dinner with your husband even if it means you are going to have to work all night, when you groggily suggest "fooling around" as a way to cure his insomnia, and when you tell him you are proud of him, suppressing your desire to tell him all the ways you think he could be doing his job better.

In many ways, you forge this private world the same way kids do on playgrounds or in tree houses. You let love take you to a more innocent time. You make sweeping statements about how there will never be anyone in the whole world who means as much to you. You have secret handshakes, or in your case, secret places only your husband knows to touch you. You spend full days apart, which seem like an eternity, all the while making mental notes of things you have to tell your best friend on the phone that night. Or you run home and throw pebbles at his window, with the assurance that your lover will answer, and give you his rapt attention.

These are the only ways my friends and I know to make time work for marriage and not against it. These are the only ways we know to safeguard the tree house and to preserve the girl who, once loosed on the world, will swing from the tree's branches.

Chapter 11
LET THE HORSE PICK HIS OWN PATH:
THE OBSTACLES OF COMMUNICATION
AND CRITICISM

It's normal to find yourself trying to squelch some of your husband's behaviors and ideas. It's normal to want to impose your life wisdom and communication skills on him. But instead, embrace his eccentricities and let your marriage grow, like a wild, unwieldy vine. It will bear unexpected and succulent fruit.

Duke and I honeymooned in the Canadian Rockies in May, when the glacier lakes were thawing and snowmelt turned streams into rivers. One morning, we set out on a three-hour horseback ride with two young Japanese couples and a guide. A half hour into our ride, we started crossing these streams-turned-rivers, the icy current of white water so high we lifted our stirrups to keep from getting wet.

The stream bottom was very rocky, so the horses often stopped altogether or faltered, trying to get a footing, which is what happened to the Japanese man in front of me. His horse stumbled and toppled him into the freezing water. Our guide circled back and helped the man, who was unhurt, and the horse to shore, where they were aided by the other Japanese man.

All of this played out in front of Duke and me while we were still haunches deep in the glacial torrent. Relieved to see the man was all right, we then became terrified for ourselves. Our horses had been patient amid the tumult, but even so, they had been pushed into deeper pockets downstream. All Duke and I could really do—besides cluck encouragingly, "Nice horsey," and succumb privately to our ensuing anxiety attacks—was give the horses plenty of rein and let them find their way to the bank of green that lay beyond.

We went on to cross fifteen comparable streams that morning. Often, our horses stumbled, recovering in the nick of time. After the first incident, I started taking pictures, documenting each time Duke and his mount arrived triumphant and *dry* on the side of the creek I had safely claimed. So that when we got our honeymoon pictures back, there were scads of almost identical photos of Duke on horseback, a virtual catalog of anxieties overcome and relief restored.

What an apt metaphor this was for marriage. In so many ways, getting married is like feeding a horse rein on a treacherous excursion. You must surrender control, you must give the animal the autonomy it needs to succeed. But the whole time, you'll be racked with the fear that you will be toppled or crushed by this unpredictable, and sometimes unreliable, behemoth.

This chapter is about that sense of being out of control, of having hitched your wagon to someone else's, most likely to a man who sees the world differently, who treats his problems differently, who talks differently, and who has constructed a life view different from yours. Mainly, this chapter addresses communication and criticism, two major sources of marital conflict, about which my friends and I offer our suggestions.

We happened upon these strategies after frequently being frustrated during the first years of so-called marital bliss by the obstinate, unmovable men we married. During this time, none of us *thought* we were really trying to change our husbands. We thought we were simply tweaking, offering wardrobe advice to husbands who were color-blind or fashion-impaired, or making teensy tiny suggestions from our wealth of experience in maneuvering office politics. And none of us thought it was unreasonable to expect a man to talk about his problems—to share his frustrations and fears with us the same way we shared ours with him.

Nonetheless, we were met with considerable resistance. Major blowups arose over minor matters. Things that hardly bothered us about our fiancés became intolerable once they were our husbands. We got to the point where we could not utter the word *men* without heaving a sigh and rolling our eyes.

Deception Defines Early Marriage

Albert Camus said, "We always deceive ourselves twice about the people we love—first to their advantage, then to their disadvantage." And in many ways, deception defines early marriage. For our weddings, we procure ice sculptures, bagpipers, and billowing tents—all of them bigger than life. We use the words *till death do us part*, often without truly letting them sink in. And we get into antique cars and ride off, not into the sunset but into the fine print of marriage, an ink that comes off on your hands, a truth as gritty as the wedding is white.

Marriage begins with a lie, or so writes Lynn Darling in a 1996 *Esquire* article entitled "For Better and Worse." She married her husband because she liked his version of herself better than her own. "I married him," she says,

... because he loved Ford Madox Ford, because he made the perfect martini, because we could fight and the walls did not fall down, because he was more at home with being a man than any man I knew, because he shouldered responsibility with deceptive ease, and because his eyes welled up with tears elicited by the everyday grace of ordinary people.

Then, Darling recounts, the first Valentine's Day they were married, her husband gave her bath towels. Even worse, they were "seconds"—flawed, snagged, and not even gift-wrapped. Darling cried when she opened them. She says, "The towels were a metaphor that blotted out the sun. . . . It was a romantic high noon, an emotional and historic accounting in which my husband was found sadly wanting."

That instant, she realized, this man on whom she had staked everything was not who she thought he was. "He is not the man who cries when he reads Ford Madox Ford. I have defined myself in terms of this choice, this man, and this is the kind of man he is, the Kind Who Gives Towels."

Darling goes to the crux of the matter because so many of us define ourselves by the choice of marriage, which is, after all, what movies, religions, and cake-topping figurines encourage us to do, setting marriage up to be the ultimate source of fulfillment—the supreme way of living life. Only it isn't. It is a splendid choice for two people who make it work, and who define themselves by other sources of fulfillment as well. But it isn't the right choice for everyone. And it can't *make* you happy if you don't know how to be happy in the first place.

Fear of Being Controlled Makes Us Controlling

And yet, it is the deception that marriage defines us, rather than us defining it, that ultimately is our undoing. Because, finally, either *we must change* or *our husbands must change* if we are to achieve this unachievable consummation.

In our quest for the Holy Grail, we start to quarrel. As psychiatrist Martin Goldberg says, "Most power struggles develop not because of a desire to control the other but because each spouse is afraid of being controlled." Thus, fear that marriage will subsume us, and disillusionment that we have married the Kind Who Gives Towels, makes us hell-bent on restoring marriage and our partners to their original gleaming pedestal.

I got out the Windex early in my marriage when I had a violent reaction to my husband's masculinity. Here I was, trying desperately to be a whole person and to jettison much of what is considered "typically female" from my life, as my husband sauntered around with John Wayne's nickname. He and his friends all had dog-eared copies of something called *The Manly Handbook*, the cover of which features a beer can and the content of which they regularly recite. In particular, Duke liked to allude to a passage about "a good wife" who picked up her husband's underwear. This, he knew, never failed to get a rise out of me.

I cannot tell you how many fights we had that first year about his blatant, verging on penis-wagging, machismo. He made me want to throw up. I'd set out floral towels, and Duke would walk past them, soaking wet and in the buff, to the linen closet to get a solid one. When we went to visit his mother, I brought Land's End monogrammed luggage, navy trimmed in kelly green. Duke, on the other hand, brought a rifle in an army camouflage bag so he could go hunting with his stepfather.

Perhaps you're thinking, What did I expect marrying a military officer? Didn't it occur to me, walking through the "arch of swords" on my wedding day, that my liberal, feminist upbringing might clash with his— steeped, as it was, in testosterone?

In my defense, I married Duke not because he read Ford Madox Ford but because he *was* a military man who *had*, on the first night we met, told me he was a feminist—a title few women I know embrace anymore, much less conservative men. I married him because he treated me better than lots of men before him, who had had far more liberal leanings. And because he accompanied me to rehearsals for a play I wrote about AIDS and held his own among a cast of gay men who were merciless teases and flirts.

Before we were married, his macho jokes seemed to be just that—jokes. But once we were hitched, I stopped laughing and started trying to reform him. I used every intelligent argument known to woman. I even threatened his manhood a few times, saying, "You doth protest too much."

Whatever You Resist Will Persist

None of it worked. In fact, the more I fought, the more obnoxious he seemed to get. That was how I learned the damning truth, "Whatever you resist will persist," as author Susan Page so wisely put it in her book *Now That I'm Married, Why Isn't Everything Perfect?*

But even if Page was on the money, her subsequent advice was unthinkable to me. When one spouse tries to change the other, she said, "the conflict is usually caused by the partner who is not willing to be more accepting." How could I be more accepting? I was on the side of right! Besides, *what would it say about me* if I conceded? *How would it reflect on me* if Duke continued to act like a Neanderthal?

Karmen, the thirty-six-year-old actress in Chicago, had to contend with a different menace—her husband's moods. All the signs were there before they were married. Once, during their engagement party, Karmen said something that angered Mark and he didn't speak to her for three days. Then, right after they were married, he went into a funk in which he'd offer only monosyllabic answers to Karmen's questions, and his mind would, decidedly, be elsewhere. "Sometimes I know he felt smothered or trapped [by the marriage]. He would say things like 'We shouldn't have gotten married,' or 'Maybe I'm not the marrying kind.' "

Of course, these curt remarks hurt far more than if Mark had slit Karmen's side with the wedding cake knife. But Karmen could not coax Mark to elaborate. And having come from a family that shared emotions, Karmen didn't know what to make of Mark's silence, or of the "snippiness" he resorted to when forced to say something—anything!—more about what he was feeling.

Several years have now passed. Mark's anxiety about marriage has eased significantly, and Karmen has learned to read his moods better. She says, "I discovered that with my husband, I can't force him to talk about something until he's ready. Often this means I introduce a subject and then have to come back to it later. This has been a big adjustment for me because I am used to being able to start and finish a discussion at the same 'sitting.' "

Self-conscious for a moment, Karmen says, "It may sound as if I'm afraid of him, but this is not the case." She has simply learned that it does no good, most of the time, to force him to do things her way. And "letting him be" hurts a lot less than it used to.

"Before, I took his procrastination as a lack of interest and took it personally that he didn't want to work things out." Now, she says, "we have both learned that sometimes we talk about things on my schedule, sometimes on his."

Like Karmen, all of us are afraid we'll look weak if we concede or accept our spouse's style. Duke and I were a textbook case of this. Duke was swaggering and posturing because he feared being "mothered" in marriage. I turned

BRIDE-TO-BRIDE

What expectations have you had to let go of when it comes to your husband?

∞ "That he will ever make much money, or that he will ever be as thin as when we met."

∞ "I thought we would live in a nice, neat, house of matrimony. I've really had to work hard at accepting that we live in a sty and that my husband is a slob."

∞ "His priorities are different from mine. I just have to relax and accept our differences."

∞ "He mothers me, because he cares. Nevertheless, it drives me crazy sometimes."

∞ "He will never be on time. And he will never be a wild bohemian type, which is probably why I married him—for the stability."

∞ "He will never be a party animal. He likes to go to sleep before one A.M. I figure this is better than the alternative but it is hard sometimes."

∞ "That he would become more detail-oriented like me. But it just ain't gonna happen."

into his worst nightmare, trying to discipline him. But I feared he was trying to turn me into his "little wife" with all his swaggering and posturing.

The more we fought, the more entrenched each of us became in our positions, so that each argument we had was a nauseating rehash of the one we'd had before. Nothing changed. And I didn't know until I started talking with other brides that all of us reach intractable, impossible positions in marriage—situations we never dreamed we'd find ourselves in before we got married.

Before, it seemed we communicated pretty well and could resolve arguments, but in marriage, we often find ourselves at wit's end. Before, our love seemed to conquer all; now, our problems loom bigger than love's resources to solve them.

Getting Past the Impasse

At this point of no return, how then do you return? How do you keep loving, honoring, and cherishing this implacable moron you married? This is a very good question. I read book after book and asked bride after bride, looking for answers, and this is what I found:

1. EMBRACE HIS ECCENTRICITIES.

There is no getting around it. You must embrace his eccentricities, and he yours. This is the nature of unconditional love.

All too often, we say to one another, "I love you but . . ." Author and psychologist Judith Sills, Ph.D., says those words rest on two assumptions: "First, if you want someone to change, you must withhold approval. Second, a criticized person will change *if he loves you.*"

These two misconceptions, according to Sills, are "the source of some of our most hopeless expectations."

Praise, she tells us, is far more apt to elicit a change in behavior. But even if it doesn't, even if he doesn't change, it does not mean that he doesn't love you. It simply means he is incapable of change. And then you have two choices: to leave him, which I wouldn't advocate doing unless his behavior is abusive, or to accept his behavior.

I can tell you none of this came easily to me, but the tactics I had used with Duke thus far had not worked. If anything, he had become more vehemently manly, smugly smoking his cigars and crusading on behalf of his ramshackle 1976 Jeep-style Toyota Land Cruiser, a vehicle we paid to insure though he never drove it. So, just because I had tried everything else, I experimented with the opposite tack.

In this experiment, the first thing I did was to buy him an expensive humidor for his birthday—not a book I prayed would enlighten him, and not a shirt I knew would push the envelope of his personal style. I picked something you'd find in a smoky, mahogany-paneled men's club, a trinket I associated with bastions of manhood.

The second thing I did was to start defending his Land Cruiser, the one we inexplicably paid for but which sat unused and rusting at his father's house. Whenever we started talking finances, one thing became unnegotiable. I would not hear of selling the Land Cruiser. And I insisted he bring it with us to San Francisco when we moved.

In this experiment, I didn't compromise my own standards. I simply humored him when he made ridiculous he-man jokes, letting them roll off my back. I stopped picking apart the things he said at dinner parties, giving him—and the good-hearted person I'd married—the benefit of the doubt even if a nuance could be deemed politically incorrect. And I encouraged the Arnold Schwarzenegger in him to do his guy things.

Nevertheless, the transformation that occurred in our relationship was startling. We stopped arguing almost altogether, flare-ups about these matters coming not weekly but every other month. Even then, we argued with more detachment, usually about politics or some news event.

Overnight, Duke was noticeably happier. I became "the cool wife" in his eyes, something that made it easier for him to become "the cool husband," someone who bragged to his office mates when I sold a magazine story, someone who did his share of the housework, and someone who cheerfully attended my Mount Holyoke alumnae events, though he often had to defend himself and his profession to my fellow women's college graduates. Later, to my astonishment, he didn't blink when I bought floral sheets for our bed.

In every important way, Duke became the feminist he told me he was the first night we met. And more so, he became my personal champion, not without flaw, but with much greater empathy and understanding of my point of view.

And yet, more remarkable than his transformation was mine. Because the instant I stopped carping at him, the minute I started accepting him and his loathsome traits, I saw him with completely different eyes. I loved him much, much more. And I empathized and really listened to him, maybe for the first time ever.

Even better was how I *felt* about myself. It made me so happy just to love him, and to stop worrying that every little thing he did or said reflected on me. He was his own man, I was my own woman. And as peculiar as it may seem, only then did we really become "one." Only then did we begin to know one another's minds, and to carry one another's burdens.

Author Naomi Wolf once said that the women's movement has made us so angry at men that we can no longer distinguish between a rapist and a man who sits while the table is being cleared. And in my case, she was absolutely right. I once told Duke that I thought every man had some animalistic tendency in him that made him capable of rape. I said this, even though I remembered that the first time I'd heard a statement to this effect—in college—I'd been adamant that my father, the gentlest soul on this planet, did not fit this bill.

Nevertheless, somewhere along the way, I had adopted this thinking, just as Duke got co-opted by a lot of white male backlash. Both of us had very pre-scribed notions of who it was we were *allowed* to love and, mostly, who it was that it would *look good* for us to love.

Even so, you must be thinking, Why must we settle for table-sitters? Why must we embrace traits that are upsetting, even abhorrent, to us? On this, my friends and I agree, you don't have to . . . unless you want to be married.

Because the truth is, if you didn't marry a table-sitter, you married the Kind Who Gives Towels, or the Kind Who Watches Sports, or the Kind Who Works Too Many Hours, or the Kind Who Clams Up. Every marriage, you see, brings two individuals together who confound and annoy each other in one way or another. (Notice we didn't say "abuse"; obviously all of us must draw the line there.) To live together, and to inspire change, our only hope is to accept, maybe even to stroke, the very tendency that sets our teeth on edge.

As I've mentioned before, my father is a Presbyterian minister, and he specializes in urban churches of mixed races and social classes. Often he works in old, downtown churches in communities where young whites have moved out as African-American families have moved in. Thus, he is usually called upon to rebuild churches whose memberships have plummeted.

In private consultation with white members, he sometimes finds them reluctant to accept the church's changing population and mission. They have grown up in a time in which the races do not mix, they tell him, or they are simply uncomfortable with the idea. But my dad encourages them to give the church a chance, to spend several Sundays "acting as if" the race factor does not exist, "acting as if" they are comfortable with the people sitting next to them in church.

The transformation, he has found, is predictably astounding, and he went on to document in his doctoral thesis the reconciliation that occurs through faith. But the more profound results are in church membership rolls that keep building and building, and draw together whites and African-Americans in fellowship.

Obviously, my dad was dealing with a more serious kind of closed-mindedness and prejudice, but what I didn't learn in my dad's church about "reframing" a situation or problem, I had to figure out in marriage. Only by letting go of fantasies and preconceived notions about who I *should* love could real love flourish.

Often, letting go of these fantasies and preconceived notions will feel like a great loss, according to psychologist and author Sills. She writes: "A husband who is a financial failure, overweight or who brags, eats with his fingers, or uses poor grammar, fill us with shame, as if the flaws are a measure of our own inadequacies. *If I love you, what does that mean about me?"*

Indeed, what it means about you is that you have what it takes to be happy, that you see the world's false promises for what they are, and that you know how to focus on beauty and integrity in life. This capacity means you can love someone in spite of, maybe even because of, his flaws.

And this may very well be the secret to successful, long-term marriages. Having studied seven hundred married couples since 1979, Robert W. Levenson, Ph.D., a professor of psychology at the University of California, says, "We found that couples who were happy companions forty years [into their marriages] were those who had been able to *embrace* each other's eccentricities along the way."

Younger couples, Levenson explains, don't reach out to one another with acceptance and affection because they are still too concerned with their own agendas. Only gradually do couples give one another room to be different. Then, over the years, the annoying differences become endearing, as couples fall in love with one another all over again, this time with the realization that their partners are lovable and flawed human beings. And their joy is often profound. Three-quarters of the couples who made it to their fiftieth wedding anniversaries described themselves as "quite happy."

Perhaps this is why Lynn Darling tells us that every Valentine's Day since that first debacle, her husband has given her bath towels. She says it has become part of their mythology. Yes, "the two people who smile at this joke are indelibly stained with each other's expectations and disappointments." And yet, in order for a couple to emerge, in order for love to really take hold, they have learned to hug these towels to themselves, to laugh rather than cry, and to accept rather than renounce.

2. AGREE TO DISAGREE.

But what if the differences between you and your husband still feel substantial? What if you've discovered that, in very important and meaningful ways, you are miles apart? How can you hope to become fond of his viewpoint when it seems to threaten your future together?

The answer is, sometimes you can't. Threats to marriage abound. But at least when it comes to internal threats, you have to learn to "agree to disagree," even about major issues, and let time bring answers that are not apparent to either of you now. My friend Elizabeth has had to do this in conflicts with her husband, Stephen, about his family. Elizabeth is from what she calls a "buttoned-up" Boston Irish family. Her husband, Stephen, is from a much more demonstrative, New York Italian family, the kind of people, Elizabeth says, who "watch TV with their arms draped over one another's shoulders, something [her] family would never do."

Stephen and Elizabeth want to have children someday, and Elizabeth has every intention of creating a more expressive family than the one she grew up in. But in the meantime, she resents the way Stephen's family seems to be trying to change her, to make her into the effusive woman they wish he had married.

In the beginning of the marriage, Stephen and Elizabeth negotiated ways to meet both families' expectations. Stephen's family vacations together for a week every summer while Elizabeth's family always spends weekends, June through August, at a house they own on Cape Cod. So Elizabeth agreed to spend Thanksgiving and

Christmas with David's family if she could skip the summer vacation to spend time on the Cape. Only this year, Stephen's family has decided to spend their summer vacation, you guessed it, on the Cape, where Elizabeth knows they expect the two families to act like "one big happy family." And she knows it will not sit well with her family to have Stephen's entourage inviting themselves over and staying beyond their welcome, as Elizabeth says they tend to do.

Stephen sees little harm in any of this. He loves his family and how open and sociable they are. He thinks Elizabeth is exaggerating how bad the summer vacation is going to be. According to Stephen, it wouldn't hurt Elizabeth's family to loosen up a little.

For now, Elizabeth has decided to agree to disagree. You can only go around and around the same argument so many times, she intimates. And without a crystal ball, Elizabeth doesn't know what conclusion they will eventually come to. She prefers to try to live through this summer's fiasco and make these major family decisions later, when they have children and need to set themselves apart more. Until then, they both want their families to be a big priority in their lives.

Neither Elizabeth nor I, nor any of the brides I interviewed, can tell you when you can afford to agree to disagree, and when you cannot. But in nearly every marriage I know of, couples have issues they cannot, in good conscience, resolve. One bride said the abortion issue divides them. Another said she doesn't like one of her husband's friends and that she's had to refrain from complaining about him. Yet another said she and her husband are so competitive that they end up being "point, counterpoint" on any given current event.

Madison, married five years and living in Tucson, Ar-

Give an example in which you have had to agree to disagree:

∞ "About where we are going to live. He wants to live in the suburbs and I am not ready for that yet. I've said my piece and then shut up. Now he's beginning to change his mind."

∞ "About spending less money on a house. He wanted to spend less, I wanted to spend what I knew we could afford. It took a year and a half but I have finally come around to his way of thinking. It's better to have extra money in the bank."

∞ "We think differently about several fundamental things. I enjoy arguing about them. But it never gets anywhere because he'll hold on to what he believes and I'll hold on to what I believe."

∞ "He goes off on tangents about what is wrong with the world, and politicians in particular. Sometimes I start to defend another position, but when he gets this way, I just let go and let him go. This is one of the few ways he shoots off steam."

izona, knows better than to offer a counterpoint to her husband Zachary's arguments. Because in their case, it does no good. Madison has learned to bide her time, even when Zachary is unreasonable or controlling, and says things like, "You didn't do the things I wanted you to do around the house. This place is a mess."

A twenty-seven-year-old working mother of two toddlers, Madison has learned to expend her energy wisely. She explains, "My husband is a verbal artist, a master at arguments, so there is no winning with him. If I react immediately, it's the kiss of death. That's what he wants, he wants me to react. But I wait until things cool down. Later, he often realizes he has been unreasonable. Or he comes to see that he's projecting issues of his, usually issues of control, off onto me."

Madison and Zachary are Mormon and have sought help with their arguments from their bishop. But in the meantime, Madison is satisfied with her approach. She lets Zachary feel as though he has had the last word, waits until his need for control passes, and then reintroduces the subject when they can talk about it rationally.

As is the case with embracing your husband's eccentricities, it may feel to you at first that you are waving a white flag by employing the strategies of "agreeing to disagree" or "postponing an agreement." Certainly, you'll feel an accompanying sense of loss that you are not simpatico with your spouse. But eventually there is a peace of sorts, a peace that is, by far, preferable to the wadded Kleenexes and wrenching words that ensue when you get into the same old argument again and again.

My biggest fear in marriage was of the so-called midlife crisis, you know, the one that makes men buy Harleys on a whim, the one that paralyzes them in front of televisions with bags of corn chips in their hands, or that drives them to affairs with pretty young things. And I decided early on that Duke was vulnerable to a midlife crisis because he was single-mindedly, hand-to-his-chest, devoted to the U.S. Navy.

You see, Duke's father is a retired captain. And Duke went to the Naval Academy at Annapolis. Since then, he has endured twelve years of incredible stress with very few rewards, in hopes of "getting command" of a ship and receiving a pension after twenty years of service. And although I always supported his pursuits wholeheartedly, I questioned the wisdom of focusing exclusively on this goal. After all, in the civilian world, a company's employees don't all vie to be the CEO, and no one expects to retire after twenty years. Mainly, I just worry about him, because cutbacks mount in the military, and friends and colleagues of his fail to be promoted in what increasingly has become a cutthroat environment.

Maybe it was the minister's daughter in me. Maybe it was the bossy older sister. But for the first year of our marriage, I made a project of persuading Duke that he define himself by something other than his job and his relationship with me. I kept pressing him with theoretical questions, "If you didn't have me, and you didn't have the navy, what would you live for?" I wanted him to find God, nature, philosophy, or some anchor in life to steady him should something happen to me or to his naval career.

This seemed to me to be an unselfish act. I felt this was my mission. Except that Duke could not be moved. He was who he was. He believed that he had to be single-minded to do his job well. He did not see the need to define himself in any other way.

He did, faithfully, go to church with me. And when he was at sea, he started going to church by himself. But he rarely had anything to say about it afterward. When pushed, he said, and wisely so, it had taken a lifetime for me to feel about faith the way I did, and it might take him forever to catch up. Meanwhile I remained frustrated that none of this sparked a passion in him, and that no bigger picture of life grabbed hold of him beyond his work and his love for me.

The arguments we had over this were excruciating, ruining quite a few weeknights and one anniversary dinner. Because he would not budge. And I was relentless. Until one day I had to ask myself that all-important question, Why is it so critical to me that he agree with me about this? And guiltily I admitted that my supposedly unselfish act—trying to gird him for the disappoint-

ments and tragedies life might bring—was entirely
selfish. *It was me* who was most afraid; *it was me* who
didn't trust the strongholds of our life to sustain us in
times of trouble.

I couldn't understand how my husband could live his
life without there being an overarcing meaning to it all.
But I wasn't living his life, he was. So it didn't have to
make perfect sense to me. I just had to love him. And
when I decided to just love him, everything made sense.
He was an earnest man who did his work, loved his wife,
and lived his life well and honorably. If that was enough
for him, I had to finally agree, it was enough for me,
too.

Now, Duke and I are in the midst of the career crisis
I so desperately feared. The cutbacks have dashed his
hopes. And although it is very hard, and Duke does not
yet know what he will do, none of my worst fears has
been confirmed. He remains the man he was, only now
he enjoys the prospect of fatherhood, too.

In this tough transition, he has latched on to prayer.
That part, for him, makes sense, even though he prays
with a kind of "you-won't-believe-who's-talking-to-
you" uncertainty. But I love him for that. And for putting up with me, when I am ridiculously demanding and
intolerant, and do not choose the wisdom of "agreeing
to disagree."

3. OFFER ADVICE ONLY WHEN ASKED, AND CRITICISM ONLY GENTLY.

I learned my lesson the hard way, because I kept offering
unsolicited advice, which I thought was my right in marriage and, for that matter, my right in life . . . until I
learned it is one of the worst things you can do to a
marriage. "The only good advice is the kind that's asked

for," says marriage and family counselor Don Childers. "You can say to your spouse, 'Look, I have an opinion or some thoughts about this if you're interested in hearing them.' But you have to be prepared that your spouse may not want your advice."

Childers says that by giving your spouse the option of hearing your advice, a secondary message is relayed, namely, "I respect you enough to ask whether or not you want my opinion." Then, if your spouse does take you up on the offer, the feeling you have conveyed from the start is one of respect and caring, making any advice easier to take.

Often, Childers says, men mistake a woman's "venting" for a request for advice or solutions. Therefore, couples have to learn to "label conversations" and to say, "Can you just hear me out on this?"—a signal to the other partner that empathy and listening will be prized, rather than advice or problem solving.

Many of us who stayed single longer before marriage have developed life and decision-making skills we think are invaluable. We are opinionated and used to advising friends and colleagues. So we wince when our partners

---

BRIDE-TO-BRIDE

How do you give your husband advice in a way that doesn't hurt or threaten him?

∞ "I try not to pound any advice into him. I pretty much wait until he's begging for it and then calmly make suggestions. And I try not to be emotional in my delivery of the advice."

∞ "Most of the time, I try to give it to him the way I would like it to be given to me, in a considerate, understanding way."

∞ "My husband's very easy going and doesn't feel threatened by advice. It bugs me sometimes because I don't take as well to 'advice.' I get uptight and defensive."

∞ "By making simple suggestions that don't insult him. And I never say something that would compare him to another man."

tell us they handled a situation at work the opposite of how we would have done it. Or we disagree with a parenting decision our partner has made in a newly blended family.

Caroline, a lawyer from Ohio, has raised her son by herself, having learned she was pregnant as she was divorcing her husband because he was involved with another woman. She recently remarried after eight years, during which she and her son, Brian, were on their own or living with her parents. Thus, Brian has never seen her in relationship to a husband, and she has never had to share parenting with anyone. For all of them, this is a whole new ball game.

First, there was the awkwardness of deciding what Brian should call Antonio, her new husband. A retired military officer and a Puerto Rican man, Antonio was uncomfortable with children calling adults by their first names. Eventually, the three of them decided on "Poppy," a Spanish term of endearment for "dad." Even so, Brian has yet to really take to the term, and Caroline has quietly squirmed through the weeks and months in which these adjustments have taken place.

In private, Caroline and Antonio have had their squabbles. Because they share parenting, Antonio wants to introduce more discipline and limits. Luckily, Caroline says, they both know the value of using "nonblaming" language so that Antonio has never come out and said Caroline is too permissive. Instead, he tries, "It doesn't work for me to have Brian do this or that." These gentle, nonaccusatory methods have helped them traverse a very stressful period of adjustment.

In general, praise is a better tool than disapproval. But when you need to address a problem, respect and caring make criticism much easier to take. Lord knows, these are tough lessons for brides. All three lessons—embracing his eccentricities, agreeing to disagree, and withholding advice—demand that we give up some degree of control, the control that makes us feel safe in the world.

As unwieldy as they seem, the vines of marriage respond to a different kind of training and yield very different kinds of fruit. That is why, on the day Duke did sell his Toyota Land Cruiser, having decided for himself that we could no longer afford to keep it, I was the one who cried. Because once I stopped ridiculing this man-toy of his, I started listening to what he said about how lonely and out-of-his-element he'd felt in graduate school, and what a refuge it was for him to take off in his open-air jeep for Big Sur, which was only a half hour away. He'd found a back road above the famed Bixby Bridge, where he'd disappear among cypress and evergreens only to emerge at the top, with a panoramic view of the crashing Pacific and cliffs that defied the onslaught of the sea.

WHAT NO ONE TELLS THE BRIDE ABOUT . . .

Communication and criticism within marriage:
∽ Deception defines early marriage.
∽ Fear of being controlled makes us controlling.
∽ Whatever you resist will persist.
∽ Everymarried couple reaches an impossible impasse.

Our brides' solutions:
∽ Embrace his eccentricities.
∽ Agree to disagree.
∽ Offer advice only when asked, criticism only gently.

Finally, I saw the fortitude that sustained him in life, long before he'd met me and at a time when his career was on hold. I began, not to understand, but to appreciate what this identity badge of his meant to him. I watched other men fawn over his car, despite the duct tape and the paint job that had gone so wrong. And finally, I loved that car like he did. I realized it didn't threaten me; it bolstered him.

Both of our eyes still well up when we talk about the Land Cruiser, although we know selling it was the right thing to do. Of course, if given the chance today, we'd buy the car back in an instant. Still, the feeling it inspired is branded onto our marriage. We know that when we let go of the controls, a trust was forged between us that will never erode.

Chapter 12

THE ENORMITY OF LOVE:
MARVELING AT THE CHANGES MARRIAGE
BRINGS AND CELEBRATING
YOUR TRIUMPHANT MOMENTS

It is normal not to feel as threatened as you once did by the changes that marriage brings. You now know that there are hundreds and hundreds of opportunities in marriage to restore balance, so stop worrying about going under and enjoy the triumph of your union instead.

It is five A.M. on July 4, a national holiday when everyone in the country has permission to sleep in, except for paper boys and girls and the man who makes the doughnuts. I am seven months' pregnant, and seven days away from my publisher's deadline for this book. And yet I am not at my desk writing.

I told Duke that if my writing went well yesterday, I would go fly fishing with him this morning. Only my writing did not go well; it went so poorly, in fact, that I forgot to call to tell him to nix the fly fishing idea. So he came home, having rented the neoprene overalls that are connected to rubber boots—what fishermen call "waders." He looked like a little boy who had caught a glimpse of Santa, so excited was he by the prospect of us having a sport we can do together. This is the same look he had on his face when he burst into my office with bamboo rods he'd found at an antiques store, the same look he got when we practiced casting together in the backyard. So, even though none of this evokes the same rapture in me that it does in him, I have granted him the four hours on this holiday weekend in which I will not be working.

We get into our 1986 Toyota Land Cruiser, not the jeep style Duke used to own but the wagon style we bought last year. There is room for us, for our dog, Lucky, for the fishing gear, and, soon, for a baby's car seat. But for now, the baby is jolted in utero, as we careen down a deeply pitted dirt road.

Duke is looking for the perfect spot on the rushing river; all the spots looking treacherous to me. This is the sport I picked instead of golf, I remind myself. This is the one that inspires glee in the husband I haven't seen for days, while I've been writing.

We find a nice fork in the river, one side of which is more my speed—in other words, slow. And because, at this point in my pregnancy, my bladder feels full all the time, I go to the bathroom several times in the deep shrubbery of the woods.

Then Duke helps me into my waders. We have to tug very hard at the rubber suit to get it up and over my belly, which looks like it is about to burst. When I am dressed, I look like the female equivalent of the Michelin man. I decide this is the stupidest thing I have ever done.

The boots are the only part of the suit that is too big on me, and I have to walk like an astronaut—heel, toe, heel, toe—to the bank where Duke helps me into the water. One misstep on these moss-covered rocks and I know I will go under, bobbing down the river like a contorted inner tube, stomach up. Duke tells me to take baby steps, which I find hilarious, until he shushes me with, "You'll scare the fish."

Then, I am alone. Duke has taken his pole to the "real river" while I am content on this side stream. The water is sun-spackled, the smoke from campfires and morning sausages giving the rays a backdrop on which to hover in the trees. I am casting, again and again, the line a lasso behind me before I set it dancing forward. It is supposed to pluck the water delicately, as a fly would, right behind some rocks where Duke has told me fish, the ones that hadn't minded my laughter, would hang out.

It is so quiet and so peaceful. I can see my husband up the river, through the trees. I know how happy I am making him. I like the repetition of this movement, the idea of having a thousand chances to get it right or make it better.

Twice, I've caught my hook on a downed tree trunk suspended over a waterfall. Duke is in shouting distance, but I go for it anyway, not sure I can really do it, afraid of deeper water, afraid of falling, afraid for the baby, pretty much afraid of everything. But then, at the crest of a waterfall, my feet firmly planted, water up to my waist, or what used to be my waist, I recover my line. And I stand there for a minute in the full force of the current, surveying my lot in life, and sucking on that feeling, that feeling of having done something I didn't know I could. It is this, and not the fish, that both Duke and I know is the point.

A New Perspective

What a difference a year or two makes in a marriage. Duke and I are both still learning, we are both still asking one another to do things we wouldn't otherwise do. And there are still times when I feel alienated from my environment, when I can't imagine what came over me that I said I would do this—be with this one man for richer and poorer, in sickness and in health, in good times and in bad.

And yet, God, I love him. Muttering as I do to myself, "Seven months' pregnant and going to the bathroom in the woods," I would not trade our life for anything. It is wacky. It is quirky. It is impossible. But I love it.

This final chapter is about looking back, marveling at the changes in both of you. It is about accepting change, craving more change, and about standing at the crest of a waterfall, the force of nature upon you, and reaffirming your decision to marry.

If you are typical of the brides I have met and come to know, you submitted yourself to this life somewhat unwittingly, your vision of marriage resembling something out of an Ethan Allen showroom. And yet what pleasure you have found in this zany, impossible existence. What deep dilemmas and soul-wrenching

BRIDE TO BRIDE

Has marriage gotten easier over time?

∞ "Trust has built for me and we both recognize dangerous spots. Our faith has changed our outlooks and helped us mature."

∞ "Now we know that fights don't threaten the relationship. We're both here to stay and so it is easier to be honest with one another."

∞ "In the beginning, I felt like I was supposed to be a different person. I just stopped thinking about this and concentrated on the routine of our lives and the weird feelings went way."

∞ "We have gotten more secure, more confortable, more relaxed with one another. It's not like a big date anymore."

∞ "Yes, you get into a groove and go with it."

∞ "Actually, marriage has been great all along. It was the first two months of living together that were killers!"

predicaments there have been, too. But you have come through them, or soon will—stronger, surer, energized, maybe even feisty.

So many things that threatened you before seem like quiet side streams now. You have graduated from baby steps. You take things in stride now that tripped you up as newlyweds. And you've realized that often, the hardest part about being married is getting over yourself— your own fears, your own stubbornness, and your own lack of imagination.

Getting Over "Myself"

Annette, a twenty-nine-year-old college administrator from Providence, Rhode Island, said this when I asked her about the toughest part of her marriage so far. "*Me*," Annette says, "I have to get over *me*. It is so easy to blame it on other people when things fail. But I am an active part in making whatever happens happen, so I have to be responsible for my actions and my attitude." Yes, Annette nods, realizing what she has just said. "*I'm* the toughest part."

Annette isn't suggesting she's to blame for everything that goes wrong in her marriage. She simply recognizes that whatever happens, she has a hand in it. And that in everything from finances to lighting the pilot light in the water heater, the power is hers to share, and the fulfillment is hers to cultivate.

This is what women in equal partnerships *do*. They understand that there are hundreds upon hundreds of minuscule opportunities in marriage in which to choose to do it differently. A woman, a bride, a wife, she always has within her the power to reject unrealistic expectations and to choose to care for herself, for her husband,

and for their union in reasonable, loving ways. Yes, the pressures on her are immense, the feelings that women are supposed to be the forerunners for love sometimes too deep and too compelling to overcome. And yes, there is always the risk that she will go under, that her happiness and independence will be the first things to go in this undertow of jumbled priorities.

And yet no bride I know has gone under for good. Again, some of us have gotten lost in crinoline, catering counts, and bridesmaid brawls for a good portion of a year. Some of us have submerged for a while, trying to do every little thing in our newlywed year absolutely perfectly, putting Vaseline on our teeth just to keep smiling. And some of us have taken on way too much, getting a dog or having a baby too soon, before we'd even gotten used to being a "Mrs." Nevertheless, all of us are still swimming upstream.

Swimming Upstream

A year ago, Duke ran in the Bay to Breakers race in San Francisco. Bay to Breakers is the world's largest footrace, a ten kilometer course that starts at the foot of the Bay Bridge and ends at the gateway to the Pacific. Eighty thousand participants—many of whom are dressed in outrageous costumes, and some wearing nothing at all, not even jockstraps, not even shoes—run or walk their way across town, up and down San Francisco's famous hills.

But even more outrageous, to Duke's way of thinking, was the team of perhaps a dozen runners dressed like salmon who jogged together in a train in the opposite direction of the other 79,988 race participants. They were, in other words, swimming upstream to spawn, going from Breakers to Bay, confounding hoards of runners who, in the midst of trying to go in the *same* direction from the starting gate on, were already tripping over one another.

As annoyed as Duke was by these salmon-people, I like thinking about them, and about all of us modern brides trying to beat the odds of divorce, trying to beat the odds of our own discontent, trying to reinvent marriage, trying to make an old idea new again. I know the struggle is exhausting. I know the temptations to give in, to go with the flow, to keep loading and unloading the dishwasher, and to keep subjecting your husband to the silent treatment are very strong. But I also know this is the condition of womanhood, and that our souls do not rest unless there is a balance to our lives. Again, swimming upstream is what women *do*.

What the world doesn't often appreciate is that good marriages make us better swimmers. My mom is the best example of this I know. She grew up in an unhappy household, one in which *her* mother was scared of her own shadow. But she grew up nonetheless and went away to college.

When my mother came home with ambitions of becoming a professional singer, her voice just one of her many notable talents, her father thought she was getting too uppity and demanded she finish school at home in Cape Girardeau, Missouri, a very sleepy Mississippi River port. My mom did what she was told and went on to get an education degree, something practical for a woman.

She married my father the day after she graduated from college. Her mother was so mortified that her hometown newspaper had published her wedding announcement a week early that she took ill and had to be coaxed from bed to come to the ceremony. A smaller snafu, my father hid their honeymoon getaway car so that overzealous groomsmen would not decorate it, only he forgot where he had stashed it. They could not have driven away from Cape Girardeau fast enough to suit my mother.

After their honeymoon, they settled in Chicago, where my dad was in seminary full-time and where my mom had too much time on her hands. She had not lived in a big city since she was six, and had certainly never had to drive in one as intimidating as Chicago. She had never been expected to make decisions on her own. She wanted my dad to tell her what to wear to the dinner parties and nights out they'd share with other seminarians and their wives. And when he didn't, when he treated her as an adult and as his equal, her world fell apart.

My mom had a nervous breakdown within months of becoming a bride and sought counseling to help her adjust to this whole new life that was her marriage. But thirty-nine years later, she and my dad are still married, and far more deeply in love than they were back then. My mom never sang on Broadway as was her dream, but she has always been a soloist in the church choir. She even took her education major to the top, winning a city-wide election and becoming president of the Board of Education in a large metropolitan school district. She became a professional woman, whose smarts were always in demand, and she put my sister and me through expensive, private colleges, largely on her salary.

The Good That No One Tells the Bride

My mom agreed to share the preceding with you because the second half of her story is what no one usually tells the bride. Women *can* emerge from forces that would stifle them, they *can* become whole people, and the love of a good marriage can do wonders, instead of harm, if you let it. Sure, her marriage is more traditional than I want mine to be. She has given up a lot for my father and for the greater good of his life's work, sacrifices that have always reminded me of Humphrey Bogart's in *Casablanca*. But these are her choices, choices she's made as his equal, and I respect them.

Women don't lose their souls to marriage. What happens is that marriage makes the yearnings of our souls all the more acute. Because we live in partnership with a husband and with the yearnings of his soul, choices are thrust upon us at a faster rate. And the choices are all the more agonizing because we are taught to believe selflessness rather than self-actualization is the key to preserving marriage.

In *SoulMates*, Thomas Moore writes that the soul of every human being experiences two yearnings, one for attachment and one for flight. In other words, all of us are, in essence, composed of competing wills, one that hopes to bond and one that hopes to distinguish itself.

Now, imagine the soul's competing wills bouncing around in an air-popper. Essentially, marriage turns up the pressure, increasing the speed and the number of times our values crash into one another and into the walls. Marriage, and lifelong companionship, is by no means the only way to increase the velocity of our vacillations between autonomy and dependence, but it heightens the chances of both rich, meaningful encounters, and individual departures, that can be healthy or devastating.

Marriage, then, is the lifelong juggling act of two people's competing tendencies. And all marriages strike different balances, according to the degrees of attachment and independence each partner and each union needs to satisfy their souls. This is not the sole domain of women or wives. Men do the same thing, only they are probably happier in marriage, because in it, they are allowed to exercise their desire for attachment, which they are not permitted to do in other realms of their lives. Women, on the other hand, are subject to more guilt and more exhaustion, determined as we are to be caretakers, determined as we are to ignore our own needs until, at various points in marriage, we come to the distinct conclusion that "something has to change!"

A friend of mine who has been married over twenty years says there comes a time in every marriage when a woman must decide if she is going to continue to be a doormat. I believe, however, that women of our generation have many points early on—before marriage and in the first years of marriage in particular—to choose not to become doormats. And many points thereafter to join with our husbands in excavating our experience of marriage from the dark ages.

Of course, with the birth of the first child, and particularly, I am told, with the birth of the second—or on a different track, with the escalating demands of two flourishing careers—it becomes almost impossible to accommodate all the competing needs without subjugating one partner's needs, at least part of the time. The challenge is to do so in a way that is either equitable or temporarily inequitable, but that is always agreed upon and talked about, mourned and celebrated, revisited and renegotiated. Because, ideally, marriage lasts forever. And therefore, it is always a work in progress.

Fear and Disbelief

Oprah Winfrey recently entertained a discussion of "marriage shock," the dramatic transition women experience when they marry and the title of the book written by Dalma Heyn. Heyn appeared on the show to talk about the way brides internalize society's expectations of the "ideal wife"—expectations that frequently undercut a woman's happiness and doom marriages.

I was enthralled by the discussion and thrilled to see newly married women talking about the tumult they experience, and all the things that no one tells the bride. But I also noticed how defensive the married women became, and how difficult it was for them to persuade the audience that it was normal and healthy to change with the advent of married life. I was left with the impression that marriage was an unbeatable foe.

Was I so wrong, I asked myself, for wanting to see a few women emerge triumphant from battle? Couldn't a few of Oprah's married-women guests have pounded their chest plates, held their swords to the sky, and shouted, "I have been to the cave of Unrealistic Expectations, I have fought the good fight, and I have returned with the head of my opponent!"

Heyn argues that society *needs* to believe that marriage is good, since it represents the last remaining structure on which we can pin our precious, tattered "family values." She says that at all costs, we avoid thinking that marriage is mortally wounded, even though there is considerable evidence that something is terribly wrong with the institution, especially for women.

Married People *Must* Believe in Marriage

There's no question that we, as a society, need to reevaluate the way we promote marriage so we don't continue to lure unsuspecting couples, and brides in particular, into disappointing marriages that end in divorce. This will take a very deep tilling of the soil, and of the deceptions about life, love, and romance that, frankly, many of us adore.

And yet, at the same time, those of us who have chosen marriage and who understand it to be a lifelong commitment and struggle *must* believe in it. We must till the soil for good, telling others about the fertile ground we find, for both women and men.

Those of us who experience triumph in marriage and try to convey it to the world end up looking a lot like the ventriloquist who, years ago, appeared on "Sonny and Cher," in a sketch in which he struggled bitterly against a pecking emu hand puppet. I'm dating myself, I know, but for those of you too young to remember, picture a talking emu on the man's left hand that attacks him regularly and draws him into wrestling matches so fierce that only occasionally can either he or the emu break free to say a word to the audience.

That is, I think, what marriage is like. In our lifelong struggle to subdue the beast of unrealistic expectations, there is hardly a moment in which we can break away from the action to say, "A great marriage is mine!" And the struggle is so often wholly internal, women pecking at themselves, feeling half-guilty, half-exhilarated, that we forget to emerge once in a while to tell others this crucial message:

"There are days, and months, and years, when I realize

this is the hardest battle I have ever fought. But I am enjoying the battle immensely. I wouldn't have it any other way. I love my life, and its blasted complexity, and sometimes, sometimes, in moments that are sweeter than I can even express, I feel I have conquered everything that stood in the way of my happiness, and I am FREE!"

It is with this important message in mind that my friends and I offer you this one last nugget of advice. It is critical, we have found, to celebrate this wonderful, complicated marriage you are forging, and to say what you are feeling about it *out loud*.

> *Say it out loud, not just the bad, but the good.*
> *By doing so, you celebrate the unique and quirky nature*
> *of your life and love.*

I went to dinner the other night with my friend Allison, the navy lawyer who is engaged to be married to the pilot stationed on Okinawa. Allison is also a triathlete, and she told me about spending last Saturday with two other elite women runners who complained all day about their marriages and their husbands. Here she is, on the brink of marriage, and all they did was heighten her fears. They spouted so much of the "prevailing wisdom" about marriage that, I suspect, Allison's imagination and her confidence in her relationship to overcome stereotypical obstacles began to wither.

Allison read the manuscript for this book before it even went to the printer, and we talked a lot at dinner about our relationships with the men we love—about the good, the bad, and the quirky. When she dropped me off at home, Allison, who isn't prone to gushing, said again and again how good it was to hear good things about marriage, not simplistic things, mind you, but good, complicated answers to difficult, complicated dilemmas.

Wouldn't it be nice if brides-to-be fed on good, complicated answers instead of gorging on movie after movie that either starts with the wedding or the day the marriage ends? Wouldn't it be better if we got some realistic and not entirely dour understanding of what lies in the middle of marriage? And wouldn't it be nice if young people grew up and aspired to have real marriages rather than fairy tales? And if young people who didn't think the competing needs of their souls could be met in marriage didn't feel they had to marry?

Be a Maker

As Thomas Moore writes, "An essential part of becoming marriageable is to be a maker, a person who cultivates a life of beauty, rich texture and creative work." Marriage, he says, works best "not by keeping the contract up to date and doing all the right things but by stamping our feet four times on the ground and saying things that touch the feelings and the imagination, not the mind."

BRIDE TO BRIDE

What do you think is the secret of your being happy in a marriage?

∞ "Never repressing feelings. You should *communicate* no matter what the issue. And think sometimes about the special nature of you as two people, having met at this particular time in history, to share your lives."

∞ "I need to have a partner who is there for me, encouraging me to grow and who nurtures my spirit. I also need a cutie. I think I've found the two in my husband."

∞ "The secret to being happy in marriage, and the secret to being happy, period, is play."

∞ "Communication and unconditional love. Strong attraction and spiritual bonds."

∞ "Using the quirks of the relationship to differentiate it from others and never comparing it to others. We both know what is important to the other and make a point to pay attention to those needs."

∞ "Don't take the other for granted—ever!"

I mentioned before that I am adopted. Being adopted and a writer, I have the freedom to peer into others' lives and to imagine what it feels like to have their roots and their identities. It is, sometimes, as if I am picking and choosing my own cells, my own characteristics, defining myself by experiences and observations much more than by destiny. This is, I think, what every woman, and every married person, ultimately must do: write your own story, make your own myths, divorce yourself of roots and identities that do not work, and bring to life your own defining passions and fulfillment.

It is good for society, and it is good for marriage itself, to write what has gone unwritten and to say what has yet to be said. *Timeless Healing: The Power and Biology of Belief*, the book I wrote prior to this, focused on the way the brain works, and how repetitive thoughts become encoded in us and in our bodies. In medicine, it turns out, there is tremendous power to be reaped from exercising our fervent beliefs in love, vitality, and God. And in marriage, too, we wire ourselves. We choose to encode ourselves with guilt, resentment, boredom, and limits. Or we can choose to bolster our immune systems and our unions with fondness, affection, and laughter.

So, for the good of us all, tell your own story. Pass on to others the magic you've made, the ideas you've hatched, and the glimpses you've had of wholeness and fusion. Talk about the exquisite joy there is, awakening every day with the same person—that same flawed person who, nevertheless, is the only person on this earth who stood up in front of a crowd of people, or a judge, and promised to love you forever.

Role Models

We all desperately need role models. Two of my parents' closest friends, a couple who had been divorced for ten years, recently married each other again. And in large part they attributed the failure of their first attempt to the fact that neither of them had had role models. Both of their childhood families had been so dysfunctional, so dragged down by alcoholism and dishonesty, that in adulthood they did not know how to forge a marriage, or even that they lacked the skills to do so. Years of counseling and of looking elsewhere for healthy role models and snapshots of life that could be good and balanced and caring have since prepared them to try again.

It's unhealthy to precisely model our marriages and our families to someone else's, but I am constantly eavesdropping on other people's lives and experiences for snippets and ideas. Just recently, a woman told me she and her family have what they call "no rules nights" in which they eat in the garage, have food fights, permit mild swearing and otherwise outlandish behavior. I have to tell you, I ate this up. Like Allison, I hadn't known until she told me this how much I craved new ideas. What a gift this mother of teenagers gave to me, a mother-to-be, saying that one of her secrets for maintaining order was to stage a minirevolution now and then—as a family.

It is good for marriages to collect ideas. And it is good for us to turn our own experiences into legends, making mythology of our foibles and our triumphs. We only do this by talking, by patting ourselves on the back, and by declaring our marriages better than any that have come before.

Audible Strokes

Sherri Suib Cohen writes in her book *Secrets of a Very Good Marriage: Lessons from the Sea* about the importance of audible strokes. She remembers:

As the first months, then years, of our marriage passed, I reveled in the way Larry told me, every day of my life, how beautiful this or that part of me was and how he loved me. I knew how imperfect my nose was, or how unglamorous my too short, broken nails, but it was those parts that he *particularly* loved, he said.

Once, with great effort, I grew inch-long nails, painted them scarlet.

"Where are those little stubbies?" asked Larry. "Bring back those adorable stubbies."

Sure, it was silly. So what? I loved him for the saying of it.

And so I got into the habit of unqualified stroking, audible stroking. You have to say it right and say it out loud. Just saying it makes you feel cherishing and cherished.

Audible strokes endear us to one another and cement our marriages. With them, we become convinced of our own truths, of the wisdom of our own choices, and of the brilliance of our creativity in marriage. The insidious expectations and the traditional models of marriage that the world offers us then become less threatening. We do not have to answer to the presumptions or perceptions of others. We sculpt our own unions. We make our own marriages, ones that work for us. As Carolyn G. Heilbrun says in her book *Writing a Woman's Life*, "The sign of a good marriage is that everything is debatable and challenged; nothing is turned into law or policy. The rules, if any, are known only to the two players, who seek no public trophies."

Triumphant Snapshots

We all come into marriage afraid of what compromise will cost and unsure of its promise to fulfill. And yet there are moments of triumph so stunning, when we settle into who we are and draw to us the men we love, that we should fish for our cameras and take snapshots of our metamorphosing marriages. Our souls need us to honor these moments, to say new and different things about marriage amid a din of dour predictions and thwarted imaginations.

This is my favorite snapshot. Duke and I had been married for seven months. It was the day the aircraft carrier to which he was assigned, the U.S.S. *Abraham Lincoln*, was to pass under the Golden Gate Bridge and into San Francisco Bay, where the long, four-month separation we'd endured during our newlywed year would end. I stood in front of my closet, as belligerent as ever, thinking to myself, "What is the least navylike outfit I can wear to his homecoming?"

As you can surely guess by now, I never wanted to be one of the women I used to see on TV, standing on a tarmac in spiked heels, chewing gum, and waving a "Welcome Home" sign. And having been raised in a liberal, pacifist home, in which military spending was derided and educational spending touted, I felt more than a little bit out of place among warships dressed in red, white, and blue bunting.

So I picked my boldest leopard blouse, velvet leggings, and black suede shoes to wear to Duke's homecoming. And I drove to the base.

But when I turned the corner of the street leading to where his ship would dock, on every streetlight for miles ahead of me, I saw that someone, undoubtedly a navy wife or a group of them, had tied hundreds of yellow ribbons, one cliché after another, to lead me to the pier. It was then that I closed ranks. And then that I started to sob, shriek, and wave like a lovesick imbecile as the ship made its slow, slow docking in our new home.

Awash in tears but nevertheless defiant in leopard and velvet, I watched Duke, never more gorgeous in his dress blues, salute the officer of the deck, dash down the stairs, and through the crowd into my arms. In that moment, I was never surer of myself. I was never surer of him. And I was never surer of our young marriage, of our great ambitions, or of the future that love held for us.

Things do indeed look very different from the inside of marriage. Sometimes the greatest obstacles to our happiness lie within. Sometimes the answers to our quan-

---

WHAT NO ONE TELLS THE BRIDE ABOUT . . .

Changes that come with marriage:

∞ Change is inevitable but not necessarily bad.

∞ Women are particularly vulnerable but need not "go under."

∞ There are hundreds of opportunities to make marriage different.

∞ There are stunning moments of triumph in marriage that are rarely conveyed to those on the outside.

Our brides' solution:

∞ Say it out loud, not just the bad but the good. By doing so, you celebrate the unique and quirky nature of your life and love.

daries are not apparent and we have to travel by faith. Often, even the stodgiest of traditions can be stretched, defied, or redesigned. In the arms of someone who loves you that much, there is a very solid assurance. And in the presence of unconditional love, there is plenty of room to grow.

Speak of this often. Tell your own story. Say out loud what this quirky marriage the two of you are making means to you. Then enjoy the way marriage surprises the soul. In these ways, you make your marriage the best it can be.

Recommended Reading

Libraries and bookstores are full of books on marriage, but these are the ones that were most useful to me and my friends. My thanks to these authors for the saving grace these books were to me and to other brides.

To better understand marriage:
- *Now That I'm Married, Why Isn't Everything Perfect? The 8 Essential Traits of Couples Who Thrive* by Susan Page (New York: Dell Publishing, 1994).
- *Marriage Shock: The Transformation of Women into Wives* by Dalma Heyn (New York: Villard Books, 1997).
- *Secrets of a Very Good Marriage: Lessons from the Sea* by Sherry Suib Cohen (Carol Southern Books, 1993).
- *The Good Marriage: How and Why Love Lasts* by Judith Wallerstein and Sandra Blakeslee (Boston: Houghton Mifflin, 1995).
- *The Marriage Survival Kit* by John Gottman, Ph.D. (New York: Crown Books, to be published).

For your own growth and nourishment:
- Any novel or short story by Laurie Colwin, perhaps starting with *Happy All the Time* (New York: Alfred A. Knopf, 1978).

- *SoulMates: Honoring the Mysteries of Love and Relationship* by Thomas Moore (New York: HarperCollins Publishers, 1994).
- *The Revolution Within: A Book of Self-Esteem* by Gloria Steinem (Boston: Little, Brown, 1992).
- *Writing a Woman's Life* by Carolyn G. Heilbrun (New York: Ballantine Books, 1988).

To empathize and communicate with your husband:
- *Loving Men More, Needing Men Less* by Judith Sills, Ph.D. (New York: Penguin Books, 1997).
- *Men Are from Mars, Women Are from Venus* by John Gray, Ph.D. (New York: HarperCollins Publishers, 1992).
- *The Hearts of Men: American Dreams and the Flight from Commitment* by Barbara Ehrenreich (New York: Anchor Books, 1983).
- *You Just Don't Understand: Women and Men in Conversation* by Deborah Tannen, Ph.D. (New York: Ballantine Books, 1990).

To inspire conversation and know one another better:
- *Getting to Know You* by Jeanne McSweeney and Charles Leocha (Hampstead, N.H.: World Leisure Corporation, 1992).

Acknowledgments

Years ago my family made me promise I wouldn't write about them until they were long gone from this earth. And yet, right away, my husband, Duke, consented to let me tell other brides our tender-most secrets. He says he has no pride, but I think he is, simply, fearless. I thank him for this, for attending to my words with laughter and love, and for once dating a chiropractor, of which the back-rub benefits are now *all mine*.

Thanks to Mom, Dad, Cathy, and Brian for relenting in the end. I hope I do you justice, as if any words could. Thanks, too, to Doyle, Carolyn, Mark, Linda, and Ada for welcoming me and my contradictory nature into your family.

Fifty incredible women, the brides who let me tell their stories, filled out exhaustive surveys, E-mailed me faithfully, welcomed me into their homes or let me linger on the phone. I marvel at and was inspired by your honesty, strength, and humor.

I am grateful for Terry Schraeder, with whom I shared sushi, yoga, and much of my initial discomfort about all the things no one tells the bride. And thank you, Sharon

Manuel, for calling me on my very vulnerable, first birthday as a bride, and for solidifying the idea of this book with one great talk.

Extraordinary thanks to Herb Benson for helping me learn to write a book and for helping me heal. And for introducing me to Patti Breitman—my agent, title maven, a champion of soul-nourishing books, and my wise friend.

The phone messages of my editor, Laurie Abkemeier, were so enthusiastic that they remain perpetually "saved" in our voice-mail system. How heartening it is to emerge from the stupor of writing and be greeted with such bright ideas and commentary.

Thanks, too, to Amy Fontanella for compiling some great bride interviews. Many friends, including Robin Bernhard, Penny Bice, Carole Lynn Duffy, Lynn Nutwell, Stacy Poe, and Robin Wild, read the manuscript with care, laughed at the right places, and fed me great feedback. Sylvia Peck did much more, becoming "my loving other," telling me pregnant women are beautiful, telling me the book was brilliant when she is, quintessentially, both of these things.

I am indebted to Madeleine Frick, Sandi Sonnenfeld, Beth and Faith Witte, and the Alumnae Association at Mount Holyoke College for poring through their Rolodexes and putting me in touch with other brides. I am also especially glad to have friends like Erin McDonough, Angie Merrill, Toni Rose, Craig and Sandi Solem, my Newport house buddies, the CCG-3 staff, and the navy wives' club who cheered me and cheered me on.

Index

absence, 226–43
  bride-to-bride on, 241
  and clinging, 233–34
  and cultivating relationship with
    the world, 235–38
  and freedom, 238–43
  girls' and guys' nights out, 71
  and holding on to ourselves, 235–
    43
  and hunger of our hearts, 229–30
  and intimacy, 247–49
  and the myth of more time, 227–
    29
  and the myth that togetherness
    equals happiness, 230–33
  and restraint, 243–47
adjustment, psychological, 20, 21–23
advice, bride-to-bride on, 270
affection, public displays of, 72
agreeing to disagree, 264–69
"all or nothing," 169–71
American Couples (Blumstein and
    Schwartz), 36, 122
anniversary, celebration of, 82–83
arguments, 7–9, 9–10
  and agreeing to disagree, 264–69
  and control, 254–56, 257–58
  and lost job, 110–11
  on money matters, 112–13
Arond, Miriam, 152, 169, 180
Atwood, Margaret, 16
audible stroking, 290–91
Austen, Jane, 10, 14
autonomy:
  healthy, 82

and money, 115–16
  struggle for, 64

"baby urge," 206, 212; see also
    family; parenthood
Blakeslee, Sandra, 105, 107, 235, 240
bliss, state of, 5
blues, after the wedding, 88
Blumstein, Philip, 36, 122
Book of Love, Laughter and Romance,
    The (Jonas and Jonas), 186
Boston Globe, Goodman's column in,
    41–42
brides:
  after the wedding, see newlyweds;
    wife
  disorientation of, 2
  expectations of, 140–41
  free rein for, 33–35
  growing pains of, 2
  identity crisis of, 19–20
  individuality of, 15
  inner turmoil of, 19–20
  overworked, 139–40
  role models of, 27–28, 289
  secrets of, 3–6
  soul of, 15
  turbulence of, 7–9
  vulnerability of, 27
  as women, 10–11
bride-to-bride:
  on accepting husband's traits, 175
  on adding excitement and
    romance, 193–94
  on becoming your mother, 142

bride-to-bride (*continued*)
on best thing about the wedding,
59
on change, 27, 34
conversation-starting questions of,
222
on disagreements, 266
on engagement fears, 44
on expectations, 99, 257
on fears, 8
on fun in marriage, 232
on giving advice, 270
on habits from single life, 165
on happiness, 287
on husbands and happiness, 106
on lessons about love, 154
on marriage over time, 277
on missing the single life, 71
on money matters, 118, 129
on old flames, 161
on parenthood, 219
on preserving aspects of single life,
77
sexual surprises of, 191
on time apart, 241
wish someone told me, 4
Brown, Helen Gurley, 179
business startup, 119–20

Cabot, Tracy, 163
Campolo, Anthony, Jr., 176
Camus, Albert, 252
career:
happiness in, 36, 40
vs. marriage, 36–37, 117
change:
bride-to-bride on, 27, 34
and control, 254–58
in cooking and eating habits, 98–
99
and culture shock, 23–24
darkness of, 23
and friendship, 67–68, 72–73
and identity crisis, 23–26, 37–38
in life goals, 25
love as catalyst for, 32
misconceptions about, 259
and money matters, 116–17, 125–
26
in name, 13, 94–95
of parenthood, 207–208
of perspective, 29–33, 228
positive, 34
resistance to, 255–58

and social life, 72–73, 78, 82
of starting a family, 25–26
taking time for, 152–56
Childers, Don, 136, 185, 269–70
Clark, Darwin "Duke":
adjustment to happiness with, 21
and "Always," 61
and arguments, 7–10, 14–15, 44–
45, 88, 166–68, 172, 257–58,
259
on being an island, 168
and career choices, 118–19
and communication, 247–48
and competitive neediness, 217–18
and the dog, 203–205
empathy of, 260
and engagement, 54, 55
and exercise, 91–93
falling in love with, 31, 167–68,
198–200, 229
and family, 74, 137–38, 198–99
fears about marriage, 28, 257–58
fly fishing with, 274–76, 277
and gourmet dinners, 98–99, 193
history revised by, 28
homecoming of, 291–92
and honeymoon, 87, 104, 250–51
and humor, 223–25
and "I love you," 107–09
and independence, 168–69
and *jamais vu*, 26–27
Land Cruiser of, 272–73
and learning about marriage, 109–
10
letters to, 30–31
long-distance relationship with,
154–56, 203, 238–39, 241–43,
246, 291–92
and loss of identity, 63–64
and machismo, 254–65, 257–58,
259–61
marriage to, 5, 60–62, 153–56,
167–68
and midlife crisis, 267–68
and money matters, 113–15, 117–
18, 120–21, 126–27, 130–32,
173
mornings with, 78, 90
and motorcycle v. china closet,
103–105
and myths, 103
and ominous signs, 47–48
outdoor activities of, 237, 274–76,
279–80

and parenthood, 215, 217–18
patience of, 170, 195–96
and pet-sitters, 150–55
and power struggles, 5
and premarital agreements, 123–24
and preparations, 44–45, 59–60
and priorities, 54–55
proposal of, 43
and reality, 32
and sex, 178–79, 189, 193, 195–96, 199–200
and silent treatment, 143–44
and social life, 68–70, 71
and teamwork, 133–34, 176, 260
and time apart, 226–27, 229–30
and unconditional love, 166–68, 177–79
and wedding service, 56
Cohen, Sherry Suib, 145, 289–90
Colwin, Laurie, 11, 12, 22–23
comfort, as aphrodisiac, 184–87
commitment:
    depth of, 49–50
    leap of faith in, 52
    lifelong, 38
    and money matters, 122–25
    and sharing a life, 227–28
communication, 250–73
    about money matters, 122–25
    about sex, 185–84, 189, 190–91
    about teamwork, 147–50
    and control, 251, 255–56, 258, 272
    and deception, 252–53
    and intimacy, 247–49
    overcoming impasses in, 258–73
    and resistance, 255–58
    and silent treatment, 143–44
    time apart and, 242–43
    waiting for, 256–58
comparison, standard of, 160–63
compensation, Emerson's law of, 175
competitive neediness, 217
compromises:
    in expectations, 97–98
    in living together, 97–98, 291
    in wedding, 52–56, 59–60
control:
    and arguments, 254–55, 237–38
    and criticism, 251, 254–55, 271
    letting go of, 151–52, 251
    and money, 115–16
conventional thinking, challenges to, 13–16

conversation-starting questions, 222
cooking and eating habits, 98–99
counselor, advice from, 50–51
couple, perfect, 101–103
criticism:
    agreeing to disagree, 264–69
    and control, 250, 254–55, 272
    and deception, 252–53
    embracing eccentricities, 258–64
    resistance to, 255–58
    strategies on, 258–73
    when to offer, 269–73
culture shock, 23–24

Darling, Lynn, 252
deception, 252–53
Deutsch, Francine, 148, 149, 152, 176
Didion, Joan, 16
divorce, 11, 17, 38, 285
Donahue, Phil, 17
Duke, see Clark, Darwin "Duke"
Dunn, Stephen, 35

eccentricities, embracing, 258–64
engagement, 43–62
    blowing your cover in, 44–45
    and calling off the wedding, 50–51
    and commitment, 49–50
    fears in, 44
    freaking out in, 48–49
    and friendships, 75–78
    ominous signs in, 47–48
    one last fling in, 48–49
    one-year, 34–35
    panic attacks of, 50
    pressures of, 7
    and relaxation, 51–53
    revisiting your decision in, 49–50
    and "This is It!," 45–46
    as turning point, 21, 66
    typical, 5
equality, as ongoing process, 152
excitement, adding, 193–94
expectations:
    changing, 257
    and dreams, 97–98
    fifty-fifty standard, 158–60
    of gender roles, 140–43
    of husband about wife, 2–3, 98
    makers and, 287–88
    of marriage, 3, 6–7, 13–16, 27, 59, 130, 233–34, 252–53

expectations (*continued*)
  of passion, 161–63, 180–81
  of perfection, 46, 96–101
  about sex, 178–84
  of society, 78–80, 141–43, 284
  standard of comparison, 160–63
  of togetherness, 238–43
  of wedding gown, 31
  of wife about husband, 96–97, 99,
    257
  see also stereotypes

fairy tale:
  end of, 87–88
  expectations of, 47
  of marriage, 6–7
faith:
  and reconciliation, 262
  and trust, 51–53
family:
  "baby urge," 206, 211–12
  breaking away from, 73–75, 78
  faux, 163–64
  vs. friends, 36, 64
  and gender roles, 138–39, 142–43
  and in-laws, 101–103, 264–65
  marriage as center of, 215–16, 244
  and money matters, 119–24
  objective view of, 82
  patterns of, 135, 152–55
  pressures of, 27–28
  pressure to start, 205–206
  and social arrangements, 70–71, 81–
    83
  starting, 25–26, 38–39, 120, 207–
    208, 211–13, 283; *see also*
    parenthood
  and thirteen bedmates, 134–35
family values, 285–293
fears, of marriage, 7–8, 27, 284
fifty-fifty standard, 158–59
finances, *see* money matters
First Year of Marriage, The (Arond
    and Pauker), 152, 169, 180
flames, old, 160–63
fling, one last, 48–49
"For Better and Worse" (Darling),
    252–53
freedom, symbols of, 37–41
friends:
  best, husbands as, 84–86, 175
  boundaries set with, 81–84
  changing relationships with, 67–
    69, 72–73

distance of, 68–69
vs. family, 36–37
honoring, 75–78
single, 77
social arrangements with, 71
weekend getaways with, 76
with women, 238
fun, 219, 220–25, 232, 233

gender roles, 10, 13–14
  and division of labor, 147–50
  expectations of, 140–41
  family patterns of, 162, 147–49
  letting go of, 150–52
  and thirteen bedmates, 134–35
  and "who cares most?," 150–52
Goldberg, Martin, 254
Goodman, Ellen, 41–42
Good Marriage, The (Wallerstein and
    Blakeslee), 105, 107, 235, 240
Gottman, John, 205, 215, 218–20,
    222, 247
Graceful Exit, 41–42
Gray, John, 158–59, 160, 173
grooms, *see* husbands

happiness:
  adjustment to, 21–23
  belief in, 11–13
  bride-to-bride on, 106, 287
  frivolity of, 21
  in one's career, 36, 40
  paranoia in, 21
  vs. serious doubts, 50–51
Happy All the Time (Colwin), 11–12
Heyn, Dalma, 14–15, 20, 27, 125,
    284
Hiding Place, The (Ten Boom), 170
home:
  husband's, 100
  sharing, 93–94
honeymoon:
  and pregnancy, 214
  time of, 3–4
humor, 220–25
husbands:
  accepting traits of, 96–101, 173
  after the wedding, *see* newlyweds
  attempts to change, 251–52, 254–
    55
  and bride's family, 74
  expectations of, 3, 98–101
  as fathers, 213–15; *see also*
    parenthood

financial dependence on, 117–19
and gender roles, 10
health and happiness of, 10
home of, 100
perfect, 96–98
secrets of, 3–6
and teamwork, 147–50
threatened manhood of, 28
as trophies, 80
as wives' best friend, 84–86, 173

identity badges, 30–31, 37–42, 172,
272
identity crisis, 19–42
adjustment to happiness in, 21–23
change and, 23–26, 37–39
and extra rein, 33–35
and the Graceful Exit, 41–42
and identity badges, 29–31, 37–42
and inner chaos, 19–20
and *jamais vu*, 26–29
and new perspectives, 29–33
priorities and, 35–37
idiosyncrasies, acceptance of, 96–101
imagination, as powerful tool, 17–18
independence:
and decision-making skill, 52,
270
vs. dependence, 226–27, 234
loss of, 13–16, 65–66, 79, 100–101
maintaining, 78–79
in time spent apart, 239–40
and unity, 260
influence, and money, 115–16
intimacy, 247–49

jamais vu, 26–29, 68
*John Rosemond's Six-Point Plan for
Raising Happy, Healthy Children*
(Rosemond), 211–12
Jonas, Barbara and Michael, 186
journals, as identity badges, 30–31

Kerouac, Jack, 37

Levenson, Robert, W., 263
life goals, changes in, 24
Lipsett, Suzanne, 209, 210
"Lone Pilgrim, The" (Colwin), 22–
23
love, 274–93
bride-to-bride on, 154
as catalyst for change, 32
centrality of, 243

at first sight, 162
and getting over "myself," 278–79
and happiness, 21–23
for love's sake, 174–77
mixed messages about, 79
obstacles to, 171–72
and perspective, 276–78
and power, 176–77
search for, 22
unconditional, 146, 168, 169–71,
172–77, 200–201, 268–69
Loving Men More, Needing Men Less
(Sills), 172

maiden name, keeping, 13
manhood, threats to, 28
Markman, Howard, 115–16
marriage:
adjustments to, 3
autonomous entity of, 84
average age at, 6
basic skills of, 88
belief in, 295–303
boring, 88–89, 164, 175, 189–90,
205
vs. career, 36–37, 116–17
celebrating the significance of, 58–
62
as center of the family, 216–17
and children, 70; *see also*
parenthood
as choice, 253
deception in, 252–53
and divorce, 11, 17, 38, 284
evolution of, 156
expectations about, 3, 6–7, 13–14,
28, 59, 129, 215, 234–53
fairy tale of, 6–7
fears of, 8, 28, 54–55, 284
freedom in, 37
fulfillment in, 3
gender roles in, 10–11, 13–14
as goal, 271
habits in sync in, 90–91
happiness in, 11–12
idea of, 6
as inadequate, 104
intimacy of, 189
juggling act of, 282–83
learning about, 89–95, 109
as lifelong commitment, 38
makeover in, 23
normal reactions to, 9–10
over time, 277

marriage (*continued*)
 parent/child relationship in, 138
 positive-to-negative ratio in, 106
 power of, 138
 renegotiation of, 228–29
 rethinking decision of, 48–49
 as reward, 174
 romance of, 6–7
 savoring reality of, 105–107
 schedules in sync in, 90–91
 second, 74–75
 and settling down, 28, 78–80, 163–64
 sex in, *see* sex
 sharing in, 90–91, 93–94, 158–60
 significance of, 66
 vs. single lifestyle, 8–9, 79–80
 as status symbol, 80
 stereotypes of, 79–80
 stress patterns in, 155
 successful, 11–18
 symbols of, 32
 taking care of each other in, 106–107
 and time apart, 226–33
 and togetherness, 229–34
 traditions of, 5–6, 284–85
 typical, 5
 uniqueness of, 16–18, 40–41, 105–106
 women and, 10–11
Marriage Shock (Heyn), 14–15, 20
Marriage Survival Kit, The (Gottman), 219
Marrying Later, Marrying Smarter (Cabot), 163
melancholy, after the wedding, 88
Men Are from Mars, Women Are from Venus (Gray), 158–59, 173–74
Molton, Warren, 82–83, 192–93, 236–37, 247
money matters, 112–32
 arguments about, 115–16
 bride-to-bride on, 118, 129
 business startup and, 119–20
 communication about, 121–25
 downside of exercising choices in, 117–19
 and family history, 120–21
 and fiscal opposites, 113–15
 and making changes, 117–19, 125–26
 milestones of economic freedom, 116–17
 power, influence, control and, 115–16
 and responsibility, 119–20, 125–27
 separate vs. joint accounts and, 121–25
 strategies for, 121–32
 trust in, 128–32
moodiness, 256–57
Moore, Thomas, 17–18, 88, 282–83, 287
mother, becoming, 143

name change, 13, 94–95
newlyweds:
 adjustments of, 3, 87–111
 arguments of, 8–10
 aura about, 4
 closeness of, 26, 233–34
 couples journal of, 186–87
 culture shock of, 23–26
 disorientation of, 3, 33
 fairy tale of, 6–7
 and girls' and guys' nights out, 71, 75
 having fun as, 220–25, 232, 233
 isolation of, 6–7, 18, 64, 235–36
 is that all there is?, 87–88
 learning curve of, 109–11
 and motorcycle vs. china closet, 103–105
 myth 1 of (license), 89–95
 myth 2 of (perfect husband), 96–98
 myth 3 of (perfect wife), 98–101
 myth 4 of (perfect couple), 101–103
 myths eliminated by, 103–11
 and normal life, 88–89
 novelty of being, 108–109
 power struggles of, 8
 secrets of, 3–6
 small wonders of, 105–107
 social life of, 69–70
 test cases of, 169
 turbulence of, 8
 typical, 5
Now That I'm Married, Why Isn't Everything Perfect? (Page), 51, 175, 181, 256

old flames, and standard of comparison, 160–63
ominous signs, 47–48

Page, Susan, 51, 175, 181, 186–87, 195, 197, 256
parenthood, 203–23
  "baby urge," 206, 212
  bride-to-bride on, 219
  changes because of, 207–208
  and competitive neediness, 217
  delaying, 214–15
  effects on women of, 208–11, 283
  entering into, 25–26, 38–39, 180, 206–207, 211–212, 283
  fertility drugs and, 220–21
  foundation for, 216–20
  and having fun, 220–25
  and marital satisfaction, 208
  obligations and sacrifices of, 211
  qualities needed for, 211–12
  reasons for, 211–13
  sharing of, 271
  strategies for, 211–25
parents, see family
passion:
  in bad relationships, 163–68
  expectations of, 161–62, 180–81
Pauker, Samuel L., 152, 169, 180
PDA (public displays of affection), 72
perfectionism, 14, 45, 96–103
personality, marriage matched to, 40–41
perspective:
  changes in, 28–33, 227
  loss of, 55–56
  love and, 276–78
positive-to-negative ratio, 106
power:
  balance of, 158–59
  and loving less, 176
  of marriage, 138
  and money, 115–16
power struggles, 8
premarital agreements, 122–25
priorities, 35–37, 53–56

Ramsey, Karen, 126
Reich, Ken, 128–29, 136
religion, rites and rituals in, 108
restlessness, 165
restraint, 243–47
role models, 27–28, 289
Rosemond, John, 211–12, 216–17

Schlessinger, Laura, 146, 174
Schwartz, Pepper, 36, 122

second marriage, 74–75
secrets, 3–6
Secrets of a Very Good Marriage (Cohen), 145, 289–90
self-image, 15, 27, 29, 65, 234
sex, 178–202
  acceptance and, 187
  comfort and knowledge in, 184–87
  communication about, 185–87, 189, 191
  creative initiatives to, 192–202
  distractions from, 187–89, 197
  engaging the senses in, 192–95, 197
  excuses and, 191–92
  expectations about, 179–84
  and fantasies, 186
  and fidelity, 201
  frequency of, 179–80
  inhibitions about, 182–84
  and laziness, 189–92
  letting go in, 197–202
  and orgasms, 185–86
  preconceived notions of, 179–84
  and pregnancy, 185, 212
  saying no to, 195–97
Sex and the Single Girl (Brown), 179
silent treatment, 143–44
Sills, Judith, 172, 258–59, 262–63
single lifestyle, 157–77
  defending, 8, 79
  dignity of, 35–37
  family and, 73–74
  and fifty-fifty standard, 158–60
  fun of, 163
  habits from, 165
  independence of, 13, 15, 52, 65–66, 79, 270
  and loving for love's sake, 174–77
  and loving more, 173–74
  mind-sets of, 158–68
  and money, 115–16, 117–18
  and obstacles to love, 171–72
  preserving aspects of, 76
  saying goodbye to, 64, 71
  solitude in, 80
  and standard of comparison, 165–68
  strategies for mind-sets of, 174–83
  and thrill standard, 163–68
  unconditional love vs., 168, 169–71
  values of, 28–29

snapshots, triumphant, 291–93
social life:
　arrangements for, 69–71, 82
　and change, 72–73, 78, 82
　as a couple, 69–70
　friends honored in, 75–78
　girls' and guys' nights out, 71, 72
　setting boundaries in, 81–84
　singles list in, 67–68
society:
　and family values, 285–93
　and gender roles, 142–43
　instant gratification in, 166
　mixed messages from, 79–80
　and pressure to start family, 206–207
　and tradition of marriage, 6–7, 284
soul, 15, 236, 282–83
soul mates, as made and not born, 179
SoulMates (Moore), 17–18, 88, 282–83
space, personal, 33–35, 92–93
spiritual life, 237
stereotypes, 78–80, 133–56
　bride's, 140–41
　gender roles and, 138–39
　patterns of, 136–38
　and the power of marriage, 138
　silent treatment and, 143–44
　societal, 141–43
　strategies to use against, 146–56
　taking time for change of, 152–56
　and teamwork, 147–50
　of thirteen bedmates, 134–35
　and unconditional love, 151–52
　and "who cares most?," 150–52
　see also expectations
Stewart, Martha, 7, 98, 141
stroking, audible, 290–93
Surviving a Writer's Life (Lipsett), 209

Tannen, Deborah, 149
teamwork, 147–50, 282–83
　and equality, 152
　and fifty-fifty standard, 158–60
　in world outside marriage, 235–38
Ten Boom, Corrie, 170–71
thirteen bedmates, 134–35
"This is It!," 45–46
Thomas, Marlo, 17
threshold, crossing, 20
thrill standard, 163–68

transitional period, 63–66
　engagement and, 66
　family's distance in, 73–75
　friends' distance in, 68–69, 84–86
　friends honored in, 75–78
　marriage as entity in, 84
　new social life in, 69–70
　not fitting in anywhere in, 64
　setting boundaries in, 81–84
　settling down in, 78–80
　singleness and, 65–66
　social life in, 67–68, 69–70, 72–73, 75–84
　spouse as best friend in, 84–86
"Traveling" (Dunn), 35
trust:
　and faith, 51–53
　and money matters, 128–32

unconditional love, 145–46, 169–71, 172–74, 200–202, 269

values, communication about, 121–25

Wallerstein, Judith, 105, 107, 235, 240
wedding bands, 61
wedding gown:
　dreams of, 1–2
　early purchase of, 34
　expectations about, 30
　fit of, 1–2
　perfect, 45–46
　white, 182
wedding jitters, 50–51
weddings:
　best thing about, 59
　as birth of the couple, 82
　calling off, 49–62
　as choice, 32
　compromises in, 53–56, 59–60
　personally meaningful, 56–58
　planning for, 33, 53–56, 99
　traditions of, 37, 56
wife:
　becoming, 20
　discomfort with word, 11
　expectations of, 96–98
　perfect, 98–101
　traditional roles of, 13–14
　working, 35
Winfrey, Oprah, 284
Wolf, Naomi, 261

women:
  biological clocks of, 213
  dignity of, 35
  and division of labor, 147–50
  as doormats, 283
  effects of parenthood on, 207–11,
    283
  fear of clichés, 13
  as friends, 238
  and gender roles, 10, 13–14, 138–
    43
  health and happiness of, 10
  and independence, 13–14
  and letting go, 150–52
  life changes for, 20, 210–11

  maiden names kept by, 13
  and marriage, 10–11
  mixed messages to, 78–80
  and money matters, 116–19, 125–
    27
  nagging, 160
  and name change, 94–95
  and perfectionism, 14
  self-images of, 15–16, 27, 29,
    65
  as "thrill whores," 163
women's movement, 261

You Just Don't Understand (Tannen),
  149

About the Author

Marg Stark is a magazine writer and author with one previous book to her credit—*Timeless Healing: The Power and Biology of Belief*, a book about the healing effects of faith, which she wrote in collaboration with Herbert Benson, M.D. Published by *Boston*, Stark's first magazine article—about two men living and dying with AIDS—was adapted into the 1994 NBC television movie "Roommates," starring Randy Quaid and Eric Stoltz.

Stark graduated from Mount Holyoke College, got her master's in journalism from Northwestern University, and spent ten decadent years single before marrying Darwin "Duke" Clark, a U.S. naval officer. Married in 1995, Stark and Clark say marriage is a wonderful, nutty work-in-progress that still feels new to them. They make their home wherever the navy sends them, with their "miracle" child, Patrick, and with Lucky, their spoiled Chesapeake Bay retriever.

6.00 11/1
300 3/4   X
2 4/4
1 7/4